高等院校立体化创新经管教材系列

国际商务函电
(第3版)

李 爽 主 编

矫 萍 胡大龙 副主编

清華大学出版社

北京

内 容 简 介

本书介绍国际经贸实务的中英文写作，紧密结合我国外经贸业务实际，总结和归纳了国际经贸业务中的常用术语、常用短语、句型结构和缩略语，内容新，实用性强。

全书分英汉两部分各十四个单元，按照实际交易程序介绍商务信函的写作方法，内容包括建立业务关系、询价、报价、还价、接受、开证、保险、租船订舱和索赔等，另外还介绍了国际商务应用文的写法和合同或合约的阅读。每个单元的内容主要包括导读、样函、注释、常用语句、写作指导和练习，书末附有各单元导读和样函主体部分的译文，以及两套模拟试卷及其答案和各单元练习题的答案。

本书适合用作大学本科和专科生，独立学院和高职高专学生及对外经济贸易工作人员的教材及自学参考书。

图书在版编目(CIP)数据

国际商务函电/李爽主编. —3 版. —北京：清华大学出版社，2023.6
高等院校立体化创新经管教材系列
ISBN 978-7-302-63610-6

Ⅰ. ①国…　Ⅱ. ①李…　Ⅲ. ①国际商务—英语—电报信函—写作—高等学校—教材　Ⅳ. ①F740

中国国家版本馆 CIP 数据核字(2023)第 094071 号

责任编辑：陈冬梅
装帧设计：刘孝琼
责任校对：吕丽娟
责任印制：宋　林
出版发行：清华大学出版社
　　　　　网　　址：http://www.tup.com.cn, http://www.wqbook.com
　　　　　地　　址：北京清华大学学研大厦 A 座　　　邮　　编：100084
　　　　　社 总 机：010-83470000　　　　　　　　　邮　　购：010-62786544
　　　　　投稿与读者服务：010-62776969, c-service@tup.tsinghua.edu.cn
　　　　　质量反馈：010-62772015, zhiliang@tup.tsinghua.edu.cn
　　　　　课件下载：http://www.tup.com.cn, 010-62791865
印 装 者：三河市少明印务有限公司
经　　销：全国新华书店
开　　本：185mm×260mm　　　印　张：17.5　　　字　数：426 千字
版　　次：2008 年 6 月第 1 版　2023 年 8 月第 3 版　　印　次：2023 年 8 月第 1 次印刷
定　　价：49.80 元

产品编号：087945-01

本书编委会

主　编：李　爽 (东北农业大学)

副主编：矫　萍 (广东财经大学)

　　　　胡大龙 (青岛大学)

编　委：李　爽 (东北农业大学)

　　　　矫　萍 (广东财经大学)

　　　　胡大龙 (青岛大学)

　　　　杨　红 (东北农业大学)

　　　　张宇慧 (海南大学)

　　　　张　鑫 (东北林业大学)

前　　言

在中国共产党第二十次全国代表大会上的报告第五部分第一条办好人民满意的教育：教育是国之大计、党之大计。培养什么人、怎样培养人、为谁培养人是教育的根本问题。育人的根本在于立德。本教材编写团队认真领会党对教育的要求，本教材符合党对高校人才培养要求，并阐释习近平新时代中国特色社会主义经济思想，深入讲述新发展阶段、新发展理念、新发展格局和"七个坚持"，坚持加强党对经济工作的集中统一领导，坚持以人民为中心的发展思想，坚持适应把握引领经济发展新常态，坚持市场在资源配置中起决定性作用、坚持推进供给侧结构性改革，坚持问题导向部署经济发展新战略，坚持正确工作策略和方法，稳中求进。引导学生充分认识到加快形成以国内大循环为主体、国内国际双循环相互促进新发展格局的重要现实意义，使学生认识到习近平新时代中国特色社会主义经济思想是党的十八大以来推动我国经济发展实践的理论结晶，是中国特色社会主义政治经济学的最新成果，开拓了 21 世纪马克思主义政治经济学的新境界。

"国际商务函电"是国际经济与贸易专业的主干课程之一。本课程旨在培养学生掌握对外贸易信函写作的基本知识，并能熟练地加以运用，这些能力是国际经济与贸易专业的学生必须具备的技能。国际商务函电作为国际商务往来经常使用的联系方式，是开展对外经济贸易业务和有关商务活动的重要工具。

全书分英汉两部分各十四个单元，按照实际交易程序组织——建立业务关系、询价、报价、还价、接受、开证、保险、租船订舱和索赔等内容，以国际商务应用文的写法和合同或合约的方式呈现。各单元的内容主要包括导读、样函、注释、常用语句、写作指导和练习，书末附有各单元导读和样函主体部分的译文，以及两套模拟试卷及其答案和各单元练习题的答案。

本书结构严谨，在层次上循序渐进、由浅入深，集国际经贸实务的中英文应用于一体，有利于学生更深入地学习，提高运用英文的能力，方便学生课后复习和自学。本书汲取了国内外同类书的一些新成果，紧密结合我国外经贸业务实际，总结和归纳了国际经贸业务中的常用术语、常用短语、句型结构和缩略语，有助于学生吸收和掌握国际经济与贸易前沿专业的知识。

本书第 3 版在第 2 版的基础上，增加了新的练习题，更换了原来的部分陈旧内容，对原有的部分注释进行了更新，使教材携带和使用更方便。

本书实用性强，针对国际经济与贸易专业的本科生、独立学院学生、高职高专学生及对外经济贸易工作人员，以实际应用为导向，增加写作实例的数量，便于学生自学。

本书由李爽教授担任主编，负责全书的设计和统稿工作，矫萍和胡大龙担任副主编。参编人员及具体的编写分工如下：李爽(东北农业大学)编写第一、二、八、九、十四单

元，杨红(东北农业大学)编写第三、六单元，张鑫(东北林业大学)编写第四、五单元，胡大龙(青岛大学)编写第七、十二、十三单元，矫萍(广东财经大学)编写第八、九、十四单元，张宇慧(海南大学)编写第十、十一单元。

　　由于编者的水平有限，书中难免有不足之处，敬请各位专家、老师和读者不吝指正。

编　者

目 录

Unit 1 Fundamentals of Business Letter Writing

【学习要点和目标】

通过本单元的学习，了解商务信函写作的基本知识，掌握商务信函写作的原则、格式、结构和方法。

Lead-in

In the business community today, the importance of good **communication** skills is even more stressed, as it is essential that employees can use the tools of the evolving information technology to communicate clearly, accurately and effectively.

Business communication is concerned with the successful exchange of messages that support the goal of buying and selling goods or other services. Business communication can be used in inquiring, ordering, negotiation, selling, marketing, complaining, etc. In international trade, most of the negotiation and contracts are signed through business letters. A business letter is legal. It is very important for both the form and the content.

So it is of very importance for students of business communication to master the skills of reading and writing a good business letter that presents ideas interestingly and clearly to enable readers to understand with least possible effort.

1. Principles of Business Letter Writing

A good business letter can play an important role in trade, increase friendship and obtain complete understanding between the parties involved. Business letter writing is one of the necessary business activities. Broadly speaking, the functions of a business letter may be said (1) to ask for or to convey information, (2) to make or to accept an offer, (3) to deal with matters concerning negotiation of business. In addition, there are letters with no other purpose than to remind the recipient of the sender's existence.

Letter-writing does not differ from any other form of creative writing. Good English is one of the important bases of good business letters. What you write should be free from grammatical blemishes, and also free from the slightest possibility of being misunderstood. There are certain essential qualities of business letters, which can be summed up in the Six Cs, as (1) **Clearness**, (2) Conciseness, (3) **Courtesy**, (4) Consideration, (5) Correctness, (6) Completeness.

(1) Clearness

First of all, make sure that your letter is so clear that it cannot be misunderstood. An **ambiguous** point in a letter will cause trouble to both sides, and further exchange of letters for explanation will become inevitable and time-wasting. Next, when you are sure about what you want to say, say it in plain, simple words. Good, straightforward, and simple English is necessary for business letters.

(2) Conciseness

Clearness and conciseness often go hand-in-hand and the elimination of wordy business jargon can help to make a letter clearer and more concise.

A concise letter is not necessarily a short one. Sometimes, a letter dealing perhaps with a multiplicity of matters cannot avoid being long. If conciseness conflicts with courtesy, make a little sacrifice of conciseness. Generally speaking, you will gain clearness and conciseness by writing short sentences rather than long ones.

A letter can be made clearer, easier to read and more attractive to look at by careful paragraphing. A paragraph for each point is a good rule.

(3) Courtesy

It should hardly be necessary to stress the importance of courtesy in your correspondence. One of the most important things is promptness, which will please your customer who dislikes waiting for days before he gets a reply to his letter.

It is nearly always wrong to doubt a statement made in good faith by the other side and even worse to contradict it. Differences are bound to occur in business, but with diplomacy and tact they can be overcome and settled without ill will on either side.

(4) Consideration

Consideration is an important rule of good business writing. The letters you send out must create a good impression. Try to put yourself in his place to give consideration to his varied wishes, demands, interests and difficulties. Emphasize the "You" attitude rather than the "I" or "We" attitude. In your letter you should always keep in mind the person you are writing to, see things from his point of view, visualize him in his surroundings, and see his problems and difficulties and express your idea in terms of his experience. Find the best way to express your better understanding and present the message.

Compare the following pairs of sentences:

(a) You-attitude

Congratulations to you on your success.

You earn a 2% discount for cash payment.

(b) I/We-attitude

I/We'd like to send my/our congratulations to you.

I/We allow you a 2% discount for cash payment.

Apparently, the "You" attitude is far better than the "I" or "we" attitude.

(5) Correctness

Correctness means not only proper expression with correct grammar, punctuation and spelling, but also appropriate tone, which is helpful to achieve the purpose. It is likely to convey the real message in a way that will not cause offense even if it is a complaint or an answer to such a letter. Business letters must have factual information, accurate figures and exact terms in particular, because they involve the rights, the duties and the interests of both sides, often as the base of all kinds of documents. Therefore, we should not understate nor overstate as understatement might lead to less confidence and hold up the trade development while overstatement would throw you in an awkward position.

(6) Completeness

A business letter is successful and functions well only when it contains all the necessary information. An outline helps for the letter to be full and complete. See to it that all the matters are discussed, and all questions are answered. Incompleteness is not only impolite but also leads to the recipient's unfavorable impression towards your firm.

He may give up the deal if other firms provide him with all the information needed, or if he would not take the trouble inquiring once again.

As you work hard for completeness, keep the following guidelines in mind: Why do you write the letter? What are the facts supporting the reasons? Have you answered the questions asked?

2. Layout of a Business Letter

It has long been customary to set it out in the semi-**indented** style (Specimen Letter 1). Many people regard this as the most attractive one of all letter styles. The **blocked** style is liked because it is compact and tidy. This style appeals to most readers. Some people like the indented paragraphing and claim that it makes for easy reading, others dislike the indentations because they claim that it wastes the typist's time. So the blocked style (Specimen Letter 2) has now come to be much more widely used than before.

The open style of punctuation in the inside name and address is often used with the modern letter style, but is not essential to it. Closed punctuation can also be used if preferred.

3. The Main Parts of a Business Letter

The business letter consists of seven principle parts: (1) the letter-head, (2) the date, (3) the inside name and address, (4) the **salutation**, (5) the message, (6) the **complimentary** close, (7) the writer's signature and official position.

(1) The Letter-head

The letter-head expresses a firm's personality. It helps to form one's impression of the writer's firm. Styles vary considerably, but they all give similar information. Besides the name and address of the firm, the letter-head may include telephone numbers, telegraphic addresses, telegraphic codes, telex numbers, and the kind of business carried on.

(2) The Date

Always type the date in full, in the logical order of day, month, year. For example: 12th October, 20×× or 12 October 20××

For the day, either **cardinal numbers** (1, 2, 3, 4, etc.) or **ordinal numbers** (1st, 2nd, 3rd, 4th, etc.) can be used, for example:

1st March 20×× or 1 March 20××

3rd April 20×× or 3 April 20××

29th October 20×× or 29 October 20××

The day can also be written after the month, for example:

March 1st, 20××

October 29, 20××

In this way, a comma must be used between the day and the year.

To give the day in figures (e.g., 12/10/20××) is in bad taste, and it may easily cause confusion because this date would mean 12th October 20×× in Britain, but it would mean 10th December 20×× in the United States and some other countries.

(3) The Inside Name and Address

The usual practice is to set out the name and address of one's correspondent at the head of the letter, as in specimen letter 1 and specimen letter 2. However, in official (i.e., Government) correspondence, it is sometimes placed at the foot, in the bottom left-hand corner.

Where the appropriate head of department is known, address the letter to him by his official title, for example:

> The Sales Manager
>
> The Hercules Engineering Co., Ltd.
>
> Brazennose Street
>
> Manchester M60 8AS
>
> England

When addressing a correspondent personally by name, take care to spell the name correctly.

English addresses may have the following parts (not all addresses have all the parts):

(a) Name of house.

(b) Number of house and name of street.

(c) Name of city or town.

(d) County or state and its postcode.

(e) Name of country.

To avoid ambiguity, when you write letters to other countries, always include the name of the country, even if the city mentioned is the country's capital. Here is an example:

> The Vice President
>
> The Eagle Press Inc.
>
> 24 South Bank
>
> Birmingham
>
> Alabama
>
> USA

In your correspondence, the use of Mr. and Messrs. as the courtesy titles is common. However, Messrs. (abbreviated from the French Messieurs) as the plural form of Mr. is used only for companies or firms, the names of which include a personal element, for example:

> Messrs. J. Harvey & Co.
>
> Messrs. MacDonald & Evans

(4) The Salutation

The salutation is the greeting with which every letter begins. The customary greeting in a business letter is "Dear Sir" or "Dear Sirs" (when a partnership is addressed). But the Americans usually use "Gentlemen" instead of "Dear Sirs". Note that you cannot use "Sirs" alone and that "Gentlemen" cannot be used in the singular. In American letters a colon is always placed after the salutation, for example:

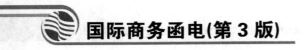
> Dear Mr. White:

Quite often now companies are owned and/or managed by women, and it is more and more customary to use the greeting: "Dear Madam" or "Sir", if the writer is not sure whether the letter will be read by a man or a woman.

(5) The Message

This forms the body of the letter and is the part that really matters. Before you begin to write, you must first of all consider the following two points:

(a) What is your aim of writing this letter?

(b) What is the best way to go about it?

Since the main purpose of the letter is to convey a message, the letter should be written in language that is easily understood. The following serves as reminders:

(a) Write simply, clearly, courteously, grammatically, and to the point.

(b) Paragraph correctly, confining each paragraph to one topic.

(c) Avoid stereotyped phrases and commercial jargon.

(6) The Complimentary Close

The complimentary close, like the salutation, is purely a matter of custom and a polite way of bringing a letter to a close. The expression used must suit the occasion. It must also match the salutation. The following salutations, with their matching closes, are the ones most commonly used in the modern business letters.

	Formal	Less Formal	Informal
Salutation	Dear Sir or Madam,	Dear Mr. Smith,	Dear Smith,
	Dear Sirs,	Dear Ms. Smith,	Dear Mary,
	Gentlemen:	Dear Mr. Green,	Dear Tom,
Complimentary Close	Yours faithfully,	Yours sincerely,	Sincerely,
	Faithfully yours,	Sincerely yours,	Cordially,
	Truly yours,	Cordially yours,	Best regards,

(7) The Writer's Signature and Official Position

The signature area mainly consists of the addresser's signature, the typed name of him immediately below the complimentary close. It is written in ink immediately below the complimentary close. To "sign" with a rubber stamp is a form of discourtesy. For example:

> Yours truly,
> *Frank W. Weston*
> Frank W. Weston
> General Manager
> Grand Resources Import & Export Co. Ltd.

4. Miscellaneous Matters

(1) Attention Line

An "attention line" leads the letter to a particular person or department when the letter is addressed to a company. It is usually typed two lines above the salutation, or underlined, and centered over the body of the letter, as shown below:

> Western Utilities, Inc.
>
> 817 West Main Street
>
> Denver, Colorado 80061
>
>
> Attention: Import Dept.
>
>
> Dear Mr. Green,
>
> …

Or

> Western Utilities, Inc.
>
> 817 West Main Street
>
> Denver, Colorado 80061
>
>
> <u>For the attention of Import Dept.</u>
>
>
> Dear Mr. Green:

(2) Subject Heading

The subject heading is regarded as a part of the body of a business letter. Usually it is in the upper case or initial capitals underlined. It is centered over the body of the letter except with the fully-blocked letter-style, and placed two lines below the salutation to call attention to what content the letter is about.

> Dear Sir,
>
> Subject: Your Order No. 1234

Or

> Dear Sir,
>
> SUBJECT: YOUR ORDER NO. 1234

Or

> Dear Sir,
>
> Subject: Your Orde No. 1234

(3) Reference

Reference numbers and letters enable replies to be linked with earlier correspondence and ensure that they reach the right person or department without delay. Many letter headings provide space for references. It may include a file number, departmental code or the initials of the signer of the letter to be followed by the typist initials. When giving the reference of a previous letter, to which the present letter is a reply, one should give the date of the earlier letter. Typical references might therefore be:

> Your ref. 23 TMR/AW/26 May 20××
>
> Our ref. 23HW/CONTRACT

(4) Enclosure

An enclosure notation should be added to the business letter, when such documents as **brochures**, **catalogues**, price lists, sales terms and conditions, etc. are attached to the letter. The enclosure notation follows two lines after the signature block. Type the word "Enclosure", or its abbreviation written as "Enc." or "Encl." with the number of enclosures or with a reference of their nature. Thus, a typical enclosure might be:

> Enclosures 2
>
> 1. Price List
>
> 2. Sales Confirmation

(5) Carbon Copy Notation

Carbon copy notation is used when copies of the letter are sent to others. Type "CC" or "cc" with the names of the persons who will receive the copies of the letter, usually positioned two lines below the signature block at the left margin. For example:

> (a) C C: The Bank of China
>
> (b) Copies to: Directors
>
> (c) CC to: CEO
>
> (d) **Copy to**: Sales Manager

(6) Postscript

When you find something forgotten to be included in the letter body before the envelope is to be sealed up, you may state it in a **postscript** with a simple signature again. The adding of a P.S.

should, however, be avoided as far as possible, since it may suggest you failed to plan your letter well before you wrote or dictated it. Sometimes it is not you really forget something, just you want to give the attention of the reader. If you forget to mention something important in the body of the letter, rewrite the letter instead of using the afterthought.

If unavoidable, write the P.S. two lines below any other notations, and flush with the left margin. For example:

> P.S. The catalogue will be sent to you tomorrow.

5. How to Address an Envelope

Envelope addressing calls for accuracy, legibility and good appearance. The envelope paper used should be the same in quality as the paper for letter and memo sheets. Stationery, format and forms adopted in business correspondence reflect the personality of a firm. Letterheads and envelopes should be imprinted with the same address and logo.

The address on the envelope and the inside address on the letter should be in the same style. It can be written in the indented style or blocked style. Block layout is mainly used in **superscription**. It is required in typing the envelopes together with open punctuation. Business stationery usually has the return address already printed in the upper left space of the envelope. The receiver's name and address should be typed on the envelope half way down leaving enough room for the stamp and postmark, and one third or one half in from the left of the envelope. Remarks of the post notation like "By Air Mail" or something like this should be placed in the bottom left-hand space.

Items below can be written on the envelope:

(1) It can be written on the left bottom of the envelope to give the remarks of the post notation.

(a) Via Air Mail (Par Avion).

(b) Via Air Mail Registered.

(c) Registered.

(d) Express.

(e) Parcel Post.

(f) Printed Matter.

(g) Sample Post.

(2) Private or Confidential letters can be remarked on the left bottom of the envelope.

(a) Private.

(b) Personal.

(c) Confidential.

(3) The following meaning should be noticed.

(a) "Attention", "Attention of" or "For the attention of" is used to express to whom the job should be done. For instance, "Attention (ATTN): Hardware Dept.".

(b) **c/o**, means "Care of".

(c) "Kind of …", "Per Kindness of …", "By Kindness of …" or "Through the Courtesy of…" means the person who transfers the letter. To give a letter by somebody, there's no necessary to write the address. It only states the name of the person who transfers the letter. For example:

> Mr. Charles Wood
> Kindness of Mr. Wang Ming

It means Mr. Wang Ming transfers the letter to Mr. Charles Wood.

B/D Corp.
123 Third Avenue
New York, NY10017
USA

(Stamp)
Registered

Mr. John Smith
c/o the Sales Manager
F & M Co., Ltd.
2000 Edward Street, Birmingham
United Kingdom

Confidential
By Air Mail

Specimen Letter 1   The Semi-indented Style

China National Import & Export Corporation, Limited

Cable address: CNIEC

Telephone No.: 123456

China National Import & Export co., Ltd.

Shanghai

China

Our Ref.: BG/1569

Your Ref.: CT-W

January 24, 20××

United Textiles Ltd.

York House

Lawton Street

Liverpool, ML3 2LL

England

Dear Sirs/Madams,

We are very pleased to receive your enquiry of 15th January and **enclose** our illustrated catalogue and price list giving the details you ask for. Also we are sending you some samples by separate post and feel confident that when you have examined them you will agree that the goods are both excellent in quality and reasonable in price.

On regular purchases in quantities of not less than 100 dozen of individual items we would allow you a discount of 2%. Payment is to be made by irrevocable L/C at sight.

Because of their softness and durability, our all cotton bed-sheets and pillowcases are rapidly becoming popular and after studying our prices you will learn that we are finding it difficult to meet the demand. But if you place your **order** not later than the end of this month, we would ensure prompt shipment.

We invite your attention to our other products such as table cloth and table napkins, details of which you will find in the catalogue, and look forward to receiving your first order.

Yours sincerely,

China National Import & Export co., Ltd.

Zhang Hong

Manager

Enclosures 2

Illustrated Catalogue

Price List

Specimen Letter 2   The Blocked Style

Brownson, Clarke & Co., Ltd

Leadenhall Street

London E. C. 4

England

Date: 26th June, 20××

China National Import & Export Co., Ltd.

Qingdao

China

Dear Sirs/Madams:

L/C No.3179

In reply to your letter of 18th June, we wish to inform you that we have instructed our bank, the Midland Bank, to amend the above L/C by inserting the following clause:

"Invoice in quintuplicate to be certified by the China Council for the Promotion of International Trade" to replace "Invoice in quintuplicate to be certified by British Consul at your end" as originally stipulated in the subject L/C.

As the amendment was made by cable, you must have received it prior to the arrival of this letter.

We trust that everything is now in order and you will be able to ship the goods in the first half of next month.

Should your goods prove to be satisfactory upon arrival are confident that further large orders will be placed.

We are looking forward to hearing from you about the shipment of the goods.

Yours sincerely,

Brownson, Clarke & Company

Manager

Notes

1. communication *n.* 交流，通讯；通信

communicate *v.* 沟通；联系；交流；表达

This communication is confidential. 这是机密信件。

All communications with foreign countries had been stopped for 2 hours. 与国外的联系已中断两个小时。

The manager communicates with his sales representative in Paris every day. 这个经理每天都要与驻巴黎的销售代表通信。

2. clearness *n.* 明晰，清楚

3. courtesy *n.* 礼貌

courtesy of 经由……提供；蒙……好意

by courtesy 礼貌起见

by courtesy of 蒙……的好意；由于……的作用

By extending the courtesy of a phone call to my clients, I was building a personal relationship with them. 通过给客户打电话这种有礼貌的行为，我渐渐地和他们建立起了私交。

4. ambiguous *adj.* 含混不清的；模棱两可的

5. layout *n.* 格式，布局；设计，安排

layout design 布局设计

general layout 总体设计

page layout 页面布局

He tried to recall the layout of the farmhouse. 他试着回忆那农舍的布局。

6. indent

(1) *v.* 缩行

(2) *n.* 缩进；凹痕；契约

Indent the second line. 第二行行首留空格。

Obviously, being able to perform operations on blocks is useful, whether it is indent/outdent, cut/copy/paste, or template. 很显然，分块执行操作会很有用，无论是缩进/突出、剪切/复制/粘贴，还是使用模板。

7. block *v.* 齐头

blocked style 齐头格式

indented style 缩进格式

semi-indented style 混合格式

8. salutation   *n.* 称呼

9. complimentary   *adj.* 问候的，称赞的；免费赠送的；祝贺的

10. cardinal number 基数

    ordinal number 序数

11. reference

    (1) *n.* 涉及，提及；参考；参考书目

    (2) *v.* 参考

    for reference 以供参考

    The firm offered to give her a reference. 公司提出给她开一封推荐信。

    The official at the American embassy asked me for two references. 美国大使馆的官员要我提供两名证明人。

    with reference to=in reference to 关于

    Please keep this sheet in a safe place for reference. 请把这张纸放在稳妥的地方以备查阅。

12. brochure   *n.* 宣传手册

13. catalogue   *n.* 目录；一览表

14. copy to   抄至……

15. postscript   *n.* 附言

16. superscription   *n.* 书写在某物外面的文字，如信封上的地址。

17. c/o(care of)   used when addressing letters to mean "at the address of" 由……转交

18. Esq. (Esquire)   *n.* 先生

19. enclose   *v.* 把……封入，把……附在信中

    We enclose herewith a price list and the latest catalog. 随信附上价格单和最新的产品目录。

20. order   *v.* & *n.* 订单；订购

    The city is going to place an order for one hundred and eighty-eight buses. 这个城市将下单订购188辆公交车。

Exercises

I. Answer the following questions.

1. How many principal parts is a business letter composed of ? What are they?

14

2. What are the principles of writing business letters?

3. What are the two layouts of a business letter?

4. What is the position of the receiver's address on an envelope?

5. What is the position of the writer's address on an envelope?

6. What is the P.S.?

II. Write a letter using the items given below, inserting the necessary capitals and punctuation.

1. Heilongjiang Textiles Import & Export Company, No.54, Youyi Road, Harbin, China

2. The New Century Trading Co., Ltd., P.O. Box No. 323, Lagos, Nigeria

3. September 5, 20××

4. Dear Sirs

5. Your ref.: WC323/20××

6. Our ref.: FH3/20××

7. Yours faithfully

8. Manager, Li Hong

III. Address an envelope in blocked style using the following names and addresses.

1. The sender: Mr. Zhang Guang, China National Chemical Corporation, No.62 West Beisihuan Road, Haidian District, Beijing, China

2. The receiver: Mr. Albert Woodrow, Managing Director, Horizon Stationery Corporation, Melbourne, Australia

Unit 1 补充练习   Unit 1 补充练习答案   Unit 1 练习答案

Unit 2　Establishment of Business Relations

【学习要点和目标】

通过本单元的学习，了解与新客户建立业务关系的重要性，以及如何获得对方的信息，掌握撰写此类信函的方法和词汇。

Lead-in

In order to open up a market to sell or buy something from the other firms or maintain or expand business activities, **establishing business relations** is the first step in a transaction in foreign trade.

Writing letters to new customers for the establishment of relations is a common practice in business communications. First, you must find out whom you are going to deal with. Anyway, to establish business relations with prospective dealers is very important, especially for some newly established firms. So, before you correspond with them you'd better do some credit investigations such as financial conditions, business activities, honesty integrity and so on.

At the same time, you should pay more attention to those old customers. Be sure not to leave them out.

There are several channels through which you can obtain the desired names and addresses of the firms to be dealt with.

1. Banks.

2. Chambers of Commerce in foreign countries.

3. Trade Directory.

4. Chinese Commercial Counsellor's Office in foreign countries.

5. Business Houses of the same trade, etc.

6. Advertisements.

7. Exhibitions and Trade Fairs.

After obtaining the information from any of the sources mentioned above you can write "First Letter" or "Circulars" to the other party.

Generally speaking, this kind of letter begins by telling the addressee how you obtained his

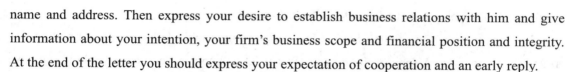

name and address. Then express your desire to establish business relations with him and give information about your intention, your firm's business scope and financial position and integrity. At the end of the letter you should express your expectation of cooperation and an early reply.

If you are interested in buying some products, you may ask for samples, price-lists, catalogues or other reference materials. No matter what you are interested in buying or selling, your letter should be written politely, simply, clearly and concisely.

The first impression matters very much. Be positive to follow the standard format and try best to avoid making mistakes. Be sure to answer in full without the least delay after you receive any letter of this nature. Only in this way can you create goodwill and leave a good impression on the reader.

Notes

1. establish business relations with 与······建立业务关系

    restore/cement/preserve/improve/promote/enlarge/interrupt/speed up business relations with 与······恢复/巩固/保持/改善/促进/扩大/中断/加快业务关系

Specimen Letter 1   Asking for Establishing Business Relations

China Textiles Import & Export Co., Ltd.

September 30, 20××

African Trading Company Ltd.

276 Whirlpool Road

Accra

Ghana

Dear Sirs,

Having learnt your name and address through the Commercial Counsellor's Office of our Embassy, we **avail ourselves of this opportunity** to write to you and see if we can establish business relations with you.

We are a **state-owned** import and export company **specializing** in cotton products such as tablecloths, and **in a position to** accept orders according to customers' samples, specifying designs, **specifications** and **packaging** requirements. We are also prepared to accept orders for goods with customers' own **trademarks** or **brand names**.

In order to give you a rough idea of our various cotton tablecloths, we are airmailing you **under separate cover** a copy of these items. Please let us know as soon as possible if you have any interest. We shall be glad to send **quotations** and samples upon receipt of your **concrete enquiries**.

We await your early reply.

Yours truly,

Liu Yun

Manager: Liu Yun

China Textiles Import & Export Co., Ltd.

Notes

1. avail ourselves of this opportunity 我们利用这次机会

2. state-owned 国有的

3. specialize *v.* 专门从事

   to be specialized in 专门经营

   We are specialized in a variety of silk piece goods. 我们专门经营各种丝绸品。

   A university professor who specializes in the history of the Russian empire. 一位专门研究沙俄历史的大学教授。

4. in a position to = be able to 可以做

5. specification *n.* 规格

6. packaging *n.* 包装

7. trademark *n.* 商标

8. brand name *n.* 品牌

9. under separate cover = by separate mail 另邮，另寄

10. quotation *n.* 报价

    quotation sheet 报价单

    price quotation 报价；价目

    Get several written quotations and check exactly what's included in the cost. 弄几份书面报价来，并查清楚成本中包含哪些内容。

11. concrete *adj.* definite; positive 明确的，确定的

12. enquiry *n.* an instance of questioning 询问；询盘

18

We're very interested in some of your products. Here is an enquiry sheet we've drawn up.
我们对你们的一些产品很感兴趣，这是我们拟订的询价单。

Specimen Letter 2   Asking for Establishing Business Relations

China National Chemicals Import & Export Corp.
Shanghai China

Telegram Address: CNCIEC Shanghai
Telephone No.: …
Telex No.: …
Fax.: (021) …

November 15, 20×　×

Messrs Wallace Kimber & Co.

40 Nsukka Road

P. O. Box 57183

Accra

Ghana

Dear Sirs,

We have your name and address from the Commercial Counsellor's Office of the Chinese Embassy in Ghana. We wish to inform you that we **specialize** in both industrial and **pharmaceutical** chemicals, and shall be pleased **to enter into** trade relations with you.

To give you a general idea of our products, we enclose **a complete set of leaflets** showing various products being handled by this cooperation with detailed **specifications** and means of packing. Quotations and **samples** will be sent upon receipt of your specific enquiries.

Business between us will be concluded on the basis of shipping quality and weight, while testing and inspection will be made by the Shanghai Commodity Inspection Bureau prior to shipment. Necessary **certificates** in regard to the quality and quantity of the shipment will, of course, be provided.

We look forward to your early reply with much interest.

Yours sincerely,

(signature)

Manager

China National Chemicals Import & Export Corp.

Notes

1. specialize   *v.* 专门从事

    specialize in   专门研究

2. pharmaceutical   *adj.* 药物的

3. to enter into/start upon/begin to take part in   开始，建立，达成

    to enter into business relations = to establish business relations   建立业务关系

4. a complete set of   一整套的，全套的

5. leaflet   *n.* 散页印刷品，小册子

6. specification   *n.* 规格

7. sample   *n.* 样品

8. bureau   *n.* 局

9. certificate   *n.* 证明书

Specimen Letter 3   Asking for Establishing Business Relations

Dear Sirs,

We are writing to you at the suggestion of our bankers, the Chartered Bank of Australia. We **take the liberty to** introduce ourselves as exporters of ox hide, which we have been exporting to Europe and Japan.

We are specialized in the above business and recall that many years ago, considerable business was done with your country on such items. Now that the diplomatic relation between our two countries has been established, we **are desirous of** establishing direct business relations with your corporation, knowing that you are the buyer of Australian ox hides.

We shall be grateful if you will let us know whether you are interested in the above hides. If so, please **advise us of** the quantity required.

Yours faithfully,

(Signature)

Notes

1. take the liberty to do… / to venture to do… 冒昧做……

   I should take the liberty of putting forward a new proposal. 我冒昧提个建议。

2. be desirous of doing… / to be desirous to do… 渴望做……

   We are desirous of being able to get the business done at a lower price. 我们渴望能以较低的价格达成此项交易。

3. We shall be grateful if… 如果……我们将非常感激。

4. to advise sb. of sth. / to inform sb. of sth. 通知、告知某人某事

   常用句型还有：

   to advise sb. that-clause; to inform sb. that-clause

   to advise sb. sth.; to inform sb. sth.

   Please advise us (of) the name of the steamer. 请告知我方船名。

   Please advise us what quantity you can supply a year. 请告知你方一年能供货的数量。

   We were informed that the shipment had arrived and been found satisfactory. 我们被告知船已到达，并且货物完好。

   Please inform us the date of sailing and the name of the steamer. 请告知起航日期和船名。

   We are informed by the local shipping company that 10 parcels of the goods are missing during transit. 我们从当地船公司获知在运输途中货物丢失 10 包。

   to instruct sb. to do sth. 通知、指示某人做……

   We have instructed our bank to open an confirmed irrevocable letter of credit. 我方已指示银行开立保兑的、不可撤销的信用证。

Specimen Letter 4　Reply to a Letter of Establishing Business Relations

China National Import & Export Corp.

Shanghai China

Telegram Address: CNIEC Shanghai

Telephone No.: ...

Telex No.: …

Fax.: (021)…

Your ref.: JM/MD

December 9, 20×.×

Messrs Ribera Y Cio

Avenida Yucatan 56

MEXICO CITY

Mexico

Dear Sirs,

　　With reference to your letter of December 2, 20×.×, we are glad to learn that you wish to enter into trade relations with this corporation in the line of canned goods.

　　In compliance with your request, we are sending you by air a **catalogue** together with a range of **pamphlets** for your reference.

　　If any of the items listed in the catalogue meets your interest, please let us have your specific enquiry, and our quotation will be forwarded without delay.

　　In the meantime, you are requested to furnish us with the name of your bank **prior to** the conclusion of the first transaction between us.

Yours sincerely,

(Signature)

China National Import & Export Corp.

Notes

1. in compliance with / in accordance with (U.S.A. to) / in line with / according to / to conform to / to comply with 与……相一致，按照，遵照

　　In compliance with your wishes, we are sending you herewith the required proforma invoice. 按照你方的要求，我们给您邮寄了形式发票。

2. catalogue

(1) *n.* 目录，a complete list of articles, usually in alphabetical order, or under special headings, and often with descriptions of the articles

(2) *v.* 编目录，make a catalogue / compile a catalogue

3. pamphlet　*n.* 小册子

4. prior to / before　在……之前

Specimen Letter 5　Reply to a Letter of Establishing Business Relations

Dear Sirs,

We thank you for your letter of April 1, from which we note that you are desirous of establishing business relations with us. As we are always willing to do business **on the basis of equality and mutual benefit** with those who desire to trade with us, we welcome you too.

Under separate cover, we are sending you **a range of pamphlets** to give you a general idea of our products. Please advise us of your specific requirements and we will make our offer promptly.

Yours faithfully,

(Signature)

Notes

1. on the basis of (equality and mutual benefit)　在(平等互利的)基础上

We do business with foreign businessmen on the basis of equality and mutual benefit.
我们与外商在平等互利的基础上做生意。

2. a range of pamphlets　一系列小册子

Specimen Letter 6　Asking to Provide Sales Agency Service

Dear Sirs,

We understand that you have no agent in China and we would like to offer services.

For the past ten years we have been selling various **durable** goods to **wholesalers** and large

retailers in all the major cities of China, and have built up a **considerable** number of well-established connections showing excellent business results.

Until recently we were not in a position to look for additional lines, as we were concentrating our efforts on sales of these lines. However, we have now enough ability to **expand our sales**, and if you agree to grant us a **sole agency** we will devote full attention to establish your products on our market.

If you are interested in our **proposal**, we should be pleased to provide our bank and trade **reference**.

Yours faithfully,

(Signature)

Notes

1. durable   *adj.* 耐用的

2. wholesaler   *n.* 批发商

3. retailer   *n.* 零售商

4. considerable   *adj.* 可观的

5. expand sales   扩大销售

6. sole agency   独家代理

7. proposal   *n.* 建议；提议；求婚

The president is to put forward new proposals for resolving the country's constitutional crisis. 总统将提出解决国家宪法危机的新议案。

After a three-weekend courtship, Pam accepted Randy's proposal of marriage. 经过 3 个周末的恋爱，帕姆接受了兰迪的求婚。

8. reference   证明书，证明人，参考

We note that you will supply references as they are quite necessary to us. 鉴于证明书的重要性，我方知悉你方将向我方提供该文件。

A market report will be sent to you for your reference. 我方将邮寄一份市场报告给您，供你方参考。

Their reference is the Bank of China. 他们的证明人是中国银行。

You may refer to our letter reference No.233 concerning your requirement. 关于你们的需求，你方可以参考我方参考号为 233 的信件。

Specimen Letter 7   Try to Resume the Old Business Relations

Dear Sir,

In **casting a retrospective glance** through our accounts for the past year, we observe that we have not had any orders from you for quite a long time.

Assuming that you are still in the market for the class of goods we handle, **we would be grateful if** you would inform us of the intentions and purposes of your **imminent** sales. If you have any comments or suggestions **in respect of placing orders** with us, please **lay your case before us** so that we may **give it our careful study**.

We **presume** that you may be interested to know that we have made a series of improvements in our products, both in workmanship and in packaging. Under separate cover, we will send you the latest samples you regularly ordered. You will find that they will meet your requirements just well and will **induce** you to **resume** and develop our friendly business connections.

We look forward to receiving your **positive response**.

Very truly yours,

(Signature)

Notes

1. cast a…glance 看……一眼

2. retrospective   *adj.* 回顾

3. assume   *vt.* (在未证实前)假定；accept without verification or proof 以为；take power or responsibility 接受(权利、责任)

   You assume his innocent before hearing the evidence against him. 在未听到对他不利的证言之前，你假定他是无罪的。

   It is a misconception to assume that the two continents are similar. 假设这两块大陆类似是种错误的概念。

   Mr. Cross will assume the role of CEO with a team of four directors. 克罗斯先生将担任由 4 位总监组成的团队的首席执行官一职。

4. We would be grateful if… 我们将非常感激……

5. imminent   *adj.* 逼近的，即将发生的

6. in respect of　关于，就……而言；涉及

7. place an order　下订单

8. lay your case before us　不吝向我方提出

9. give it our careful study　我方慎重研究

10. presume　*v.* 以为；认定，推测，假定

In Britain an accused man is presumed (to be) innocent until he is proved guilty.　在英国，被告在未证实有罪以前，仍被认作是无辜的。

I presume you're here on business.　我想你是来这出差的吧。

"Had he been home all week?"　"他整个星期都在家吗？"

"I presume so."　"我想是。"

11. induce sb. to do sth. = persuade or influence / lead or cause　诱导；促使(某人做某事)

12. resume　*vt.* 停止后续续；重新开始；恢复

After the war he resumed his duties at Wellesley College.　那场战争之后，他恢复了在韦尔斯利学院的任职。

13. positive / active / energetic / vigorous　*adj.* 积极的

positive response　积极的答复

Useful Sentences

1. We avail ourselves of this opportunity to write to you and see if... 我们利用这次机会向您写信，看看是否能……

2. We are a state-owned import and export company specializing in... 我们是国营的进出口公司，专营……方面的业务。

3. Accept orders according to customers' samples, specifying designs, specifications and packaging requirements. 接受根据客户的样品定做或有特殊的设计、规格和包装要求的订单。

4. In order to give you a rough idea of..., we are airmailing you a copy of... under separate cover 为了让您对……有一个大致的了解，我们正另空运寄给您……

5. We are willing to enter into business relations with your firm on the basis of equality and mutual benefit. 我们正准备与你公司在平等互利的基础上建立业务联系。

6. We have come to know the name of your corporation and have the pleasure of writing this letter to you in the hope of establishing business relations with you. 我们已获知您公司的名称，并且非常高兴写这封信，希望同你公司建立业务关系。

7. Your letter expressing the hope of entering into business connection with us has been received with thanks. 感谢您此前来信表示愿意与我方建立业务关系。

8. We owe your name and address to…through which we learn that you were seeking partners in China for selling your…products. 我们从……获知你公司的名称和地址，并得知你公司正在中国寻求……产品销售的合作伙伴。

9. We have been in the line of…for many years. 我们已从事……行业很多年了。

10. Our competitive prices, superior quality and efficiency have won confidence and goodwill among our business clients. 我们的产品价格具有竞争力，品质上乘，我们的工作效率也很高，这使我们在商业客户中赢得了信誉。

11. Our market survey informs us that you have a keen interest in the import of… 我们的市场调研显示您对进口我们的……产品非常感兴趣。

12. We are writing to you in the hope that we can open up business relations with your firm. 我们写信给您，希望与你公司开展贸易往来。

13. We shall be grateful if you will reply at an early date. 如果您能及早回复，我们将非常感激。

Letter-writing Guide

The steps and expressions to write a letter for establishing business relations are as follows. (建立业务关系的信函的写作步骤及常见表达方式如下。)

Writing steps (写作步骤)	Examples of expressions (表达方式举例)
1. 说明信息来源(告知对方你从何种渠道得知对方公司的情况)	Your company has been kindly introduced to us by… 贵公司由……介绍给我们。
	We learn through/from…that… 我们通过……得知……
	We have your name and address from… 我们从……获知你公司的名称和地址。
	On the recommendation of… 由……推荐……
2. 对你的公司做简单的介绍(例如公司的业务范围等)	We wish to introduce ourselves to you as a… 我们把自己作为……介绍给你们。

续表

2. 对你的公司做简单的介绍(例如公司的业务范围等)	We have been in the line of…for many years. 我们从事……行业已经很多年。
	We wish to inform you that we specialize in… 我们希望告知您我公司从事……业务。
	…fall within our business activities. ……属于我们的经营范围。
3. 表达写信目的	We are willing to enter into business relations with you. 我们愿意和贵方建立业务关系。
	We express our desire to… 我方愿意……
	We are writing to you in the hope that we can open up business relations with your firm. 我们写信给贵公司,希望同你公司建立业务关系。
	We are desirous of… 我方愿意……
4. 表达与对方合作及早日收到回复的愿望	We look forward to receiving… 希望早日收到……
	Hope to receive… 希望收到……
	Your early reply is appreciated. 盼早回复。
	We are anticipating your answer. 盼早回复。

The steps and expressions to reply for establishing business relations are as follows. (回复建立业务关系的信函的写作步骤及常见表达方式如下。)

Writing steps (写作步骤)	Examples of expressions (表达方式举例)
1. 感谢对方对你公司的兴趣	Your letter expressing the hope of establishing business connection with us has been received with thanks. 非常感谢你方关于愿意同我方建立业务关系的信。
	Thank you for your interest in… 感谢你们对……的兴趣。
	We note with pleasure from our Commercial Counsellor in…that you are interested in establishing business relations with us on the supply of… 我们高兴地从驻……商务参赞处得知你方对供应……而与我方建立业务关系感兴趣。
	Your letter of August 8 has been received with thanks. 感谢贵方8月8日的来信。
2. 表示愿意与对方建立业务关系	Your wish of establishing business relations coincides with ours. 你们建立业务关系的愿望和我们不谋而合。
	This is also our desire. 这也是我们的愿望。
	We shall be very glad/pleased to enter into direct business relations with you. 我们将非常高兴与你们建立直接的业务关系。
3. 下一步将要进行的工作	We are sending you our catalogue and price list. 我们将给你方寄去我们的目录和价格表。
	We shall be glad to have your specific inquiry. 我们将很高兴得到你方的具体询价。

Exercises

I. Put the following English phrases into Chinese or Chinese phrases into English.

1. up to date   2. bottom/favorable price   3. have extensive connections with

4. in the line of business   5. in compliance with   6. 另外邮寄   7. 在国外的商会

8. 中国驻国外商务处   9. 同业商行   10. 贸易行名录

II. Fill in the blanks of the following letter with the words given below, and change the form when necessary.

| inform   establish   reputation   proposal   specialized |
| opportunity   purpose   interest   owe |

Dear Sirs,

We ___1___ your name and address from ABC Company, who has ___2___ us that you are ___3___ in entering the market in China. We hope to ___4___ business relations with you for the ___5___ of marketing your products here.

We like to take this ___6___ to introduce ourselves as one of the leading companies in China mainly ___7___ in electronic products, with high ___8___ and reliable outlets.

To give you a general idea of our company, we are sending you separately a copy of our brochure. Any ___9___ concerning cooperation will be given our immediate consideration.

We are looking forward to your early reply.

Yours faithfully,

(Signature)

III. Translate the following English into Chinese or Chinese into English.

1. Our company is one of the leading manufacturers of silk products in China, with the headquarter based in Beijing, China.

2. Silk products fall within the scope of our business activities.

3. Please send us your samples and the price list, as well as information about terms of payment and time of delivery.

4. Your prompt reply is highly appreciated.

5. The firm enjoys the fullest respect and unquestionable confidence in the business world.

6. 我们很高兴与贵方建立直接的贸易关系。

7. 如能收到贵公司有关商品说明书，我们将不胜感激。

8. 对贵方所提供的任何资料，我们都予以保密。

9. 按照你方要求，我们附上一套小册子(说明书)连同价格单，供参考。若你方对所列商品感兴趣，请告知具体需求。我方收到询价后，将立即寄送报价单。

10. 为了使贵方对我们经营的产品有一个概念，兹附上一整套注有规格和包装要求的活页说明书。

IV. Writing practice.

Write a letter with the following hints.

1. 从中国驻美国使馆商务处得知贵公司。

2. 贵公司从事纺织业。

3. 我公司出口纺织品。希望建立业务关系，并附寄产品目录和价格单。

Unit 2 补充练习   Unit 2 补充练习答案   Unit 2 练习答案

Unit 3　Inquiries and Replies

【学习要点和目标】

通过本单元的学习，掌握询价和答复信函的写作要点。

Lead-in

Inquiries are made when a businessperson intends to purchase certain goods or obtain desired services. The buyer usually sends an inquiry to invite a quotation or an offer from the seller; therefore inquiries mean potential business for both the buyer and the seller.

Based on the inquired contents, inquiries can be divided into general inquiries and specific inquiries. The writer of a general inquiry, asks for general information, a catalogue, a price list, or a sample book, while that of a specific inquiry focuses on the detailed information about the specific target goods or services. A satisfactory inquiry will include the following:

1. Source of information, asking for a catalogue and a price list.

2. Introduction of the seller or the buyer's general information and business scope, statement of the products of interest.

3. Quantity discounts and terms of payments (such as FOB, CIF etc.).

4. Terms of delivery.

5. Hope for reply.

As mentioned above, an inquiry means potential business to be established; therefore the reply to it should be prompt and courteous and cover all the requested information. A reply to an inquiry and especially to a first inquiry should be handled with special care to create goodwill. When the goods inquired are out of stock, the seller should inform the buyer of the reason and when the goods will be available. If the goods asked have no longer been produced, or special request cannot be met, the seller needs to answer the inquiry with care and avoids making direct refusal that may offend the other party. Besides, the seller must make sure that all the questions asked in an inquiry have been answered in the reply, and if there are many questions to reply to, bullets or numbers are recommended to enumerate them. A satisfactory reply will include the following:

1. Pleased to receive the inquiry.

2. Mention that the product catalogue and price list asked for in the inquiry are enclosed in

the letter.

3. Emphasize the competitive quotation and tell clearly available discount.

4. Declare terms of payment and delivery service available.

5. Hope for early reply.

Specimen Letter 1   Make an Inquiry after Reading an Advertisement

Dear Sirs,

We have obtained the information of your company from *21 Century* and are pleased to know that you are one of the **principal producers and exporters** of Chinese Cotton. We **are desirous of** entering into direct business relations with you. We assure that this happens to **coincide** with your desire.

At present, we are interested in ramie cotton printed shirt and shall be pleased to receive catalogues, samples and all necessary information **regarding** these goods from you by airmail so as to acquaint us with the quality and workmanship of your supplies. Meanwhile please **quote** us your **floor price**, CIF Vancouver, **inclusive of our 5% commission**, stating the earliest date of shipment.

Provided your price is found competitive and delivery date is acceptable, we intend to **place a large order with you**.

We trust you will give us an early reply.

Sincerely yours,

(Signature)

Notes

1. inquiry *v.* 询盘，又作 enquiry，指交易一方准备购买或出售某种商品，向对方询问买卖该商品的有关交易条件，又称询价。

We thank you for your inquiry of Aug. 23rd for ground nut kernels. 感谢你方 8 月 23 日关于花生仁的询盘。

They promised to transfer their future enquiries to China corporations. 他们答应将今后的询盘转给中国各公司。

We can not make offers without specific enquiries. 没有具体询盘我们无法报盘。

Your enquiries will receive our prompt and careful attention at all times. 你方询盘随时

都会得到我们立即并认真的关注。

2. principal producer and exporter 主要的/最大的生产商和出口商

They are the principal producer and exporter of this class of goods here. 他们是本地此类商品最大的生产商和出口商。

3. be desirous of 渴望，想要

desire 期望，渴望，要求，请求

We are desirous of entering into direct business relations with you. 我们热切盼望与你方建立直接的贸易关系。

What do you desire to buy at present? 你方目前想要买些什么？

It is desired that the catalogues shall be airmailed to us within one week. 热切盼望在一周内给我们航空邮寄目录本。

4. coincide *v.* (意见等)一致；(时间上)相同

We are glad that our ideas coincide. 很高兴我们双方意见一致。

Your inquiry coincided with our offer. 你方询盘正好与我方报盘同时发出。

5. regarding *prep.* 关于，与 with regard to 和 in regard to 同义

We have already written to you regarding this matter. 关于此事我们已致信你方。

Regarding the balance, we will advise you of the position in a few days. 关于剩余数量的情况，我们将于几日内告知你方。

6. quote *v.* 报价

quote sb. a price for sth.

quote sb. for sth.

Please quote us your lowest price for walnuts. 请向我方报核桃最低价。

Please quote us for walnuts. 请向我方报核桃价格。

7. floor price = rock-bottom price 最低价；其反义词为 ceiling price 最高价。

8. inclusive of our 5% commission 包括我方 5%的佣金

This offer is inclusive of your 2% commission. = This offer includes your 2% commission. 此报盘包括你方 2%的佣金。

9. provided *conj.* 如果，假若，词义相当于 if，但强调"以……为条件"。

Provided (that) you can guarantee regular supplies, we may place bulk orders with you. 如果你方能保证经常供货，我们就能大量订购。

We accept your order provided shipment is made in March. 如能三月装船，我们就接受你方订单。

10. order

(1) *v.* 订购，订货

If you allow us 10% discount, we will order 10,000 dozen. 如果你方给予10%的折扣，我们将订购10000打。

place a large order with you 向你方大量订货

(2) *n.* 作为名词时，order 常与动词 make，send，place 等连用，表示订购某项货物，其后接介词 for。

If your price is in line, we will send you an order for 5,000 sets. 如果你方价格与市场相符，我们将订购5000台。

Specimen Letter 2   Customers Interested in the Displayed Products

Gentlemen:

As one of the largest textile companies in Pakistan, we are interested in the machine you **displayed** at **the Spring Commodities Fair**. We **are in urgent need of** the machines for **replacement** of our outdated ones. Please let us have your latest CFR **Karachi** prices, together with your terms of payment and the earliest delivery date. Thank you **in advance** for your close attention to this matter.

Yours truly,

(Signature)

Notes

1. display   *v.* 展览；展示；陈列

   a fashion display 时装展览

   the exhibition display 陈列的展览品

   Department stores display their goods in the window. 商店在橱窗陈列商品。

2. The Spring Commodities Fair 春季商品交易会

   The Chinese Export Commodities Fair 中国出口商品交易会

   mini fair 小型交易会

3. be in urgent need of sth. 急需某物

   be in need of sth. 需要某物

   be in badly need of sth. 急需某物

be in dire need of sth. 急需某物

be in great need of sth. 急需某物

Please do your utmost to expedite the shipment of our order as our buyers are in urgent need of the goods. 请尽快装运我方所订购货物，因为我方买主急需该货。

4. replacement　*n.* 替换物；更换

We request your replacement of the goods as it is stipulated in the contract. 要求你方按合同规定更换货物。

5. Karachi　*n.* 卡拉奇港，是巴基斯坦最大、最繁忙的港口，处理大约 60% 的全国货运。

6. in advance 尽早；预先；事先；提前

Please keep us fully informed as far in advance as possible. 请尽早详细告知我们。

We thank you for your close cooperation in advance. 我们对您的密切合作预致谢意。

Specimen Letter 3　Asking for the Catalogue and Price List

Dear Sirs,

Seeing your advertisement in the *American Trade Directory*, will you kindly send us as soon as possible your latest price list of Men's Coats, and synthetic fiber goods, with the lowest **quotations**, **discounts** and **terms** of payment, together with an illustrated **catalogue**.

We shall be pleased to be informed of your financial condition and business standing. Ours is the American City Bank, Hong Kong.

Your early reply will be **appreciated**.

Sincerely yours,

(Signature)

Notes

1. quotation　*n.* 报价，与动词 make，send，give，cable，fax 连用，后接介词 for，有时也接 of。

   quotation sheet 报价单

   Please quote us your most favorable price CIF Seattle for the above goods, including 5% of our commission. 请就上述货物向我方报 CIF 西雅图的最优惠价，含佣金 5%。

   We are going to give you a quotation which is based upon the prevailing international market price. 我们准备按当前的国际市场价格给您报价。

Your quotation of Men's Shirts is too high to be acceptable. 你方男士衬衫的报价过高，不能接受。

2. discount *n.&v.* 折扣，打折

The highest discount we can allow (give, make, grant) on this article is 10%. 我们对这项商品最多只能打九折。

The rate of discount in London is now 5%. 现在伦敦的贴现率是 5%。

If you can discount your price by 10%, we are ready to take 300 bales. 如果你方价格能予以九折处理，我方即订购 300 包。

Bills can be easily discounted in London. 汇票在伦敦贴现毫无障碍。

3. term *n.* 期间；条款；条件

It is not our practice to accept term L/C. 我们一般不接受远期信用证。

The rights of agent are clearly defined in Term No.7 of the Agreement. 代理人的权利在协议的第七条中已明确定义。

We can not do business on your terms. 我们不能按照你方的条件进行交易。

4. catalogue *n.* 目录

classified catalogue 分类目录

descriptive catalogue 带有说明的目录

illustrated catalogue 有插图的目录

catalogue of industrial products 工业产品目录

5. appreciate *v.* 感谢，感激

We highly appreciate your kind cooperation. 对您的友好合作，我方表示衷心的感谢。

We shall appreciate you sending us a sample book soon. 若你方邮寄来样品册，我们将不胜感激。

Specimen Letter 4   Sending Catalogues and Price Lists

Dear Sirs,

　　We welcome your inquiry of 26 December and thank you for your interest in our hand-made artificial leather gloves. **As requested**, we are enclosing our illustrated catalogue and price list giving the details you asked for. Also under separate cover, we are sending you a full range of samples and, when you have a chance to **examine** them, we feel **confident** that you will agree that the goods from **stock** are both excellent in quality and very reasonable in price.

On **regular** purchase in quantities of not less than five gross of individual items, we would allow you a trade discount of 30%.

We also export a wide range of hand-made leather shoes in which we think you may be interested. They are fully illustrated in the catalogue and are of the same high quality as our gloves.

We hope the samples will reach you in good time and look forward to your order.

Yours truly,

(Signature)

Notes

1. request   *v.&n.* 请求，要求

   as requested   按照要求

   on request   一经要求就

   at the request of; at one's request   应某人要求

   As requested, we send you our latest price list. 按照要求，我方寄上最新价格单。

   Sample books and catalogues will be sent on request. 样本书和目录册一经要求就会寄出。

   At your request we make you the following quotation. 应你方要求，我方做出以下报价。

2. examine   *v.* 检验，检查；审查，核查

   The goods were carefully examined before shipment. 货物在装运前已经过仔细检查。

   The issuing bank shall have a reasonable time to examine the documents. 开证行应有合理的时间来审核单据。

3. confident   *adj.* 自信的，有信心的

   We are confident that we can push the sales of your products in our market. 我方对在本地市场推销你方产品很有信心。

   We are confident of being able to ship the goods to you by the end of this month. 我方有信心在本月底前将货物送抵你方。

4. stock   *n.* 库存；存货

   a stock of   一批现货

   from stock   动用库存

in stock　库存中

out of stock　无货；缺货

There is no more stock on hand. 手头已无存货。

We can supply from stock. 我们可以现货供应。

The type you required is out of stock, but the similar type is in stock. 你方询购的型号无货，类似的型号有货。

Our stock will be exhausted soon. 库存将售罄。

5. regular　*adj.* 经常的

If your prices are competitive, our company will be pleased to place regular orders with you. 如果你方价格更为优惠，我公司乐意经常向你方订货。

As your purchases are regular and numerous, it would be advisable for you to open a revolving L/C in our favor. 因你方多次大量订货，故请向我方开具循环信用证。

Specimen Letter 5　Asking for Quotations

White Crystal Sugar

Dear Sirs,

We have just received an inquiry from one of our Japan clients who **is in the market for** 10,000 metric tons of the white crystal sugar and shall appreciate your quoting about your **rock-bottom prices of the same** at the earlier date.

For your information, the quality required should be superior white crystal sugar packed in new gunny bags of 100 kg each. Meanwhile, the goods should be **surveyed** by a public surveyor as to their quality and weight before shipment. For this inquiry, the buyers will arrange shipping and insurance, therefore the price to be quoted by you should be on an FAS Dalian basis.

As there is a critical **shortage** of sugar in Japan, the goods should be ready for shipment as early as possible. Please be assured that if your price is **acceptable**, we will place an order with you right away.

Your early reply to this inquiry is requested.

Sincerely yours,

(Signature)

Notes

1. be in the market for　想要购买(如果去掉介词 for，表示要买或要卖)

We note from your letter of 16th this month that you are in the market for textiles. 从你方本月 16 日信中得知你们想要购买纺织品。

Please let us know when you are in the market. 如果你方想买(或卖)，请告知。

2. rock-bottom price 最低价

类似的表达方式还有：minimum price；lowest price；bedrock price；floor price 等。

As we have quoted you our rock-bottom price, we can not do better. 我们已报给你方最低价，不能再减让了。

3. the same 或 same 在书信中常用作代词来指前面所说的人或事。这是商业信函中的一种陈旧的用法。

If you require further information, we can supply the same. 如需进一步的资料，我方可以提供。

4. for your information 顺告你方

For your information, the tendency of the leather market is still uncertain. 顺告你方，皮革市场的趋势仍难肯定。

5. survey *n.&v.* 检查，调查，鉴定

public surveyor 公证检验行，是指站在独立公正(independent and impartial)立场上的社会检验机构，接受委托对商品的品质、规格、数量进行检验并出具检验证书。

customs surveyor 海关检验人员

marine surveyor 海事鉴定人

survey report 鉴定报告

surveyor's report 鉴定行报告

6. shortage *n.* 不足；不足之量

Please do your utmost to ship shortage by the next available steamer. 请尽力把短交之数由下次船运来。

7. acceptable *adj.* 可接受的，合意的

Your offer is not acceptable. 我方无法接受你的报盘。

The quality is acceptable, but the time of shipment is not. 质量可以接受，但船期不行。

July shipment is acceptable to our customer. 我们的客户同意 7 月发运。

Specimen Letter 6   Reply to the Inquiry

Dear Sirs,

Your inquiry for pens has been passed on to us for **attention** by our Commercial

Counsellor's Office in your country.

We **specialize** in producing **Hero Brand Pens** of various types, with a history of 64 years. The enclosed catalogue will make you acquainted with some of our products.

In particular, we recommend and quote for the following types which have **met with warm reception** in the Middle East market and, we are sure, they will be of interest to you.

Art No.	Name of Commodity	Specifications	Prices(per dz)
Type 200	Twin Gift Set	A fountain pen of 14k gold nib matches a ball pen	US $89
Type 13	High Grade Golden Pen	12k gold nib, stainless steel cap	US $52
Type 251	High Grade Iridium Pen	Exposed nib, Aluminum cap, plastic barrel	US $36

It is understood the above prices are quoted **on FOB Shanghai basis** and are **without engagement**, **subject to our final confirmation**. We'd appreciate payment by confirmed, irrevocable **L/C at sight**. The goods would be ready for shipment one month from receipt of your written order.

We look forward to your trial order.

Sincerely yours,

(Signature)

Notes

1. attention   *n.* 注意，处理

   Your letter addressed to our Head Office has been passed on to us for attention and reply. 你方致我总公司的信已转交我方处理并作答。

2. specialize   *v.* 专门经营(后跟介词 in)

   Being specialized in the export of light industrial products, we express our desire to trade with you in this line. 因我方专营轻工产品出口，故期待与你方在此行业进行贸易往来。

   They specialize in dyestuffs. 他们专营染料。

3. Hero Brand Pens 在商业信函中，某某牌的产品通常用大写。

4. meet with warm (favorable) reception 受到欢迎，在商业信函中引申为"畅销"；还可以说 well received。

   We are glad that our handicrafts have met with warm reception at your end. 我们很高兴我们的手工艺品在你处畅销(深受欢迎)。

We are pleased to note from your letter that our products are well received in your market. 由你方信中得悉我们的产品在你们的市场上很受欢迎，甚感高兴。

5. Art No. 是 article number 的缩写，表示"货号"。

6. specifications *n.* 规格，指产品规格，常用复数。

7. It is understood... 不言而喻，毋庸讳言……类似的表达方式还有 needless to say; it goes without saying 等。

It is understood that the L/C should be opened on time. 不言而喻，信用证应及时开立。

It is understood that as soon as we receive your confirmation, a Letter of Credit will be opened through the Bank of China, Shandong Branch. 毫无疑问，一旦收到你方确认，我方即通过中国银行山东分行开出信用证。

It is understood that this is a special treatment not applicable to future business. 不言而喻，这是一个特殊待遇，下不为例。

8. on FOB Shanghai basis 以 FOB 上海作价

FOB 是外贸业务中的价格术语，它是 free on board 的缩略语，译作"装运港船上交货价"。后面接指定装运港(named port of shipment)，此信中指定装运港是上海。

Please make us an offer for the above goods on FOB Qingdao basis. 请按青岛装运港船上交货价给我方报上述商品。

9. without engagement 无约束力，不承担义务，不承担责任。类似的表达方式还有 without obligation。

The above are offers without engagement. 上述均为虚盘(无约束力的报盘即为虚盘)。

10. subject to our final confirmation 以我方最后确认为准，表示此交易是否成立，要由卖方最后确认来决定，又如：subject to goods being unsold 以货物未售出为有效；subject to prior sale 以货先售出为准。

As requested, we are making you an offer as follows, subject to our final confirmation. 按照要求，我方报盘如下，以我方最后确认为准。

11. L/C at sight 即期信用证，还可以表述为 sight L/C。

L/C 是 letter of credit 的缩略语，它是一种银行在买方的要求下开立的有条件的承诺付款的书面文件。即期信用证是开证银行或付款银行收到符合信用证条款的跟单汇票或装运单据后，立即履行付款义务的信用证。

We require payment by an L/C at sight. 我们要求用即期信用证付款。

Useful Sentences

1. Your name was given to us by London Chamber of Commerce and we should like to inquire whether… 通过伦敦商会得知你公司名称，现询问是否……

2. We would like to purchase your Silver Spoon as advertised in the June 5 *New York Times*. 我方愿购买你方在 6 月 5 日《纽约时报》上宣传的银勺。

3. Today we received an inquiry from a buyer in Singapore. He wants to import chinaware of the best quality. 今天我方收到来自新加坡进口商的一封询价函。他欲进口质量上乘的瓷器。

4. One of our clients takes interest in your products and wishes to have your quotations for the items specified below. 我们的一位客户对你们的产品很感兴趣，并向你们索要以下指定商品的报价。

5. We should be pleased to receive your illustrated catalogue and price list of Plastic Kitchenware. 非常荣幸收到你方带有图解的塑料厨房用品目录表和价格单。

6. Please quote us your lowest prices for the following goods FOB London. 请报贵方下列货物 FOB 伦敦的最低价。

7. The quality must be exactly the same as that of the enclosed samples. 质量一定与随函附上的样品完全相同。

8. If you are in a position to meet our demand, we shall place a large sum order from you. 如果能够满足我方要求，我们将向你方下大笔订单。

9. How much discount will you allow us if we order 500 sets? 如果我们预订 500 台设备，你方将给我们多少折扣？

10. You will please let us know how long it will take for delivery. 请告知可能最早的交货期。

Letter-writing Guide

The steps and expressions of an inquiry are as follows. (询价函的写作步骤及常见表达方式如下。)

Writing steps (写作步骤)	Examples of expressions (表达方式举例)
1. 说明如何得知这家公司名称，并要求对方寄来商品目录及价目表	Your name was given to us by London Chamber of Commerce… 从伦敦商会得知你公司名称……
	We would like to purchase…in the June 5 *New York Times*. 我们想购买你方刊登在 6 月 5 日《纽约时报》广告上的……
	We hear that you are the exporter of… 据悉，你方系……的出口商。

2. 介绍本公司的情况和经营范围，说明感兴趣的产品	We are supplying about 1000 stores with their import needs. 我们向大约 1000 家商店供应进口货。
	One of our clients takes interest in your products。 我方一客户对你们的产品感兴趣。
	We want to import chinaware of the best quality. 我们想进口质量上乘的瓷器。
3. 询问可以给予的折扣及要求的支付条件(例如 FOB、CIF 等)，询问对方能够提供的发货服务	How much discount will you allow us if we order 500 sets? 如果我们购买 500 台，能给多少折扣？
	It is not our practice to accept term L/C. 接受远期信用证不是我们的习惯做法。
	You will please let us know how long it will take for delivery. 请告知可能最早的交货期。
4. 表达与对方合作及早日收到回复的愿望	We should like to have further particulars. 我们需要进一步了解细节。
	Kindly give this matter your prompt attention. 请尽快办理此事。
	We look forward to hearing from you soon. 盼佳音。

The steps and expressions of writing a reply to an inquiry are as follows. (回复询价函的写作步骤及常见表达方式如下。)

Writing steps (写作步骤)	Examples of expressions (表达方式举例)
1. 询价函已经收悉，提及已将所索要的商品目录及价目表附于信中或另函寄送	Your inquiry of June 11 is greatly appreciated. 感谢你们 6 月 11 日的询价。
	…receive your letter requesting a catalogue of our products. 收到你方索取产品目录的信。
	We are enclosing our illustrated catalogue and price list. 随信附上带图目录册及价格单。
2. 清楚地介绍有关商品的种种优点	It illustrates various kinds of silk goods of the best quality. 本目录有各种优质丝织品图片。
	Our instruments are the product of the finest materials. 我们的乐器产品原料优良。
	The product is guaranteed long wear, attractiveness and real comfort. 产品保证耐用、美观、舒适。
3. 强调所报价格具有竞争性，说明要求的支付条件及能提供的发货服务	Our prices are competitive enough to attract your customers. 我们的价格具有竞争性，足以吸引你们的顾客。
	Payment should be made under an irrevocable letter of credit. 货款应开立不可撤销信用证。
	…effect shipment within four weeks from receipt of your order. 收到订单后四周内可装运。
4. 希望得到对方的答复	We look forward to hearing from you soon. 盼佳音。
	We are expecting a reply at your earliest convenience. 盼早日回复。

Exercises

I. Put the following English phrases into Chinese or Chinese phrases into English.

1. regular supply   2. be in receipt of   3. in large quantities   4. at a discount   5. out of season

6. 合理的价格   7. 激烈竞争   8. 一旦请求就   9. 廉价出售   10. 供你参考

II. Fill in the blanks of the following letter with the words given below, and change the form when necessary.

| place   sight   popular   shipment   separate   discount   requested   inquiry |

Dear Sirs,

We are pleased to receive your ___1___ of April 10. As ___2___, we are enclosing our illustrated catalogue and price list. We are also sending you by ___3___ post some samples and feel confident that when you have examined them you will agree that the goods are both excellent in quality and reasonable in price.

On regular purchases in quantities of not less than 1000 gross of individual items, we would allow you a ___4___ of 2%. Payment is to be made by irrevocable L/C at ___5___.

Because of their softness and durability, our cotton bed, sheets and pillow cases have rapidly become ___6___, and after studying our prices you will not be surprised to learn that we are finding it difficult to meet the demand. But if you ___7___ your order not later than the end of this month, we would ensure prompt ___8___.

We look forward to your early reply.

Yours faithfully,

(signature)

III. Translate the following English into Chinese or Chinese into English.

1. What quantities of the specified item can you regularly deliver on short notice?

2. We can not trim anything off the price.

3. If the prices are within your expectation, we shall reply to your enquiry with our firm offer.

4. He negotiated a $250, 000 loan with the City Bank.

5. We can assure you of our regular supply.

6. 正如你们所知，我们是经营此类商品多年的国有企业。

7. 你们在本月《中国对外贸易》上刊登的广告，我们很感兴趣，现请告知该商品的详细情况。

8. 如贵公司的报价具有竞争力，机器的质量令人满意，我们会向贵公司订购。

9. 除非你方在 3 月订货，否则我们无法在 6 月送货。

10. 我们已向波音公司订购 30 架中型新客机。

IV． Writing practice.

Write a letter of a general inquiry asking for all the information you need.

1. 从 ABC 公司得知贵公司为主要棉质内衣出口商。

2. 我方欲进口该货物，如有可能请寄送目录册及样本。

3. 请报 CIF 大连价、折扣和支付条件。

Unit 3 补充练习   Unit 3 补充练习答案   Unit 3 练习答案

Unit 4 Offers and Counter-offers

【学习要点和目标】

通过本单元的学习，掌握发盘和还盘信函的写作要点，并理解实盘和虚盘的区别以及实质性还盘和非实质性还盘的区别。

Lead-in

According to ***United Nations Convention on Contracts for the International Sale of Goods***, a proposal for concluding a contract addressed to one or more specific persons constitutes an offer if it is sufficiently definite and indicates the intention of the offer or to be bound in case of acceptance. A proposal is sufficiently definite if it indicates the goods and expressly or implicitly fixes or makes provision for determining the quantity and the price.

A satisfactory offer will include the followings:

1. An expression of thanks for the enquiry, if any.

2. Name of commodities, quality and specification.

3. Details of prices, terms of trade, discounts and terms of payments.

4. Packing and date of delivery.

5. The period for which the offer is valid.

6. Hope for reply.

A reply to an offer purports to be an acceptance. But when it contains additions, limitations or other modifications, it is a rejection of the offer, which constitutes a counter-offer.

However, if a reply to an offer contains additional or different terms which do not materially alter the terms of the offer, the reply constitutes an acceptance, unless the offer is without undue delay, objects orally to the discrepancy or dispatches a notice to that effect. If he/she does not so object, the terms of the contract are the terms of the offer with the modifications contained in the acceptance.

Additional or different terms relating, among other things, to the price, payment, quality and quantity of the goods, place and time of delivery, extent of one party's liability to the other or the settlement of disputes are considered to alter the terms of the offer materially.

A satisfactory counter-offer will include the followings:

1. An expression of thanks for an offer.

2. Regret to be unable to accept what has been offered and state your reasons.

3. Make a counter-offer or suggest other opportunity to do business together.

4. Hope for early reply.

Specimen Letter 1 Make an Offer Based on Enquiry: A Firm Offer

Dear Sirs,

Thank you for your enquiry dated July 5th, asking us to **offer** 5000 metric tons of rice, and we **appreciate** very much your interest in our product. **As requested**, we **take pleasure in** making you a firm offer **as follows**, **subject to** your reply reaching here on or before July 30th.

1. Commodity: superior rice, Heilongjiang Origin.

2. Quantity: five thousand (5000) metric tons.

3. Price: **U.S. dollars … (U.S. $...) per metric ton, FOB Dalian.**

4. Packing: in new **gunny bags**, each **containing** 100 kg.

5. Shipment: during October, 20××.

6. Payment: by **irrevocable and confirmed Letter of Credit payable by draft at sight** for the full invoice value to be **opened** 30 days before the date of shipment.

Please **note** that we have quoted our most **favorable** price and we cannot **see our way** clearly to **entertain** any **counter-offer**.

We are **awaiting** your early reply.

Yours sincerely,

(Signature)

Notes

1. offer

(1) *n*. 发盘

Please make us a firm offer CIF London for 20 metric tons of groundnuts. 请向我方报 20 公吨花生实盘，贸易条件为 CIF 伦敦。

The offer is firm (valid, open) for two weeks. 本发盘两周有效。

firm offer 实盘：受盘人在有效期内表示完全同意，交易立即达成的报盘为实盘。

non-firm offer 虚盘：发盘人没有肯定的订立合同的意旨，例如发盘内容不是很明确，或者主要条件不完备，这种发盘对发盘人无约束力。

We offer…subject to our final confirmation. 本发盘以我方最后确认为准。

The offer is subject to the goods being unsold. 本发盘以货未售出为准。

(2) *v.* 发盘

We offer the goods at the current season's prices. 我们按本季行情报价。

2. appreciate

(1) *v.* 涨价，increase in value

The price has appreciated. 价格已经上涨。

(2) *v.* 感谢(后接名词或动名词)，put a high value on

Your immediate attention will be appreciated. 感谢你方给予的及时关注。

重要句型：We shall appreciate it if you… 如果您……我们将不胜感谢。

3. as requested=as is requested 正如所要求的

类似的短语还有 as expected 如所预料的那样；as reported 据报道；as said above 如上所述；as well known 众所周知。

4. take pleasure in = take the pleasure of 乐于

5. as follows 如下

6. subject to 以……为准

We offer you firm, subject to your reply reaching here before or on Sept. 30. 我方向贵公司报实盘，以你方答复在 9 月 30 日或此日期之前到达我方为准。

7. 英文报价的表达方法：

计价货币+单价金额+计量单位+贸易术语，如：$124.00 per dozen CIF Hamburg

8. gunny bag 麻袋

9. contain *v.* 装有

The bag contains two books. 包里装有两本书。

10. Letter of Credit 信用证

Irrevocable Letter of Credit 不可撤销信用证

Confirmed Letter of Credit 保兑信用证

Letter of Credit payable by draft at sight 即期信用证

Letter of Credit payable by draft…d/s after sight… 远期信用证

11. draft *n.* 汇票，又称 bill of exchange，是指出票人签发的，委托付款人在见票时或者在指定日期无条件支付确定的金额给收款人或持票人的票据。

12. open an L/C 开立信用证，另外还可以用 issue an L/C 或 establish an L/C 来表示。

13. note　*v.* notice, pay attention to　注意

We note that your order stipulates direct shipment. 我方注意到你方的订单规定直航。

14. favorable　*adj.* 优惠的，有利的

If your prices are favorable, we can place the order right away. 如你方价格优惠，我方可立即订货。

A deeper understanding will be favorable to our business. 进一步的了解对我们的业务有利。

15. see one's way (clear) to do sth.　能够

We are regretful that we just cannot see our way clear to accept your counter-offer, as the price we quoted is quite realistic. 我们很遗憾不能接受你方的还盘，因为我方报出的价格是十分合理的。

16. entertain　*v.* 考虑接受

We are not in a position to entertain your claim. 我们不能接受你方的索赔。

17. counter-offer　还盘

Much to our regret, we are not in a position to accept your counter-offer. 很抱歉不能接受你方还盘。

18. await = wait for　*v.* 等待

Specimen Letter 2　Make an often Based on Enquiry: A Non-firm Offer

Dear Sirs,

We are in **receipt** of your letter of October 20th, inquiring for our Men's Shoes Style No.456. We greatly appreciate your interest in our products.

To **comply** with your request, we are offering you 500 pairs of Calf Men's Shoes Style No. 456 at USD 50 per pair FOB Shanghai, subject to our final confirmation. Shipment will be **effected** within 30 days after receipt of the **covering** L/C **in our favor** issued by your first class bank.

We are a company manufacturing various styles of Men's Shoes and Women's Shoes for exportation, and we are sending you a brochure of our products **under separate cover for your information**. We hope some of them will meet the need of your customers.

We are looking forward to your early reply.

Yours truly,

(Signature)

Notes

1. receipt   *n.* 收到

    (1) in receipt of 收到

    We are in receipt of your letter dated June 6th. 我方收到你方 6 月 6 日的来信。

    (2) on receipt of 一收到

    The goods will be sent on receipt of your remittance. 一收到你方汇款即发货。

    (3) after receipt of 收到……之后

    The seller should check it carefully after receipt of the L/C. 卖方在收到信用证后应该仔细审证。

2. comply   *v.* 依照，依从，符合(后接介词 with)

    Your offer does not comply with our requirement. 你方发盘不符合我们的要求。

3. effect   *v.* 实现，完成

    Insurance will be effected by the seller. 由卖方投保。

    Shipment is to be effected during June. 20××. 20××年 6 月装运。

    Payment is to be effected by L/C. 用信用证方式付款。

4. covering   *adj.* 相关的

    Please open the covering L/C at the early date. 请早日开出相关信用证。

5. in one's favor 以……为受益人。在信用证业务中，出口方即为信用证的受益人。

6. under separate cover 另邮寄

7. for your information 供你方参考

    同义的表达法还有：for your reference；for your study

8. meet the need of... 满足……的需要

    It is our responsibility to meet the need of our customers. 满足客户的要求是我们的责任。

Specimen Letter 3   Counter-offer: Ask for a Price Cut

Dear Sirs,

Your offer of June 4th and the **samples** of the cotton shirts have been received with thanks.

In reply, we are **regretful** to say that our customers find your price is **on the high side** and **out of line with** the **prevailing** market, although we appreciate the high quality of your shirts.

Such being the case, we are not **in a position to** persuade our customers to accept this price, as the products of the same quality can be obtained at a much lower price. **Should you be**

prepared to make a price reduction by, say 10%, we might put the deal through.

We trust that you will find our counter-offer reasonable and we are awaiting your prompt reply.

Yours faithfully,

(Signature)

Notes

1. sample   *n.* 样品

   We have sent you by separate mail a sample of(for) the goods. 我方已经另邮寄货物样品一件。

   counter sample 对等样品

   sample for reference 参考样品

   duplicate sample 复样

2. in reply 此复

   In reply, we are sorry that we cannot do business on your terms. 此复，我方很抱歉不能按你方的条件成交。

3. regretful   *adj.* 对某人感到抱歉的

   We are regretful that we just cannot see our way clear to entertain your counter-offer, as the price we quoted is quite realistic. 由于我方报价合理，我方不能接受你方还盘，对此表示抱歉。

   表示"我方很抱歉"的表达有：

   We are regretful that…

   We regret that…

4. on the high side 偏高

   We learn from your letter of 10th October that our price for the subject article is found to be on the high side. 从你方 10 月 10 日来信得知，你方认为我方对标题货物报价偏高。

   类似的表示价格高的方法还有：

   Your price is a little high. 你方价格有点高。

   Your price is too high. 你方价格太高。

   Your price is excessive. 你方价格过高。

5. out of line with 不符合

   in line with 符合

Since your price is out of line with the prevailing market, we can not come to terms.
由于你方价格与现行市场价格不符，因此不能成交。

While our price is in line with the prevailing international market rate, we are not in a position to consider any concession in our price, much to our regret. 由于我方价格符合现行国际市场价格，我方不会对价格做出让步，对此我们十分抱歉。

6. prevailing   *adj*. 现行的

We very much regret to state that our customers here find your price too high compared with the prevailing market level. 我们本地的买主认为，与现行市场价格相比，你方报价过高，对此我们深表遗憾。

7. such being the case 事实既然如此

Your L/C calls for an insurance amount for 130% of the invoice value. Such being the case, we would request you to amend the insurance clause. 你方开来的信用证要求按照发票金额的130%投保。像这种情况，我方要求你方修改保险条款。

8. in a position to 能够

We are not in a position to entertain your claim. 我方不能接受你方的要求。

We are now in a position to supply this article from stock. 我们现在能为你方提供该商品的现货。

9. Should you be prepared to make a price reduction by, say 10%, we might put the deal through. 如果你方能降低价格，比方说10%，我们就可能成交。

当 if 条件句中含有助动词 should、were 或 had 时，则可以省略 if，而将 should、were 或 had 置于句首，从而构成倒装虚拟句，意思不变。

注意：

(1) If I were you 不能倒装成 Were I you。

(2) 如果 had 不是用作助动词，则句子不能倒装。如：If I had time 不能倒装成 Had I time.

10. put the deal through 达成交易

表示"达成交易"的表达还有：come to terms; close a deal; conclude a business.

Specimen Letter 4   Counter-offer: Ask for a Smaller Quantity

Dear Sirs,

Thank you for your offer of Oct. 10 and the sample of calf shoes.

We agree that the quality of your shoes is **up to the standard**, and the prices you offered are **satisfactory**. But **with regard to** the **minimum** quantity of 10,000 pairs which you asked for in your letter, we have to point out that in your **previous** letter of Sept. 20th the minimum was 5000 pairs. We ask you to accept this lower minimum.

Please let us have your confirmation **at your earliest convenience**.

Yours faithfully,

(Signature)

Notes

1. up to the standard 符合标准

   The goods are up to the standard. 此货物符合标准。

   above standard 超过标准

   below standard 低于标准

2. satisfactory *adj.* 令人满意的

   Sales are up 20% from last year, which is very satisfactory. 销售额比去年增加了 20%，非常令人满意。

3. with regard to 关于

   With regard to Contract No.123, we are agreeable to D/P payment terms. 关于 123 号合同，我们同意用付款交单方式付款。

   以下表达也可以表示"关于"：regarding，with reference to，as to，covering。

4. minimum

   (1) *n.* 最低限度，最小量，least possible or recorded amount, degree

   We have cut our price to the minimum. 我方价格已经降到最低限度。

   (2) *adj.* 最小量的，最低额的，最低程度的，of least possible or recorded amount, degree

   The minimum quantity should be 1000 metric tons. 最低量应当是 1000 公吨。

5. previous *adj.* 在前的，早先的

   Thank you sincerely for your kindness and assistance in the previous cooperation. We feel quite pleased to work with you. 感谢你方在以前合作中的友好和给予的帮助，与你方合作十分愉快。

6. at one's earliest convenience 尽早

   We will appreciate it if you could effect shipment at your earliest convenience. 如果你方能尽早安排装运，我方将不胜感激。

   表示类似意思的短语还有 at an early time, at an early date。

Specimen Letter 5   Counter-offer: Ask for Alternation of Terms of Payment

Dear Sirs,

We appreciate your offer of June 5th for 5000 pairs of Women's Shoes. We find your price and quality satisfactory. However, we would suggest that your terms of payment should be **altered**.

Generally speaking, D/P at sight is the **usual practice** with all our customers in your country, and therefore we cannot **make an exception** of your case.

In view of our long term business relations, we suggest you accept payment by D/P at sight. We are awaiting your early reply.

Yours faithfully,

(Signature)

Notes

1. alter   *v.* 改变

   The design of this machine must be altered to meet the new requirements. 这台机器的设计必须改动一下，以适应新的要求。

2. generally speaking   一般说来

   Generally speaking, there was no resistance to the idea. 一般说来，没有人会反对这个观点。

3. usual practice   惯例

   customary practice   习惯做法；惯例

   standard practice   通常惯例

4. make an exception   破例

   We shall make an exception of your case. 我们会将你的情况作为例外处理。

5. in view of   鉴于，与 considering 同义

   In view of the small amount of this transaction, we have decided to accept your D/P payment terms. 鉴于这笔交易额很小，我们决定接受你方用付款交单方式付款。

Specimen Letter 6　Reject the Price Reduction

Dear Sirs,

We learn from your fax of 15th October that our price for the Men's Shirt is found to be on the high side.

Much as we would like to cooperate with you in expanding sales, we are regretful that we just cannot see our way clear to entertain your counter-offer, as our quoted prices are the best possible prices if you **take** the quality **into consideration**.

Despite our inability to offer you lower prices, we still hope we may receive an order from you. **On account of** a limited supply **available** at present, we would ask you to act quickly.

We look forward to hearing from you.

Yours faithfully,

(Signature)

Notes

1. much as　尽管，虽然，引导让步状语从句

   Much as we are interested in your products, we cannot place an order with you because of the high price. 尽管我方对贵公司产品很感兴趣，但由于价格过高，我方不能订货。

2. take...into consideration　把……考虑进去

   同义短语：take...into account

   Price is not the only factor; you have to take the quality into account. 价格不是唯一的因素；你也应该考虑质量。

   Taking the transport condition at your end into the consideration, we have improved our packing so as to avoid any damage to the goods. 考虑到你地的运输条件，为避免货物破损，我们已经改进了包装。

3. despite　*prep.* 尽管

   Despite the pressure from many countries, the trade negotiation goes smoothly. 尽管有来自许多国家的压力，贸易谈判仍然进展顺利。

4. on account of　由于

   On account of lack of direct steamer, please allow transshipment in your L/C. 由于缺少直达船只，请在你方信用证中允许转船。

5. available   *adj.* 可利用的；可供应的

We will ship by the first available steamer next week. 我方将用下周可订到的第一条船装运。

Specimen Letter 7   Make a Concession

Dear Sirs,

We thank you for your letter of March 30. Your counter-offer of our shirts has had our great **attention**.

Although we are **keen** to meet your requirements, we are regretful that we are unable to reduce the price as you request because our prices are precisely calculated. **Even if** there is a slight difference between our prices and those of other suppliers, you will find it profitable to buy from us because the quality of our products is **superior** to that of other makers available in your area.

However, in order to develop the business relations between us, we are prepared to allow you a **discount** of 5% provided that the minimum quantity of your order is 5000.

If our suggestion is **acceptable** to you, please let us have your order at an early date.

Yours faithfully,

(Signature)

Notes

1. attention   *n.* 注意

   We'd like to draw your attention to the fact that the delivery date is approaching, but we haven't received your L/C up to now. 请你方注意，装运期临近，我方仍未收到你方开来的信用证。

2. keen   *adj.* 刺激的，激烈的，热切的，低廉的

   keen smell 刺鼻的气味

   keen competition 激烈的竞争

   Please quote keen price. 请报低价。

   be keen on doing/to do 热切希望

   Buyers are keen to have your offer. 买方热切期盼你方发盘。

   Buyers are keen on having your offer. 买方热切期盼你方发盘。

3. even if=even though 即使，尽管

   I wouldn't lose courage even if I should fail ten times. 即使要失败十次，我也绝不灰心。

4. superior   *adj.* 优于的

be superior to 优于

inferior   *adj.* (质量等)低劣的

be inferior to 劣于

This machine is superior (inferior) to that in many respects. 这台机器在很多方面优于 (劣于)那台。

5. discount   *n.* 折扣

The highest discount we can allow on this article is 10%. 这件商品我们能给的最高折扣是 10%。

6. acceptable   *adj.* 可接受的

For future deal, D/P will be acceptable to us if the amount involved is not up to RMB 1000. 在今后的交易中，如果金额不到 1000 元人民币，我们可以接受付款交单。

Specimen Letter 8   Accept the Counter-offer

Dear Sirs,

We have for acknowledgement for your letter of May 17, asking us to **make a 10% reduction in our price** for Men's Shirts.

In reply, **much to our regret**, we find it **intolerable** to meet your request because our price leaves us with a small profit and if it were not for the regular orders we receive from various sources, we could not have quoted even at those prices.

However, in order to develop our market in your place, we have decided to accept your counter-offer as an **exceptional** case.

We hope we can come to terms and await your prompt reply with great interest.

Yours faithfully,

(Signature)

Notes

1. We have for acknowledgement for your letter of... 我方收到贵方……(日期)的来信。
   同样含义的表达法还有：

   We receive your letter of...

   We are in receipt your letter of...

   We acknowledge receipt of...

2. make a ...% reduction in the price 降价……%

We cannot meet your requirement for making a 10% reduction in our price. 我方不能答应贵方的要求，把价格降低 10%。

3. much to our regret 令我方非常遗憾的是

"to+形容词性物主代词/名词所有格+表示情感的名词" 表示 "令某人……的是"，例如：

to my surprise 令我吃惊的是

to his anger 令他生气的是

to his father's disappointment 令他父亲失望的是

4. intolerable *adj.* 不能容忍的

They felt this would put intolerable pressure on them. 他们觉得这会给他们带来无法承受的压力。

5. exceptional *adj.* 例外的

This is an exceptional case. 这是例外情况。

Useful Sentences

1. Thank you for your enquiry dated July 5th, asking us to offer... 感谢贵公司 7 月 5 日的询盘，让我方对……报盘。

2. As requested, we take pleasure in making you a firm offer as follows, subject to your reply reaching here on or before... 按贵公司要求，我方很高兴地报出以下实盘，以贵方在……或之前答复为有效。

3. To comply with your request, we are offering you...at..., subject to our final confirmation. 按贵公司要求，我方以……价格向你方报……(货物)，以我方最终确认为准。

4. In reply, we are regretful to say that our customers find your price is on the high side and out of line with the prevailing market. 此复，我方的客户认为贵公司报价偏高，不符合现行市场的价格水平，对此我方深表遗憾。

5. Should you be prepared to make a price reduction by, say 10%, we might put the deal through. 如果贵公司能够降价 10%，我们可能成交。

6. Much as we would like to cooperate with you in expanding sales, we are regretful that we just cannot see our way clear to entertain your counter-offer, as our quoted prices are the best possible prices if you take the quality into consideration. 尽管我方愿意与贵公司合作扩展贸易，但是我方很遗憾，不能接受贵公司的还盘，因为如果把质量考虑进去的话，我方所报

的价格是最优惠的。

7. In order to develop our market in your place, we have decided to accept your counter-offer as an exceptional case. 为了在贵地拓展我公司的市场，我方决定破例接受贵公司的还盘。

Letter-writing Guide

The steps and expressions of writing an offer letter are as follows. (发盘信函的写作步骤及常见的表达方式如下。)

Writing steps (写作步骤)	Examples of expressions (表达方式举例)
1. 如果有对方的询盘，首先要对对方的询盘表示感谢	We thank you for your enquiry for…dated… 感谢贵方于……对……的询盘。
	We thank you for your letter dated…enquiring for…. 感谢贵方于……来函对……的询盘。
	We are in receipt of your letter of…asking us to offer…and appreciate very much your interest in our product. 我方收到贵方……的来函，让我方对……进行发盘，感谢贵公司对我产品的兴趣。
2. 具体说明商品的名称、质量和规格，对价格、贸易术语、折扣、付款方式、包装和交货日期等做出详细规定	To comply with your request, we are offering you…at… 按照贵公司要求，我方向你方报出……，价格为……
	Payment is to be made by… 货款支付方式为……
	Shipment is to be made during… 装运在……期间进行
	The goods are to be packed in… 货物用……包装
3. 写明发盘的有效期	We offer firm, subject to your reply reaching us on or before… 我方报出实盘，以贵公司的答复在……或之前到达我方为有效。
	The offer is open/valid for… 此盘有效期为……
4. 表达与对方合作及早日收到回复的愿望	We are awaiting your early reply. 盼早回复。
	We are looking forward to your early reply. 盼早回复。
	Your early reply is appreciated. 盼早回复。

The steps and expressions of writing a counter-offer letter are as follows. (还盘信函的写作步骤及常见表达方式如下。)

Writing steps (写作步骤)	Examples of expressions (表达方式举例)
1. 对对方发盘表示感谢	Your offer of…and the samples of… have been received with thanks. 我方已经收到贵方……的发盘以及……样品，非常感谢。
	We thank you for your offer of…and the sample of…, for which we thank you. 我方已经收到贵方……的发盘以及……样品，非常感谢。
	We appreciate your offer of…for… 感谢贵方于……对……的发盘。
2. 对不能接受对方发盘表示抱歉并说明理由	We are regretful to say that our customers find your price is on the high side and out of line with the prevailing market, although we appreciate the high quality of your shirts. 我方很遗憾地告知贵方，尽管我方非常欣赏衬衫的优良品质，但我方的客户认为你方价格过高，不符合现行市场的价格水平。
	While appreciating the good quality of your shirts, we find your price is rather too high. 尽管贵方衬衫质量很好，但是我方认为价格过高。
	We find your price and quality satisfactory, however we would suggest that your terms of payment should be altered. 我方认为贵方所报的价格以及产品的质量都很令人满意，但是我方建议对付款方式进行修改。
3. 做出还盘或提出其他的贸易机会的建议	We have to ask you to consider if you can make reduction in your price, say… 请贵方考虑是否能降低价格，比方说……
	We ask you to accept this minimum of… 希望贵方接受……的最小订货量。
	We suggest you accept payment by… 建议贵方接受……的付款方式。
4. 希望对方早日答复	We are awaiting your early reply. 盼早回复。
	We are looking forward to your early reply. 盼早回复。
	Your early reply is appreciated. 盼早回复。

Exercises

I. Put the following English phrases into Chinese or Chinese phrases into English.

1. final confirmation   2. in our favor   3. prevailing market   4. put the deal through

5. up to the standard   6. 实盘   7. 虚盘   8. 保兑信用证   9. 还盘   10. 惯例

II. Translate the following English into Chinese or Chinese into English.

1. The offer is valid within five days.

2. Shipment is to be effected within 30 days after receipt of your L/C.

3. If you can allow us a discount of 10%, we will place an order of 3000 dozen.

4. Our goods are excellent in quality and reasonable in price.

5. Such being the case, we have to ask you to consider if you can make reduction in your price, say 10%.

6. 我方向你方报出特惠盘，以你方的答复在 9 月 30 日之前到达有效。

7. 非常遗憾，我方不能接受贵方发盘，我方现已经低价从其他供应商处购进。

8. 此复，很遗憾我方客户认为你方价格太高，与现行的市场水平不一致。

9. 鉴于我们之间长期的业务关系，特做此还盘。

10. 请报你方最优惠的 CIF 上海价，包括我方 3% 的佣金。

III. Translate the following letter into Chinese.

Dear Sirs,

We wish to thank you for your letter of March 2, offering us 1000 pairs of cotton socks at RMB¥15 per pair FOB Dalian.

Although we are interested in your products, we find your price is so high that our margin of profit would be very little. Information indicates that the socks of similar quality are available at present on the market and at a price 10%～15% lower than yours.

We hope, therefore, you will reduce your price so as to put the deal through.

We are awaiting your reply.

Yours faithfully,

(Signature)

IV. Write a letter offering the followings.

1. 商品：牛皮鞋(AA121)。

2. 数量：1000 双。

3. 价格：每双 20 美元 CIF 纽约价。

4. 装运期：20×× 年 12 月。

5. 付款方式：不可撤销即期信用证。

6. 包装：纸箱装。

7. 有效期：本月底前答复有效。

Unit 4 补充练习　　Unit 4 补充练习答案　　Unit 4 练习答案.

Unit 5　Orders and Fulfillment of Orders

【学习要点和目标】

通过本单元的学习，掌握订购信、确认订货信以及拒绝订货信函的写作要点。

Lead-in

An order is a request to supply a specified quantity of goods. Accuracy and clarity are the essential qualities of an order or an order-letter. A satisfactory order or order-letter should include the following:

1. The name and specification of the commodity.

2. The quantity to be ordered.

3. The unit price and total value.

4. The mode of packing.

5. The date and method of shipment.

6. Terms of payment.

When the seller agrees to the clauses of the order from the buyer, the seller should send a letter of confirmation to the buyer. However, sometimes, the seller cannot accept the buyer's order because the goods required are not available or prices and specifications have been changed. In such circumstances, letters declining the order must be written with the utmost care. It is advisable to recommend suitable substitutes and persuade the buyer to accept it.

Specimen Letter 1　Making a Trial Order

Dear Sirs,

Thank you for your letter of June 23. Having studied your **illustrated** catalogue and price list, we have chosen five models among them, for which we would like to **enclose** our order.

We would like to stress the fact that this is a **trial order.** If we are **satisfied** with both the quality of goods and shipment, you can expect our regular **repeated orders**. In order to avoid any difficulties with the **customs authorities** here, please make sure that our **shipping instruction**s are carefully **observed**.

For our financial and credit **standing**, we refer you to the **Chamber of Commerce** in your country.

Yours faithfully,

(Signature)

Notes

1. illustrated *adj.* 带图解的

We are very pleased to receive your enquiry of 15th January and enclose our illustrated catalogue and price list giving the details you ask for. 我们非常高兴地收到你方 1 月 15 日的询盘，并随函寄去带图解的商品目录和价目单以向你方提供所需详情。

2. enclose *v.* 随附

We are enclosing herewith our commercial invoices in duplicate. 随函附寄商业发票一式两份。

Enclosed are our commercial invoices in duplicate. 随函附寄商业发票一式两份。

Enclosed please find our commercial invoices in duplicate. 随函附寄商业发票一式两份。

enclosure *n.* 附件

3. trial order 试销订单

duplicate order 重复订单

initial order 初次订单

repeat order 重复订单

We should be grateful for your trial order. 如尝试订货，不胜感激。

4. satisfied (with) *adj.* 对……感到满意

We very much regret to learn from your letter of 2nd May that you are not satisfied with the dress materials supplied to your order No.87. 我们非常遗憾地从你方 5 月 2 日的信中得知，你方对第 87 号订单所提供的布料不满意。

5. customs authority 海关当局

An accurate description will help the customs authority of import country to clear the products quickly. 准确的货物名称有助于进口国海关快速清关。

6. shipping instructions 装运须知，是买方发给卖方的装运须知。

辨析：shipping advice 指装船通知，是卖方在 FOB、CFR 价格术语条件下，完成装货后，发给买方的通知，以便买方能及时安排保险。

Our shipping instruction must be observed. 必须要按照我方的装运须知行事。

7. observe   *v.* 遵守

You must be aware that the terms and conditions of a contract once signed should be strictly observed, failure to abide by them will mean violation of contract. 你必须知道，一旦合同签署，合同的条款和条件就必须遵守，不遵守就意味着违约。

8. standing   *n.* 地位，身份，名誉，名望

credit standing 资信状况

financial standing 财务状况

Anyhow, we should look into your credit standing, and then make a decision. 然而，我方要对贵公司的资信状况进行调查，然后再做出决定。

9. Chamber of Commerce 商会

We owe your name and address to the Chamber of Commerce that you are in the market for textiles. 我方从商会得知贵方名字和地址，并得知贵方欲购纺织品。

Specimen Letter 2   Enclosing an Order Form

Dear Sirs,

Thank you for your letter of July 6, and we are very glad to **inform** you that the quality and the prices of the products are both satisfactory. We are enclosing **herewith** a copy of our order form No.1234 for the items.

We are pleased to have transacted this first business with your corporation and look forward to the further expansion of trade to our **mutual benefit**.

> Yours faithfully,
>
> (Signature)

Order Form

> Order No.: 1234
>
> Date: July 20, 20××

Dear Sirs,

We have the pleasure of **placing with you our order** for the **under-mentioned** goods on the **terms and conditions** stated **as follows**:

Item	Quantity	Unit Price (CIF NEW YORK)	Total
Men's Shoes Model 121	500 pairs	US$35	US$17 500
Women's Shoes Model 223	400 pairs	US$30	US$12 000
Children's Shoes Model 312	500 pairs	US$20	US$10 000
		Less 5% discount	US$37 525

Packing: in new strong **cartons** suitable for long-distance **ocean transportation**.

Shipment: to be effected during September, 20××

Payment: by irrevocable L/C available by draft at sight.

We are going to instruct our bank to open a letter of credit for the amount of this order. You will soon hear from your bank.

Yours sincerely,

(Signature)

Notes

1. inform *v.* 通知

   inform sb. of/about sth. 通知某人某事

   Please inform us of the market situation on your side. 请向我方告知你方的市场状况。

   inform sb. that… 通知某人……

   We wish to inform you that business has been done at $200 per metric ton. 现通知你方以每公吨 200 美元的价格成交。

   Please be informed that 兹通知你方

   Please be informed that we are an importing company with a good reputation. 兹告知你方，我公司是一家拥有良好声誉的进口公司。

   keep sb. informed of/that 随时向某人告知

   We hope you will keep us informed of the market condition at your end. 希望你方随时向我方告知你方的市场状况。

2. herewith *adv.* 同此，随附

   We enclose herewith our catalogue and price list for your information. 我方随函附上商品目录和价目表供贵方参考。

3. mutual benefit 互利

   Our relationship is based on the principle of equality and mutual benefit. 我们的关系建立在平等互利的基础上。

4. place an order with… 向……订购货物

   We have decided to place a large order with you on the following conditions. 我公司决定

按下列条件向你方进行大宗订货。

5. under-mentioned　*adj.* 下述的

   above-mentioned　*adj.* 上述的

   We have not received the under-mentioned goods. 我们尚未收到下述货物。

   Samples for the above-mentioned goods will be sent on request. 上述货物样品承索即寄。

6. terms and conditions 条款；条件

   This contract is made by and between the Sellers and Buyers, whereby the Sellers agree to sell and the Buyers agree to buy the following goods on the terms and conditions stipulated below. 本合同由买卖双方共同拟定，根据本合同，卖方同意出售并且买方同意购买下列货物，条款如下。

7. as follows 如下

   这是一个习惯用语，不论前面的主语是单数或复数都要用 as follows。

   It is as follows. 如下。

   We state as follows. 兹陈述如下。

8. carton　*n.* 纸板箱

   When the postal clerk delivers your order, check the carton before signing it. 你方订购的货物由邮政人员送达时，签收前请先检查包装。

9. ocean transportation 海洋运输

   Ocean transportation is most widely used in international trade. 海洋运输是国际贸易中最广泛应用的运输方式。

Specimen Letter 3　Place an Order

Dear Sirs,

　　We acknowledge with thanks the receipt of your offer dated Jan. 3 and the sample leather shoes you send us. After **examining** your samples we found both the quality and the **workmanship** are **up to our requirement** and we are pleased to place an order with you for the following:

Item	Quantity	Unit Price (CIF NEW YORK)	Total
Men's Shoes Model 121	500 pairs	US$35	US$17 500
Women's Shoes Model 223	400 pairs	US$30	US$12 000
Children's Shoes Model 312	500 pairs	US$20	US$10 000
			US$39 500

Please **make delivery** within the next six weeks. The payment is to be made by **D/P** 30 days after sight. If this order proves satisfactory, we shall be happy to place further orders with you.

Yours faithfully,

(Signature)

Notes

1. examine   *v*. 检验；审核

The goods should be examined carefully before shipment. 货物在装运之前应仔细检查。

2. workmanship   *n*. 工艺

Our buyers insist on high standards of workmanship and materials. 我们的买主对工艺和材料坚持要高标准。

3. up to the requirement 达到标准

Our products are up to the requirement. 我们的产品达到了标准。

4. make delivery 交货

take delivery 提货

When we made delivery to the buyers, they refused it on seeing the damaged condition. 当我们向买方交货时，他们看到货物破损，拒绝接受。

We will take delivery of the goods as soon as they are released from the Customs. 货物一从海关放行，我方就会提货。

5. D/P，即 Documents against Payment (付款交单)。这种付款方式是跟单托收的一种，采用这种支付方式时，必须在进口人付清全部货款后，代收行才把货运单据和其他单据交给进口人。根据货款支付时间的不同，付款交单又分为即期付款交单(D/P at sight)和远期付款交单(D/P after sight) 两种。即期付款交单是指出口人发货后，开具即期汇票，委托托收行向进口人收取货款，进口人见票后要立即付款，付清货款后领取货运单据。远期付款交单是出口人发货后，开具远期汇票，通过银行向进口人提示，先由进口人承兑，于汇票到付款期限时再由进口人付清货款，领取提货单据。

D/A，即 Documents against Acceptance (承兑交单)。这是跟单托收的另一种形式，采用这种付款方式时，进口人只要承兑汇票，便可从银行取得货运单据，承兑汇票到期时进口人付款。这种支付方式对卖方风险较大。

Specimen Letter 4   Decline an Order

Dear Sirs,

Thank you very much for your order of 5000 pairs of black leather shoes on August 19. However, much to our regret, we have to **decline** your order, because at present we have no **stock** of shoes in the color required and do not expect further deliveries for at least another one month.

But now we can supply the brown and white ones from stock, and they are of the same quality and also fashionable. If they are of **interest** to you, you can consider them as an **alternative**.

Thank you again for your order, and we hope you can give us the opportunity to **fill your order** when the black leather shoes are available. **Meanwhile**, we shall be **only too** pleased to have other inquiries from you.

Yours sincerely,

(Signature)

Notes

1. decline

(1) *v.* 下降，become less

Computer sales declined 2% this year. 计算机的销售今年下降了 2%。

(2) *v.* 婉言谢绝，say no

After careful consideration on your request, we have come to the conclusion that we cannot but decline your order. 经过对你方的要求认真研究后，我们认为不得不谢绝你方订单。

2. stock   *n.* 存货

There is no stock at hand. 手头上无存货。

in stock 库存，现货

out of stock 缺货，无货

from stock 从库存中供应，供现货

3. interest   *n.* 兴趣

We have no interest in the leather goods. 我们对皮革货物不感兴趣。

The leather goods are not of interest to us. 我们对皮革货物不感兴趣。

4. alternative

(1) *adj.* 可选的

(2) *n.* 替代品

It seems clear that he has no reasonable alternative. 他没有其他合适的选择，这一点似乎很清楚。

5. fill your order 履行订单

类似的说法还有 carry out your order、fulfill your order、execute your order。

6. meanwhile *n./adv.* 同时

We trust the above information serves your purpose. Meanwhile we await your reply. 我们相信上述的信息能合你们的愿望。同时，我们静候佳音。

7. only too

too 前面如果有 only、all、but 修饰时，结构表示肯定。Only too pleased to…相当于 to be very glad to… 十分乐于做······

We would be only too glad to go with you. 我们很乐意与你同行。

Specimen Letter 5   Confirm an Order

Dear Sirs,

We are pleased to receive your order of 5 April for Men's Shoes. We **confirm** supply of 1000 pairs of the shoes at the prices **stated** in your order No.123. It is our honor to have the opportunity of serving you and we are sure that you will be satisfied with the quality of our goods.

Our **Sales Confirmation** No.ABC111 in two **original**s were **airmailed** to you. Please sign and return one copy of them **for our file**.

It is understood that a letter of credit in our favor **covering** the goods should be opened immediately. We wish to point out that **stipulations** in the **relative** L/C must strictly **conform** to the stated in our Sales Confirmation so as to **avoid subsequent amendments**. **You may rest assured that** we will effect shipment **without delay** on receipt of your letter of credit.

We appreciate your cooperation and look forward to receiving from you further orders.

Yours truly,

(Signature)

Notes

1. confirm *v.* 确认，证实

We confirm having purchased from you 1000 tons of the captioned goods on the following terms and conditions. 我们确认已经从你处购买 1000 吨的标题货物，条件及条款

如下。

Please confirm this order by return. 烦请回函确认此订单。

2. state   *v.* 陈述，说明

Please quote us your lowest price FOB NEW YORK, stating the earliest shipment and the packing. 请报最低 FOB 纽约价，并说明最早装运期和包装情况。

3. Sales Confirmation 售货确认书

Purchase Confirmation 购货确认书

4. original

(1) *n.* 正本

This contract is made out in two originals in both Chinese and English. 本合同制成中英文正本各两份。

(2) *adj.* 正本的

These are original documents. 这些是正本单据。

5. airmail

(1) *n.* 航空邮件

We shall be pleased to receive from you catalogue and samples by airmail. 我方很高兴收到你方航空邮寄来的目录和样品。

(2) *v.* 用航空邮件寄送

Please airmail us your catalogue and samples. 请把贵方的商品目录和样品航空邮寄给我方。

6. for our file 供我方存档

Please sign and return one copy for our file at your earliest convenience. 请尽快签退一份以供我方存档。

7. covering 有关，关于

We enclose our Sales Contract No. 66 covering this transaction. 我方随函附上这笔交易的 66 号销售合同。

8. stipulation   *n.* 条款

The transaction is concluded on the stipulation that L/C should be opened 30 days before the commencement of shipment. 这笔交易是以在装船前 30 天开出信用证达成的。

9. relative   *adj.* 有关的，关于

We are anxiously awaiting the relative L/C. 我方在急切盼望相关信用证。

10. conform   *v.* 使一致，符合

It is necessary to conform the specifications to the requirements. 规格必须与所需相符。

11. avoid   *v.* 避免

   We want to avoid disappointing our customers. 我们希望避免让我们的客户失望。

12. subsequent   *adj.* 以后的

   The story will be continued in subsequent issues of the magazine. 小说将继续在以后几期杂志上连载。

13. amendment   *n.* 修改

   After we have checked the L/C carefully, we request you to make the following amendments. 经认真审核信用证，请贵方修改如下。

14. You may rest assured that… 你方可以放心……

   You may rest assured that we will arrange for dispatch by the first available steamer without any delay upon receipt of your L/C. 你方可以放心，一收到你方开来的信用证，我方即用可订到的第一班船来安排装运。

15. without delay 毫不迟延

   We will send you a quotation without delay. 我方会立刻向贵方报价。

Specimen Letter 6   Confirm a Repeat Order

Dear Sirs,

   We thank you for your letter **duplicating** your order of Dec. 12 for 5000 pairs of Leather Shoes.

   Much as the prevailing prices are a little higher, we will accept the order on the same terms as before **with the view of** encouraging business.

   As requested in your previous letter, we have **made out** our Sales Confirmation No.123 in duplicate and shall thank you for sending back one copy **duly countersigned**.

   We are glad to know that a letter of credit will be established in our favor immediately. However, we would like to draw your attention to the fact that the stipulations in the relative credit should strictly conform to the terms in our Sales Confirmation in order to avoid subsequent fax amendments.

   We appreciate your cooperation and trust that the shipment, which is to be **dispatched** after receipt of the relative Letter of Credit, will turn out to your entire satisfaction.

                                                            Yours faithfully,

                                                            (Signature)

Notes

1. duplicate

(1) *v.* 使重复，使加倍，make an exact copy of

If you would like to duplicate your last order, we can give you the same price reduction. 如果你方愿意重复上次的订单，我方可给予同样的价格减让。

(2) *adj.* 复制的，成对的，副本的，copied

duplicate documents 单据副本

(3) *n.* 复制品，副本，an exact copy of something

in duplicate 一式两份

2. with the view of 目的是……

We take the liberty of writing to you with the view of establishing business relations with you. 我方冒昧与您通信，希望能与你方建立业务关系。

3. make out 缮制

We will make out our Sales Contract in two originals. 我方将缮制合同正本，一式两份。

4. duly *adv.* 及时地

We have duly received your Sales Contract No.1234 covering 50 metric tons rice we have booked with you. 我方已经及时收到向你方订购 50 公吨大米的销售合同 1234 号。

5. countersign *v.* 会签

When the Sales Contract has been signed by the seller, it should be countersigned by the buyer. 销售合同经卖方签署后，应由买方会签。

6. dispatch

(1) *n.* 发送

As we need the articles we ordered to complete deliveries to our new customers, we must ask you to arrange for the dispatch of replacements at once. 因我方需订购货物以向我方新客户完成交货，故我方要求你方务必立刻发送替换的货品。

(2) *v.* 发运

Please note that as these goods are urgently required here, we should be most grateful if you could dispatch the goods as soon as possible. 请注意，由于此地急需这些货物，如果你方能尽快发运这批货物，我方感激不尽。

Specimen Letter 7   Recommendation of a Substitute

Dear Sirs,

We are glad to receive your letter of Dec.15, ordering 200 sets of electric heater Art No. 113. However, we are regretful to tell you that the **article** you order is not available because the **demand** for this article has fallen to such an **extent** that we have **ceased** to produce it.

In order to meet your requirement, we would recommend an excellent **substitute**. It is superior to your inquired article in quality, but the price is almost the same. It has already found a ready market in Europe. We are sure it will meet with warm reception in your country as well.

Enclosed please find an illustrated catalogue and **sales literature**, from which you can know the full details of the product.

We are looking forward to your order.

Yours sincerely,

(Signature)

Notes

1. article

   (1) *n.* 物品，a thing, especially one of a group of things

   We learn from your letter of 10th October that our price for the subject article is found to be on the high side. 我方从你 10 月 10 日的来信中得知我方上述产品的价格偏高。

   (2) *n.* 文章，论文，专论，a piece of writing about a particular subject

   (3) *n.* (契约的)条款、条目，clause or item in an agreement

   The article of the contract must be observed completely. 必须完全遵守合同条款。

2. demand

   (1) *n.* 需求(后接介词 for)

   There is a demand for... 对……有需求。

   There is a great demand for textiles in Europe. 欧洲对纺织品有很大的需求。

   Many reports have been received from our selling agents in Hong Kong, that there are very heavy demands for the captioned garments. 从我方香港销售代理人处收到的报告表明标题服装的需求旺盛。

   There is steady demand in Europe for leather gloves of high quality. 欧洲对高品质的皮手套有稳定的需求。

(2) *v.* 要求(后面接从句时要用虚拟语气)

The exporter demanded that the buyer (should) open the irrevocable L/C immediately. 出口方要求买方立即开出不可撤销信用证。

3. extent   *n.* 程度

to some extent 在某种程度上

to such an extent that… 达到此种程度以至于……

4. cease   *v.* 停止

The factory has ceased making bicycles. 该工厂已经停止生产自行车。

5. substitute

(1) *n.* 代替品，something new or different that you use instead of something else that you used previously

This is an excellent substitute for leather. 这是一种极好的皮革代替品。

(2) *v.* 替代，to use something new or different instead of something else

"用 A 替代 B" 可以表达为 substitute A for B 或 substitute B with/by A。

As Art No.111 is out of stock, we will substitute No.112 for No.111. 由于 111 货号产品没有存货，所以我们将用 112 货号产品代替它。

6. sales literature 文字说明，印刷的商品资料的总称

Useful Sentences

1. We are enclosing herewith a copy of our order form No.××for the items. 我方随函附寄一份货物订单……号。

2. We are pleased to have transacted this first business with your corporation and look forward to the further expansion of trade to our mutual benefit. 我方很高兴与贵公司达成第一笔交易，希望能够为双方共同的利益进一步扩展贸易。

3. We have the pleasure of placing with you our order for the under-mentioned goods on the terms and conditions stated as follows. 我方很高兴按照以下条款向贵公司订购以下货物。

4. After examining your samples we found both the quality and the workmanship are up to our requirement and we are pleased to place an order with you for the following. 在检验过贵公司的样品后，我方认为质量和工艺都符合要求，愿意向贵公司订购如下货物。

5. Much to our regret, we have to decline your order, because… 十分遗憾，我公司不得不

拒绝你方订单，原因是……

6. We confirm supply of…at the prices stated in your order No.××. 我方确认按照你方……号订单中的价格订购……货物。

7. The stipulations in the relative L/C must strictly conform to the stated in our Sales Confirmation so as to avoid subsequent amendments. 相关信用证中的条款必须严格符合销售确认书中的条款，以避免日后的修改。

Letter-writing Guide

The steps and expressions of writing an order letter are as follows. (订货信的写作步骤及常用表达方式如下。)

Writing steps (写作步骤)	Examples of expressions (表达方式举例)
1. 感谢对方的来函，决定订购货物	Thank you for your letter of… Having studied your illustrated catalogue and price list, we have chosen five models among them, for which we would like to enclose our order. 感谢贵方……的来信。在仔细研究了你方的图解目录及价目表之后，我方从中选择了五个型号的产品，并随函附上了我方订单。
	Thank you for your letter of…and we are very glad to inform you that the quality and the prices of the products are both satisfactory. We are enclosing herewith a copy of our Order form No.×× for the items. 感谢贵方……的来函。我方很高兴地告知贵方，我方对贵方产品的价格及质量都十分满意，特随函附寄……号产品订单一份。
	We acknowledge with thanks the receipt of your offer dated…and the sample you send us. After examining your sample we found both the quality and the workmanship are up to our requirement and we are pleased to place an order with you for the following: 收到贵方……的发盘以及样品，十分感谢。在检验样品后，我方认为质量和工艺都符合我方的要求，因此很高兴地向贵方订购以下货品：
2. 订购商品的名称、规格、数量、单价、总值等	为使内容更明晰，这部分可列表。
3. 包装、装运及付款方式等	The goods should be packed in… 货物应用……包装。
	The goods should be delivered in… 货物应在……装运。
	The payment is to be made by D/P 30 days after sight. 用30天远期付款交单方式支付货款。
4. 表示若对本次交易满意，以后会继续订购	If this order proves satisfactory, we shall be happy to place further orders with you. 如果这次订货令我方满意，我方会再次订购。

The steps and expressions of writing a letter to decline an order are as follows.(拒绝订货信的写作步骤及常用表达方式如下。)

Writing steps (写作步骤)	Examples of expressions (表达方式举例)
1. 感谢对方订购货物	Thank you very much for your order of... 感谢贵方……的订单。
	We are glad to receive your order of... 很高兴收到贵方……的订单。
2. 拒绝订货的原因，并表示歉意	Much to our regret that we have to decline your order because there is no stock of the goods you order. 很遗憾不能接受贵方的订单，因为您所订购的货物无货可供。
	We are regretful to tell you that the article you order is not available because the demand for this article has fallen to such an extent that we have ceased to produce it. 很遗憾地告知贵方，您所订购的货物目前无货可供，因为对这种产品的需求下降，我方已经停止生产了。
3. 若有可提供的替代货品，可加以推荐	Now we can supply the...from stock, and they are of the same quality and also fashionable. 但是目前我方可供……，它们和贵方订购的货品质量相同而且同样流行。
	In order to meet your requirement, we would recommend an excellent substitute. It is superior to your inquired article in quality, but the price is almost the same. 为满足贵方要求，我方推荐一种非常好的替代产品。它在质量上优于贵方订购的产品，但是价格几乎相同。
4. 希望收到对方的订单	We are looking forward to your order. 期望收到贵方订单。
	We hope to receive your order again. 期望再次收到贵方订单。

The steps and expressions of writing a letter to confirm an order are as follows.(确认订货信的写作步骤及常用表达方式如下。)

Writing steps (写作步骤)	Examples of expressions (表达方式举例)
1. 感谢对方订购货物，并确认订单	Thank you very much for your order of...and we confirm having sold you the following goods on terms and conditions as below. 感谢贵方……的订单，我方确认按以下条款供下列货品。
	We are glad to receive your order of...and we confirm supply of ...on the following terms and conditions. 很高兴收到贵方……的订单，我方确认按以下条款供货。
2. 说明货物名称、规格、数量、价格、包装、装运、付款等内容或附寄合同	Our Sales Confirmation No××.... in two originals were airmailed to you. Please sign and return one copy of them for our file. 我方……号销售确认书正本一式两份已经航寄你方。请会签并寄回一份供我方存档。
	We will effect shipment within one month after receipt of your relative L/C. 装运在收到你方开来的相关信用证后一个月之内进行。

Writing steps (写作步骤)	Examples of expressions (表达方式举例)
3. 提醒对方注意的事项	Please open the covering L/C in our favor immediately. 请立即开立以我方为受益人的信用证。
	We wish to point out that stipulations in the relative L/C must strictly conform to the stated in our Sales Confirmation so as to avoid subsequent amendments. 我方要指出的是，相关信用证条款必须严格遵照合同条款开立以避免日后的修改。
4. 请对方放心己方会很好地履行订单，并希望再次收到对方的订单	You may rest assured that we will effect shipment without delay on receipt of your Letter of Credit. 贵方可放心，一收到信用证，我方立刻安排装运。
	You may rest assured that you will be satisfied with our goods. 贵方可放心，您会对我方所交货物感到满意。
	We appreciate your cooperation and look forward to receiving from you further orders. 感谢贵方的合作，期望再次收到贵方的订单。

Exercises

I. Put the following English phrases into Chinese or Chinese phrases into English.

1. illustrated catalogue   2. price list   3. trial order   4. repeated order   5. D/P

6. 财务状况   7. 信用状况   8. 商会   9. 装运须知   10. 海运

II. Translate the following English into Chinese or Chinese into English.

1. The L/C in our favor covering the said shoes should be opened immediately.

2. You may rest assured that we will effect shipment without delay on receipt of your L/C.

3. Please refer to Bank of China, London for our credit standing.

4. On receipt of your confirmation of order, we will make delivery without delay.

5. If you can allow us a 3% commission, we are prepared to place a trial order with you.

6. 随函寄去我方第 123 号售货确认书一式两份，请会签后退回一份以供存档。

7. 请你方注意，信用证的条款必须与我方销售确认书的条款完全相符，以避免日后修改。

8. 由于双方共同努力，我们达成了交易，希望这是我们双方之间贸易的良好开端。

9. 请向我方告知你方最早装船日期，以便我方及时通过中国银行给你方开出信用证。

10. 关于我方向你公司订购的 500 台缝纫机，我们已经收到你方 484 号销售合同。

11. 可以肯定，我们会非常认真地履行你方订单，使你方完全满意。

III. Translate the following letter into Chinese.

Dear Sirs,

We have duly received your Sales Contract No.563 covering 50 tons rice we have booked with you. Enclosed please find the duplicate with our counter-signature. Thanks to mutual efforts, we were able to bridge the price gap and put the deal through.

The relative L/C has been established with the Bank of China, London, in your favour. It will reach you in due course.

Regarding further quantities required, we hope you will see your way clear to make us an offer. As an indication, we are prepared to order 80 tons.

Yours sincerely,

(Signature)

IV. Writing practice.

Write a letter according to the following particulars.

1. You have received S/C No.123 in duplicate.

2. You countersigned and returned one copy.

3. You have opened an L/C.

4. If the goods are satisfactory, you prepare to place further orders.

Unit 5 补充练习   Unit 5 补充练习答案   Unit 5 练习答案

Unit 6　Sales Promotion

【学习要点和目标】

促销信的文体风格与其他商业信函完全不同。许多促销信都旨在为客户提供全面的销售信息，其中必须包括各项有关内容。因此，必须预计收信人可能会提出哪些问题，并在信函中做出相应的解答，同时也要注意信文不能写得太长，以免读来令人乏味。本单元介绍各种促销信的写作方法。

Lead-in

The purpose we write a sales correspondence is to persuade the readers to buy what we sell. Writing a sales correspondence, we should try to present the offer from the point of view of the buyer but not from the seller himself so as to promote sales of the goods. In order to reach this goal, we should learn about the potential customers. What kind of goods or service do they need? What are their interests? What is the most crucial factor they concern? Before writing, careful analysis should be made by writers so as to present answers the customers want to know in the sales correspondence. A satisfactory sales correspondence will usually include the followings:

1. Arousing buyers' interests.

2. Creating buyers' buying desire.

3. Persuasion.

4. Action.

In order to make a good impression on the goods you wish to promote you have to remember the following points:

1. Keep the correspondence as short as possible.

2. Catch the reader's interest in the opening paragraph.

3. Give the correspondence an attractive look and make it as personal as possible.

Specimen Letter 1　Introducing Commodities

Dear Sirs,

The Sunrise Trading Co., Ltd. has **informed** us that you are searching for high grade Wool Sweaters to be shipped to London. We'd like to offer you our "Comfort" lines which reach a standard sufficiently high to redound your **credit**.

"Comfort" brand Wool Sweaters are exclusively made from superior **quality** export grade Australian pure new wool, which has unique features giving natural warmth and comfort with proper elasticity and soft feeling. They are also ideal for those with rheumatic, arthritis and back suffering, and already have a good market in over 25 countries and regions.

Because of its successful sales in these countries and gratifying profits **dealers** get from it, we think you will also share the success.

We enclose a catalogue of the goods **for your reference** and look forward to your early reply.

Sincerely yours，

(Signature)

Notes

1. inform   *v.* 告知；通知。其基本句型是 inform sb. + 宾语从句和 inform sb. of sth.。

    We shall inform you of the date of shipment, name of steamer. 我们将把装运日期、船名通知你。

    Please inform us that which one of the three types is of interest to you. 请告知你对这三种类型中的哪种感兴趣。

    We wish to inform you that business has been done at $200 per metric ton. 我们已以每公吨 200 美元的价格成交，特此告知。

2. credit   *n.* 信用，信誉，信贷；赊欠(期)。多用于商人间的出口信贷、买方信贷和卖方信贷。

    I would like to know exactly how their credit stands. 我们想确切地知道他们的信用状况怎样。

    Our services are in high credit with the customers in Europe. 我方服务在欧洲客户中享有盛誉。

    The bank refused further credits to the company. 银行拒绝再贷款给那家公司。

    No credit is given at this shop. 本店概不赊欠。

3. quality   *n.* 质量

    Quality is the essence of this order. 质量是这笔订货的关键。

    If the quality of your initial shipment is found satisfactory, large repeats will follow. 如果你们第一批运来的货令人满意，随后将有大批续订。

    The goods are available in various qualities. 此货有各种不同的质量可以供应。

4. dealer   *n.* 又称 distributor，经销商或商号。他们通常与贸易商或厂商有着长期买卖的密切关系，有时有独家的经销权。dealer 也可指在证券、外汇及黄金市场上从事证券、外汇及黄金交易的交易商或交易员(经纪人)，前者自己负责盈亏风险，后者仅赚取佣金。

They are among the leading dealers of this city in these products. 他们是这个城市中经营这些产品的主要商号之一。

dealer in toilet articles 化妆品商

small dealer 小商贩

securities dealer 证券商

5. for your reference 供你方参考。该短语是外贸信函中提供情况信息时常用的一种表达方式，也可说 for your information。

We enclose an analysis of the test we have made for your reference. 兹附上化验结果以供你方参考。

We shall appreciate it if you will send us some up-to-date patterns for our reference. 如能寄给我们一些最新的花样作参考，我们将不胜感激。

Specimen Letter 2   Offering a Discount

Dear Sirs,

We are a well-organized **exporter** with experienced salesmen who have a comprehensive knowledge of the **requirements** and preferences of your market. In order to show you the excellence of our products, we are sending you our free **sample under separate cover**. Please find our price list and illustrated catalogue for reference.

The enclosed price list shows that we can offer you our products at 5%～10% reduction in prices than those of our competitors. Although the **prices** we offered are exceptionally low, the **quality** is still very good.

With these advantages you can develop your market without worrying about competition. We therefore trust that we will be able to receive your order soon.

Yours faithfully,

(Signature)

Notes

1. exporter

(1) *n.* 出口商

They are leading exporters of computers. 他们是电脑的主要出口商。

(2) *v.* 出口

We export a large quantity of textiles now. 我们目前出口大量纺织品。

export control 出口管制

export drawback 出口退税

export documents 出口单据

export subsidies 出口补贴

export dumping 出口倾销

2. requirement   *n.* 需要，要求

Good quality is the major requirement. 质量好是主要的要求。

Please let us know your annual requirements for walnuts. 请告你方对核桃的年需量。

We have noted your requirement of samples. 我们已注意到你们需要样品。

3. sample   *n.* 样品

The sample is for reference only. 样品仅供参考。

The business is not done on the basis of sample. 这笔交易不是根据样品成交的。

free sample 免费样品

full range of sample 全套样品

random sample 随意取样

sample for reference 参考样品

4. under separate cover 另邮。在平时的业务中，样本或目录等业务文件体积比较大，和业务信一起寄显得不方便，因此通常分开邮寄。这样，我们就经常使用这一短语。还可以说 by separate post，by separate mail，by separate airmail。例如：

We are pleased to send you by separate post our revised catalogue. 我们高兴地另行寄上修订后的目录。

We are airmailing you under separate cover our latest sample books. 我们另航空邮寄最新样本。

We are sending you the contract under separate cover. 我们将合同另邮寄给你方。

We have forwarded to you under separate cover a full range of samples for the coming season. 我们另邮寄给你方一批供下季销售的货物样品。

5. price   *n.* 价格；定价

Business is possible if you can raise (increase/lift/improve) the price by 5%. 如果你方出价能提高5%，则可能成交。

We have stretched the price to the highest price we can do. 我方已将价格出到最高限度。

6. quality   *n.* 质量，品质

average quality 平均品质

common quality 一般品质

fair quality 尚好品质

standard quality 标准品质

fair average quality (F.A.Q) 大路货

Specimen Letter 3   Sales Promotion Correspondence

Leaking Window Frames?

Until recently, the only cure for seriously leaking window frames was to strip out the entire window frame and replace all defective parts.

Now there is a superior alternative which **represents** much better value for money. That alternative is thermobond insulation.

With thermobond, no scaffolding is needed. So, thermobond is far cheaper than conventional treatment. Yet thermobond leads to greater insulation and security for your house or flat, and is **guaranteed** for 10 years. Thermobond is made of the highest grade aluminum, and is **assembled** by skilled craftsman in Malaysia.

So if you're fed up with winter draughts and leaking windows, send off the **postage-paid** card enclosed, and we'll send you a full-colour brochure giving all **range** of product details you need to help you choose thermobond insulation.

The sooner you write, the sooner you'll be sitting pretty!

Notes

1. sales promotion 促销。促销是指把企业的出口产品向客户宣传并介绍，使他们认识和了解该产品，引起他们的注意和兴趣，激发他们的购买欲望，促使他们采取购买行动，从而达到开发市场、扩大产品销路的目的。促销信函的特点是以明确、简练、生动的语言介绍产品的性能、优点和用途，内容必须充实、可靠，使人感到亲切可信，有吸引力。

    Our efforts in sales promotion turned out to be a success. 我们在促销方面所做的努力取得了成功。

    We have specially raised the commission to 4% so as to enable you to cover the advertising expenses you may incur in sales promotion. 我们特别把佣金提高至4%以使你方能支付在促销活动中可能发生的广告费用。

2. represent   *v.* 代表，代理；再提示，再提交

We are willing to represent you for the sales of Chinese Men's Shirts in our country. 我公司愿意代理你方在我国销售中国男式衬衫。

represent a cheque at the bank 再向银行兑支票

represent a bill for payment 再提交账单或票据要求付款

3. guarantee   *v.* 担保，保证

If you guarantee payment, we will forward them the shipment on D/P basis. 如果你们担保付款，我们将按付款交单把这批货发运给他们。

It is not possible for us to guarantee the time of arrival. 我们不可能保证到达的时间。

We are ready to allow you a 3% commission provided if you can guarantee a yearly turnover of $75, 000 for a start.

倘若作为开端，你方能保证一年营业额达 75 000 美元，我方乐于给予 3%的佣金。

4. assemble   *v.* 装配

assembling with components 来件装配

assembling shop 装配车间

a processing and assembling line 加工和装配线

assembly industry 装配工业

5. postage-paid 邮资已付

6. range

(1) *n.* 系列(产品)，货物

As soon as we are in possession of details and samples of your range, we shall be in a position to advise you on their suitability for this particular market. 一旦我们收到你方产品的详细资料和样品时，我们就可告知你方这些产品对此地市场的适应性如何。

We can supply carpets in a wide range of designs. 我们能供应花样繁多的地毯。

We send you a full range of samples covering this article. 兹寄去这种商品的全套样品。

(2) *v.* (在……范围)变动

Wholesale prices rang from 25 to 35 percent off retail prices. 批发价是按零售价减少25%～35%。(此句也可以表述成 Wholesale prices range between 65 to 75 percent of the retail prices。)

Regarding sewing machines, stock is available in various types, prices ranging from USD60 to USD180 per set. 关于缝纫机，各种型号均有货供，每辆价格自 60 美元至 180 美元不等。

Our scope of business ranges over an extensive line of light industrial products. 我们的经营范围包括多种轻工业品。

Specimen Letter 4   Comparison of Goods

Gentlemen:

We are pleased to learn from China Council for the Promotion of International Trade who informed us that you are in the market for honey. We wish to inform you that we are **specialized** in the export of the commodity. Chinese honey is popular with European customers with its special flavor. As requested, we now **enclose** our quotation sheet with samples and catalogues to be sent under separate cover. We trust that the quoted price is acceptable to you, which is 10% lower than that of the similar article of Indian origin. A fair **comparison** in quality between our products and those of other suppliers will convince you of the reasonableness of our quotations. We would suggest that you send us your **trial order** as soon as possible, as there is a brisk demand for this article.

Yours faithfully,

(Signature)

Notes

1. specialize   *v.* 专门经营。后接 in

   We are a state-operated corporation specializing in the import and export of Chemicals. 我们是国有企业，专门经营化工产品的进出口业务。

2. enclose   *v.* 把……封入；把……附在信中，随函附寄

   We are enclosing our commercial invoice in duplicate. 随函附寄商业发票一式两份。

   We enclose (are enclosing) a price list for our exportable items. 随函寄去我方可供出口商品的价目表。

   Enclosed please find a full set of shipping documents. 随函寄去全套装船单据。

   表示附在某封信内时用介词 with 或 in。

   Please refer to the price list enclosed with (in) our letter of Aug. 5. 请查阅 8 月 5 日去信所附的价目表。

3. comparison　*n*. 比较。其动词形式为 compare，注意该词在下列例句中的用法。

If you compare our products with theirs, you will agree that our quality is much more superior. 如果你将我们的产品和他们的货物比较，你会同意我们的质量要高得多。

The price is some what on the high side as compared with those of the rival goods. 同竞争对手货品价格相比，此价格有些高。

If you make a comparison between the two, you will see the difference. 如对两者做一比较，你将看出差别。

You will find that our prices are moderate in comparison with those of competitors. 和竞争者的价格比较，你将发现我们的价格是公道的。

4. trial order　试订单，试订货。一般新品上市，买主对其销售情况不了解，先试订小数量，等销售情况看好时，再大量订货；或新客户初次订货时，没有把握，一般先试订一批货。试订单一般数量小，而且价格上有优惠。

Please try your best to execute this trial order as it will lead to more businesses. 请尽力执行这一试订单，因为它会带来更多的业务。

We suggest you place a trial order to see how it goes. 我们建议你方试订一批看看怎样。

Specimen Letter 5　Recommendation of a Substitute

Dear Sirs,

　　We are delighted to receive your letter of October 18 asking whether we can supply you with computers Model 210. However, we regret to tell you that the said article is not **available** owing to the rush of orders. In order to meet your demand，we would **recommend** an excellent **substitute**.

　　We have a residue **stock** of Model 330 and we can **supply** you with that. You are well **aware** that it is efficient and durable, economical and practical in use for middle school students. It is as good as the inquired article in quality. We are prepared to clear the stock by allowing you a generous discount. Say:

　　9% for an order for 100 sets to 199 sets;

　　12% for an order for 200 sets to 299 sets;

　　15% for an order for 300 sets and above.

on the current price of HK$ 280 per set CIF Hong Kong. This offer is subject to your reply reaching here on or before 20th June.

We hope you will take advantage of this exceptional offer.

Yours truly,

(Signature)

Notes

1. available   *adj.* 可利用的，可供应的；可支付的

Please ship the goods by the first available steamer. 请用第一艘可订到舱位的船只装运此货。

There are no such Men's Shirts available for export. 没有这种男式衬衫可供出口。

Our usual terms of payment are by confirmed, irrevocable L/C available by sight draft. 我方通常的支付方式是凭保兑的、不可撤销的信用证，即期汇票付款。

2. recommend   *v.* 推荐；劝告；建议。其后可接双宾语，也可接动名词和 that 从句。

They request you to recommend them some material that suits the African market. 他们请你方推荐一些适合非洲市场的商品。

We recommend buying a small quantity for trial. 我们劝你们购买少量试用。

We recommend that you try the Scandinavian markets. 我建议你方可尝试北欧市场。

3. substitute   *n.* 代用品，它还可以用作动词(*v.*)和形容词(*adj.*)。以 A 代替 B，可以说 substitute A for B，substitute B by(with)A。

As Art No.756 is no longer available in stock, we have substituted Art.No.757. 由于货号 756 没有存货，我们已用货号 757 代替。

If agreeable to you, we will substitute Type A for Type B. 如你们同意，我们将用 A 型来代替 B 型。

In this shipment, as agreed, we have substituted the portion undelivered with Type No.15. 如所商定的，在这批货中，我们已用十五型代替了未交货部分。

Enclosed please find our substitute order No.123 for order No.120. 寄去我方第 123 号订单以代替第 120 号订单，请查收。

We suggest you accept Pattern No.45 as a substitute. 我们建议你方接受四十五型作为代用品。

This is an ideal substitute for leather. 这是一种很好的皮革代用品。

4. stock   *n.* 存货。用单复数均可，表示所存具体商品时，stock 后接介词 in 或 of 再接商品；指储存时，stock 为不可数名词，常用于一些介词短语中。

There is/are no more stock(s) on hand. 手边无存货。

Spot stocks are insufficient to meet demand. 现货不够满足需要。

At the moment, we have only a limited stock in/of linen goods. 我们目前仅有有限的亚麻织品存货。

in stock 库存，现货

out of stock 缺货，无货

from stock 自库存中供应

5. supply v. 作动词时可以用 supply sb. with sth. 的句型(如本信中)，也可以用 supply sth. to sb. 的句型。

We can supply Art No.6024 to you. 我们可以供应 6024 货号商品。

supply 也用作名词，如：Supply for this article exceeds demand on our market。我方市场这种商品供大于求。

Owing to short supply, we can not make you an offer at present. 由于缺货，目前我们不能给你方报盘。

This article is in short (scarce/light/free/abundant/ample) supply. 这种商品供应缺少(稀少/量少/量大/丰富/充分)。

We are glad we have been able to supply your needs to the full. 我们很高兴，我们能供应你们的全部所需。

6. aware adj. 知道的。后接介词 of 或 that 引起的从句；后接 how、what、where、why 引起的名词从句时，介词 of 常常省略。

We are aware of the change in the market. 我们看到市场的变化。

We are aware that the market has changed. 我们看到市场已有变化。

We are not aware (of) why you have not opened the L/C. 我们不知道你方为什么还没有开出信用证。

Specimen Letter 6　Promotion to a Former Client

Dear Sirs,

Looking through our records, we note with regret that we have not had the pleasure of an order from you since last August. As you are one of our regular clients, we are concerned very much about whether you have been dissatisfied either with our goods or with our service. Would you fill out the enclosed reply card if you have encountered some problems with us? We will give your comments immediate attention.

We think you may be interested to know that we have recently been **appointed agents** for the sale in this country of the computers of four leading American **manufactures**. Our stocks now include a wide range of first-class personal computers at very **competitive** prices. You will see from the catalogue enclosed that our prices are much lower than those of other importers. In addition, we are offering very generous terms of payment. We look forward to the pleasure of your renewed order.

Yours faithfully,

(Signature)

Notes

1. appoint   *v.* 任命，委派，委任

   appoint sb. for a post 派某人任某职

   We have appointed an agent for our china ornaments in your city. 我方已在你市委派了陶瓷装饰品的代理人。

   We have appointed ABC Co. our agent for china ornaments in your city. 我方已委派 ABC 公司为我方在你市陶瓷装饰品的代理人。

2. agent   *n.* 代理人

   If you would appoint us as your agent, we could give you a reasonable guarantee to sell US $ 100 000 a month, because yours is a line we can handle well. 假如你们委任我们为你方代理，我们保证每月销售 10 万美元，因为你方所经营的商品是我们最善于经营的。

   The exporter may employ an agent living in the buyer's country to push the sales of his products. 出口商可以雇用居住在买方国家的一位代理人，以推销其产品。

   agent service 代理业务

   buying agent 采购代理人

   chartering agent 租船代理人

   selling agent 销售代理人

3. manufacture

   (1) *v.* 制造，生产

   In order to meet your requirements, we are test-manufacturing something new. 为了满足你方需要，我们正在试制一种新产品。

   Your order is being manufactured and will soon be ready for shipment. 你方的订货正在制造中，不久即可备妥装船。

   (2) *n.* 制造，制造品

   manufactured goods/products 制成品/工业品

They are engaged in the manufacture of plastics. 他们从事塑料品的制造。

4. competitive   *adj.* 可竞争的

Please cable us an offer at competitive price. 请电告我方有竞争性价格的报盘。

We believe our price is competitive enough to induce business. 我们相信我们的价格不逊于别家，是可招来业务的。

Useful Sentences

1. We avail ourselves of this opportunity to write to you and see if... 我们利用这次机会给你写信，看看是否……

2. We are a state-owned import and export company specializing in... 我们是一家国有进出口公司，致力于……

3. In order to give you a rough idea of..., we are airmailing you under separate cover a copy of... 为了使你大致了解……，我们正以航空邮件的方式另函寄给你……

4. We are willing to enter into business relations with your firm on the basis of equality and mutual benefit. 我们愿意在平等互利的基础上同你公司建立贸易关系。

5. We have come to know the name of your corporation and have the pleasure of writing this letter to you in the hope of establishing business relations with you. 我们已经获悉您公司的名字，并且怀着与你确定贸易关系的希望给您写这封信。

6. Your letter expressing the hope of entering into business connection with us has been received with thanks. 您希望与我们建立业务联系的来信已经收到，非常感谢。

7. We learn that you were seeking partners in China for selling your products. 我们获悉您正为出售您的产品在中国寻找合伙人。

8. Our competitive prices, superior quality and efficiency have won confidence and goodwill among our business clients. 我们具有竞争性的价格，上乘的质量和卓越的效率已经在我们的客户中赢得信誉。

9. Our market survey informs us that you have a keen interest in the import of... 从我们的市场调查中得知你方对进口……感兴趣。

10. We are writing to you in the hope that we can open up business relations with your firm. 我们写信给您，希望能与您公司建立业务关系。

11. We shall be grateful if you will reply at an early date. 如果您尽早答复，我们将不胜感激。

Letter-writing Guide

The steps and expressions of writing sales promotion are as follows. (促销信函的写作步骤及常用表达方式如下。)

Writing steps (写作步骤)	Examples of expressions (表达方式举例)
1. 介绍所促销的产品，使对方了解并对该产品产生兴趣	to be made of… 由……制成
	to be popular with customers… 受到顾客欢迎
	to sell well… 销路很好
	to meet with warm reception… 很受欢迎
	to be moderate in price, elegant in style, matching in colors and skillful in workmanship… 价格合理，式样优美，款式典雅，色泽和谐，做工考究……
2. 进行商品比较，体现本产品的优势	to compare favorable with… 优于……
	to be+形容词比较级+than… 比……要……
	to make a comparison of…in respect to… 做有关……的比较
3. 优惠条件(价格或数量方面)	to give…the first chance… 给予……优先
	to offer/allow/give/grant…a…discount 给……折扣
4. 劝导客户最终行动	to be acceptable to… 可以为……接受
	to deem it to one's advantage to do… 认为对……有利
	to advise…to work fast… 劝……尽早做决定

Exercises

I. Put the following English phrases into Chinese or Chinese phrases into English.

1. a sale to celebrate   2. pre-paid postage envelope   3. be completely satisfied

4. from stock   5. for your reference

6. 受到顾客欢迎   7. 密切关注   8. 提供有竞争性的价格

9. 追加订货   10. 免费样品

II. Fill in the blanks of the following letter with the words given below, and change the form when necessary.

receiving   quality   respected   number   attend   invitation   pleasure   range

Dear Sirs,

As one of our most __1__ customers, Double Star Company takes great __2__ in inviting you to our annual winter sale which will take place from 12-19 December at our showroom in

Marine Parade Road. There will be great savings to be made on all Double Star Company' products, including our full ___3___ of digital audio and high ___4___ video equipment.

Simply cut out the entry badge below and wear it when you ___5___ the sale. This ___6___ entitles you to bring one guest, too. If you phone the telephone ___7___ above within seven days of ___8___ this letter, your name will also be entered in a special lottery with some great prizes. The winners' name will be read out at the showroom on 19 December.

Ms. Janice Lai

Sales Executive

III. Translate the following English into Chinese or Chinese into English.

1. We understand from your letter of May 15 that you would give us an order if we allow you a 10% discount from the listed price.

2. We are sending you by this post a catalogue, containing quotations for large orders taken from our existing stock.

3. We have received your samples, with a price-list, also your scale of rebate and terms of settlement, all of which we find satisfactory.

4. Our products have been enjoying fast sales in Europe.

5. To encourage you to place orders with us, we would allow for a 3% special discount for any order received at the end of September.

6. 我方还可采用对你方有利的支付条件。

7. 为了向你方说明商品的优越性，我方另寄免费样品。

8. 我们的货物价格公道，比竞争对手的价格低约10%。

9. 我方产品在质量上和价格方面都优于您现在所用产品。

10. 由于所需型号脱销，我们将用下列型号代替。

IV. Writing practice.

Write a letter with the following hints.

1. 推销新款电脑桌。

2. 电脑桌质量上乘，价格合理，颜色多样。

3. 尽快交货，支付方式有利。

Unit 6 补充练习　　　Unit 6 补充练习答案　　　Unit 6 练习答案

Unit 7　Terms of Payment

【学习要点和目标】

通过本单元的学习，了解不同的国际贸易付款方式，掌握信用证的申请、开立、延期以及修改等信函的写作方法和写作词汇。

Lead-in

Payment in international trade is much more complicated than that in domestic trade. There are many **modes of payment**. The most widely used are three ones, namely, remittance, collection and letter of credit (abbreviated to L/C).

Remittance means that the importer remits the amount of money to the exporter through banks. There are mainly three types of remittance: Mail Transfer (M/T), Telegraphic Transfer (T/T) and remittance by banker's Demand Draft (D/D).

Payment can also be made by collection through banks under the terms of Documents against Payment (D/P) or Documents against Acceptance (D/A). Documents against Payment requires actual payment against shipping documents. There are D/P at sight and D/P after sight. Documents against Acceptance requires **delivery of documents** against **acceptance of the draft** drawn by the exporter.

Letter of credit (L/C) is the most often used method of payment in international trade. It is reliable, safe and flexible. L/C can **be defined as** a conditional undertaking by a bank, issued **in accordance with** the instructions of the buyer, addressed to or **in favor of** the seller. The bank promises to pay, accept, or negotiate the beneficiary's draft up to a certain sum of money, in the stated currency, within the prescribed time limit, **upon** the presentation of the stipulated documents. In international trade, the applicant is the importer, the beneficiary is the exporter and the issuing bank is the importer's bank. In an L/C transaction, banker's credit replaces the commercial credit. As long as the seller complies with all conditions stipulated in the L/C, such as submitting the documents required in the L/C within the time limit, the seller is safer in terms of being paid than in any other modes of payment. In a word, bank functions as the credit provider for both the exporter and the importer in L/C transaction, where both parties' interests are assured.

It is usual practice in our export trade that the L/C is to be established and to reach the seller at least one month prior to the date of shipment so as to give the seller adequate time to make preparations for shipment, such as making the goods ready and booking shipping space. For prompt shipment, urging the establishment of L/C is absolutely necessary.

If any discrepancies or some unforeseen special clauses to which the seller does not agree are found in L/C, the seller should send an advice to the buyer, asking him to make amendment. The L/C must be **in complete conformity with** the sales contract and the related documents.

In order to leave sufficient time to the seller to produce the shipping documents and to the bank to make their negotiation, the date of shipment and the expiry date of the L/C should be at least two weeks apart. Sometimes the seller may fail to get the goods ready for shipment in time or the buyer may request the shipment be postponed for one reason or another, then the seller will have to ask for extension of the expiry date as well as the date of shipment of L/C.

As far as the exporter's benefit is **concerned**, L/C is better than D/P. D/P at sight is better than D/P after sight while D/P is better than D/A. Sound choice of modes of payment depends very much on the credit situation of the business partners involved.

Notes

1. modes of payment 付款方式

2. delivery of documents 提交单据

3. acceptance of the draft 汇票的承兑

4. be defined as 定义为

   It can be defined as a responsibility for all parties involved. 可将其定义为参与各方的责任。

5. in accordance with 与……一致

   Everything should be in accordance with what is prescribed. 所有的都应与所规定的一致。

6. in favor of 以……为受益人

   The draft should be drawn in favor of you. 应开具以你方为受益人的汇票。

7. upon 一……就……

   Upon presentation of your document, payment will be made. 提交单据即付款。

8. in complete conformity with 与……保持严格一致

   The regulations within your organization should be in complete conformity with the law. 您组织内部的规定应符合法律的规定。

9. as far as … concerned 就……而言

   As far as the payment is concerned, we'd like to propose L/C. 就付款而言，我们建议使用信用证。

Specimen Letter 1　Asking to Establish L/C as the Terms of Payment

Dear Sirs,

We appreciate your order No.12 for 5000 pieces of tablecloth but regret being unable to accept your terms of payment mentioned.

In our last letter we sent you a copy of our specimen contract stating clearly our **general sales terms and conditions**. If you have read the specimen contract you will notice that our usual terms of payment are by **confirmed, irrevocable letter of credit in our favor**, available by **draft at sight**, reaching us one month ahead of shipment, remaining valid for **negotiation** in China till the 21st day after the **prescribed** time of shipment, and allowing **transshipment** and **partial shipments.**

We also mentioned in our letter dated on 15th of August that some European companies had already done business with us **in accordance with** the **above-mentioned** terms. We hope that you will come to agree with us **in this concern** and successfully conclude the first deal between us as soon as possible.

We will send you the contract upon your **favorable reply** in order to allow enough time to prepare the goods.

We await your early reply.

Yours truly,

(Signature)

Notes

1. general sales terms and conditions　一般销售条款

2. confirmed, irrevocable letter of credit　保兑的、不可撤销的信用证

3. in our favor　以我方为受益人　in favor of　以……为受益人

4. draft at sight　即期汇票

   You may draw a draft at sight on us.　您可以向我们开立一个即期汇票。

5. negotiation　*n.* 议付

   Adequate time should be left for the bank negotiation.　应留出足够的时间给银行议付。

6. prescribed　*adj.* 规定的

   类似的词语还有 stipulated，set forth，stated。

Anything prescribed in our contract should be abide by. 应遵守合同中规定的所有内容。

7. transshipment *n.* 转船

8. partial shipments 分批装运

9. in accordance with 与……一致

10. above-mentioned 以上提到的

11. in this concern 在这方面

类似的短语还有 in this regard、in this issue、at this point。

Your accommodation in this concern is highly appreciated. 非常感谢您在这方面的关照。

12. favorable reply 肯定的回复，有利的回复

Specimen Letter 2 Advice of Establishment of L/C

Dear Sirs,

We write to inform you that we have now opened a confirmed, irrevocable, letter of credit in your favor for USD 15 000 with the Commercial Bank of Africa, **valid until** October 15th. You **are authorized to** draw at 60 days' draft through the bank in Ghana for **the amount of invoice** after shipment is made. The bank will require you to **present** the following documents before accepting the draft:

1. Bill of Lading **in triplicate**.

2. Commercial Invoice in 5 copies.

3. **Packing List**.

4. Certificate of Insurance in 2 copies.

5. **Certificate of Origin**.

We are looking forward to your shipment at the end of September.

Yours sincerely,

(Signature)

Notes

1. valid until 有效至……

2. are authorized to 经授权做……

类似的词语有 be authorized to、be entitled to、be given the power to。

3. the amount of invoice 发票金额

4. present　*v.* 提交

　　类似的词语有 put in、submit、hand in documents。

5. in triplicate　一式三份

6. packing list　装箱单

7. certificate of origin　原产地证

Specimen Letter 3　Asking for Amendment to L/C

Dear Sirs,

　　We are **in receipt of** your letter **dated** September 19 informing us about the establishment of the L/C No. L89 **against** our S/C No. 56. However, we regret to find that there are some discrepancies, which are not **in conformity with** the contract. We hereby list these discrepancies as follows **for your attention**:

　　1. The name of the beneficiary should **read** "Qingdao Arts & Crafts Imp. & Exp. Co." instead of "Qingdao Crafts Imp. & Exp. Co." as appeared on the current L/C.

　　2. Please change the "with partial shipments and transshipment prohibited" to "with partial shipments and transshipment allowed".

　　We suppose that the above mistakes are clerical and hope you will make necessary amendments **without delay** by fax in order for us to make the shipment in time.

　　Your early reply is highly appreciated.

Yours faithfully,

(Signature)

Notes

1. in receipt of　收到

2. dated　*v.* 于……天

　　Your email dated November 19 has been received. 收到你方 11 月 19 日的电邮。

3. against　*prep.* 对，针对

　　(1) 相反：against the law　违法

　　(2) 反对：No one is against the proposal. 没人反对这个建议。

　　(3) 靠着，倚着：lean against the wall　靠在墙上

　　(4) 与……成对照：against a dark background　与黑色背景成对照

　　(5) 以……相抵：income against expenditure　收支相抵

4. in conformity with　与……保持一致

　　类似的表达还有 in accordance with、be consistent with、be identical with。

5. for your attention 提请您注意

6. read   *v.* 读作

The banner reads "Welcome to China." 横幅上写着"欢迎来中国"。

7. without delay 没有任何延误

Specimen Letter 4   Ask for Extension of L/C

Dear Sirs,

We **regret** to inform you that we did not receive your L/C covering the above Sales Confirmation until today. It is clearly stated in the above contract that the related L/C should **reach** us **no later than** the end of November. Although it is already very late for your L/C to arrive, we are still going to make the shipment for your order **recognizing** the long-term business relationship with your company.

Nevertheless, we are unable to ship the goods in accordance with the date specified in the S/C due to the delay caused by the L/C. You are supposed to extend the L/C as follows:

1. To extend the time of shipment to the end of January next year.

2. To extend the **validity** of the L/C to February 15, 20××.

Please make sure this time that the above-mentioned amendment to L/C should be made before the end of December this year since otherwise we will be unable again to **effect shipment** according to the extended time limit mentioned above.

We await your prompt reply.

Yours sincerely,

(Signature)

Notes

1. regret   *v.* 遗憾

类似的短语有 regret/feel sorry to do sth、regret doing sth.。

I regret doing that to you. 很遗憾那样对你。

2. reach   *v.* 到达，送达

Your letter did not reach us until yesterday. 直到昨天才收到您的信。

3. no later than 不迟于

4. recognizing   *v.* 鉴于

in view of/in consideration of/in regard to/seeing our long term relationship 鉴于我们长期的合作关系

5. validity   *n.* 有效期

The validity of the L/C has to be extended in order for us to make the shipment. 必须延期信用证使我们得以装运。

6. effect shipment 装运

in effect, in fact 事实上

It is in effect the same thing. 实际上是一回事。

take effect, come into force 生效

The new regulation will take effect on the first day of next month. 新规定下月首日生效。

to the effect, with the general meaning 意思大概是

We have received your cable to the effect that shipment is to be held pending your instructions. 我们已收到您的电报说即将装运。

to the same effect, with the same meaning 相同的意思

We sent a telegram and wrote a letter to the same effect. 我们发了个电报，也写了封同样意思的信。

Specimen Letter 5　Reply to the Letter of Asking for Extension of L/C

Dear Sirs,

We have received your letter on December 11 asking us to **extend** the related L/C to February 15, 20××and the shipment to be effected to the end of January 20××.

We **are aware of** the fact that if we cannot send you the L/C by the end of December **at the latest**, you will not be able to **catch** the shipment **deadline** stipulated in the related S/C. However, since we have to go through certain procedures in order to apply for the **import license**, we could not open the L/C earlier. The import license will only be valid until the beginning of January 20××.

We will try our best to provide support but as there is no possibility to extend the import license **under the current circumstances**, we regret having to say that it is **beyond** us to make any extensions to the above L/C.

Please try your best to effect the shipment in time and we appreciate your effort made **in this concern**.

Yours faithfully,

(Signature)

Notes

1. extend   *v.* postpone/defer/put off shipment date 延期

2. be aware of   意识到，认识到

3. at the latest   最晚

   You are supposed to make the shipment on December 12 at the latest. 您最晚应在 12 月 12 日发货。

4. catch   *v.* 赶上

5. deadline   *n.* 最终期限

6. import license   进口许可证

7. under the current circumstances   在目前的情况下

8. beyond   *prep.* 超过

   It is beyond us now to accept such a big order. 我们现在无法接受这么大的订单。

9. in this concern   在这方面

Specimen Letter 6   Reply to Urging to Establish L/C

Dear Sirs,

We have received your letter dated on September 16 **urging** us to establish the covering L/C for the above-mentioned order.

We are very **sorry for** the delay in establishing the L/C and for the **consequent** trouble caused. The delay is mainly due to the communication error happened within our organization. Nevertheless, we have immediately opened the relative L/C with the Bank of China upon our receipt of your last letter. We believe that you should **get hold of** one copy of the L/C by now.

Please allow us to express our apology again and we promise that such mistakes will not take place in our future transactions. Thank you again for your understanding **in advance**.

Yours faithfully,

(Signature)

Notes

1. urging   *v.* 催促

   We have received your letter urging/asking/enquiring/us for establishing L/C. 信中催促/请求/要求我们开信用证。

2. to be sorry for   对……感到抱歉

I am very sorry for the inconvenience caused in this issue. 我对在这个问题上造成的不便深感抱歉。

3. consequent

(1) *adj.* 所造成的

(2) consequence *n.* 后果

You are liable for any consequences resulted from your behavior. 你要对你的行为造成的后果负责。

4. get hold of 得到，抓住

类似的词语还有 seize、catch、catch hold of、obtain。

5. in advance 事先

Thank you in advance. 先表谢意。

Specimen Letter 7 Request for D/A Payment

Dear Sirs,

Thank you for your letter dated on July 7.

We are pleased that you have effected shipment in time but we are surprised that you still require us to make the payment against document. After many years of **sound cooperation**, we have the feeling that we **are entitled to** easier terms. In fact, many of our old business partners have **adopted** D/A 60 days as terms of payment with us. We will **appreciate** it very much if you could follow suit **in this regard**.

We are looking forward to your favorable reply.

Truly yours,

(Signature)

Notes

1. sound cooperation 良好合作

2. are entitled to = be authorized to = give authority to 有权

You are entitled to draw a 60 days' draft. 您有权开具 60 天的汇票。

3. adopt   *v.* adopt policy/method/attitude/technique/manner 采用

4. appreciate   *v.* 感谢

Your prompt reply is highly appreciated. 如您尽快回复将不胜感激。

5. in this regard 在这点上

Specimen Letter 8   Urging Establishment of L/C

Dear Sirs,

We wish to inform you that the goods **under S/C No.76** have been ready for quite some time. According to the stipulations in the covering S/C, shipment is to be made during May/June. We sent you an email two weeks ago asking you **expedite** the relevant L/C. But much **to our disappointment**, we have not received any reply **up to now**. We, therefore, again ask for your attention **in this issue**.

The shipment date is **approaching**. We must **point out** that unless your L/C reaches us by the end of this month, we shall not be able to effect shipment within the stipulated time limit.

We hope this letter will **receive your prompt attention**.

Truly yours,

(Signature)

Notes

1. under S/C NO.76   第 76 号销售确认书项下

2. expedite   *v.* accelerate；quicken up；speed up 加快，加速

   You need to expedite your production process in order to catch the shipment date. 您需要加快生产来赶上交期。

3. to our disappointment 让我们感到失望

   类似的短语还有 to our surprise、to our pleasure、to our sadness。

4. up to now 到现在

5. in this issue 在这件事上

6. approaching   *adj.* 接近的，临近的

   Spring is approaching. 春天将至。

   approach   *v.* 接洽

   Did he approach you about a loan? 他有否就货款一事找您？

7. point out = indicate 指出

8. receive your prompt attention 得到您及时的关注

   We hope this issue will receive your prompt attention. 我们希望贵方及时关注此事。

Useful Sentences

1. Our terms of payment are by confirmed, irrevocable letter of credit in our favor, available by draft at sight, reaching us one month ahead of shipment, remaining valid for negotiation in China for another 21 days after the prescribed time of shipment, and allowing transshipment and partial shipments. 我们的付款条件是用保兑的、不可撤销的、以我方为受益人的信用证，凭即期汇票付款，在装运前一个月抵达我处，在中国议付有效到规定的装运期后第 21 天，并且允许转船和分批装运。

2. In view of the small quantity you have ordered, we are in a position to accept payment by D/P at sight for the value of the goods shipped. 鉴于您所订购的数量比较小，我们准备接受即期付款交单作为货值的付款方式。

3. In compliance with your request, we will make an exception to our rules and accept D/P at sight, but this should not be regarded as a precedent. 按照您的要求，我们破例接受即期付款交单，但这不应被看作一个先例。

4. We regret having to inform you that although it is our desire to pave the way for a smooth development of business between us, we cannot accept payment by D/A. 我们遗憾地通知您，虽然我们努力想达成交易，但我们无法接受承兑交单作为付款方式。

5. We regret our inability to make any arrangement contrary to our usual practice, which is payment by confirmed, irrevocable letter of credit payable against presentation of shipping documents and valid for at least 15 days beyond the promised date of shipment. 我们很遗憾无法违反我们的一贯做法，即使用保兑的、不可撤销的信用证，凭提交货运单据付款，在规定的装运日期后至少 15 天保持有效。

6. Your L/C No.×× calls for shipment to be made in June/July while it is explicitly stipulated in the S/C No.×× that the shipment is to be made in two equal lots in July/August. Please amend the L/C accordingly. 你的……号信用证要求在 6 或 7 月份进行装运，而在第……号销售确认书中有明确的规定，装运应该在 7 或 8 月份两批同等数量进行。请据此修改信用证。

7. It has been found in your L/C that the amount is USD 1,000 short against the total value of the S/C. We hope you will immediately approach your bank to increase the L/C amount by USD 1,000. 在您的信用证中发现所示金额比销售确认书的金额少了 1000 美元。我们希望您能立即联系您的银行将信用证金额增加 1000 美元。

8. We wish to refer you to our letter of…in which we asked you to extend the time of

shipment and time of negotiation to 31 October and 15 November respectively. However, up to now, we have not heard from you. Please note that unless we could receive your amendment advice by the end of this month we shall be unable to ship the goods before 31 October and an extension of another month will be unavoidable. 我们请您参考我们……号的来信，信中我们要求您分别将装运期和议付期延至 10 月 31 日和 11 月 15 日。然而，直到现在，我们没有收到您的任何消息。请注意，除非我们在本月底前收到您的改证通知，否则我们将无法在 10 月 31 号之前装运，而需要再延长一个月。

9. As there is no direct vessel sailing for your port this month, please amend your L/C No. ×× to allow transshipment, instead of "transshipment not allowed" as laid down in the L/C. We must have the amendment in the first half of this month as otherwise we shall be unable to effect shipment, and an extension of one month for the time of shipment and negotiation will be necessary. 由于本月没有到您港口的直达船，请修改第……号信用证，改成允许转船而不是在信用证中规定的"不允许转船"。我们必须在本月上旬收到修改通知，否则我们将无法装运，而只能要求再将装运期和议付期延长一个月。

10. We promise to pay by D/A at 30 days. 我们承诺按照承兑 30 天付款方式进行付款。

11. Please draw on us for the amount of your invoice and attach the documents listed below to your draft. 请向我们开具一个您发票金额的汇票，并将下列单据附在您的汇票上。

12. It would be advisable for you to establish the covering L/C as early as possible so as to enable us to effect shipment in due time. 建议您尽快开立相关信用证以便我们按时发货。

13. Considering the small amount involved, we are prepared, as an exception, to accept payment by D/P at sight for the value of your first trial order. 考虑到数额较小，我们破例准备接受即期付款交单作为你方试订单的付款方式。

Letter-writing Guide

The steps and expressions of writing terms of payment are as follows. (有关说明付款方式的信函的写作步骤及常用表达方式如下。)

Writing steps (写作步骤)	Examples of expressions (表达方式举例)
1. 感谢对方订货/来信，并指出我方所采用的付款方式	We thank you for your order No. ×× 感谢您第……号订单。
	We are in receipt of your letter on... 我们已收到您……号的来信。
	Thank you for you letter of... 感谢您……号的来信。

2. 指出我方所要求的付款 方式(例如按照所寄样 函等)	In our last letter we sent you a copy of our specimen contract in which are contained the general sales terms and conditions. 我们给您的上一封信中附有一个样本合同，其中说明了一般的销售条款。
	We'd like to refer you to our last letter. 我们请您参考我们的上一封信。
	Our general business practice is by... 我们通常的付款方式是……
3. 不同付款方式的表达 方法	Our usual terms of payment are by confirmed, irrevocable letter of credit in our favor, available by draft at sight, reaching us one month ahead of shipment, remaining valid for negotiation in China till the 21st day after the prescribed time of shipment and allowing transshipment and partial shipment. 我们通常的付款方式为保兑的、不可撤销的、以我方为受益人的、以即期汇票开立的信用证，并应于装船前一个月到达我处，而且一直到所规定的装船时间的第 21 天在中国保持有效并允许转船和分批装运。
	Most of our suppliers are drawing on us at 60 days D/A... 我方大多数供货商跟我们都采用 60 天承兑交单的付款方式……
	We call for 1/3 down payment with the order and the balance to be paid against a confirmed irrevocable L/C. 我方要求首付该订单的 1/3 押金，剩余部分通过保兑的不可撤销信用证进行付款。
	We'd like to pay by T/T. 我们乐意使用 T/T 付款。
4. 表达与对方合作及早日 收到回复的愿望	We look forward to your favorable reply. 希望早日收到您肯定的答复。
	Hope to receive...　希望收到……
	Your early reply is appreciated. 盼早回复。
	We are anticipating your answer. 盼早回复。

The steps and expressions of writing L/C amendments and extension are as follows. (信用证修改和延期信函的写作步骤及常用表达方式如下。)

Writing steps (写作步骤)	Examples of expressions (表达方式举例)
1. 表达遗憾，对方在信用 证中出现偏差，或者由 于对方延误，需要延期 信用证	We regret to have found that there are certain clauses which do not conform to those of the contract. 我们遗憾地发现有一些条款与合同不符。
	We regret to inform you that we did not receive your L/C covering the above S/C till today. 我们遗憾地告知您我们直到今天都没收到您有关上述销售确认书的信用证。
1. 表达遗憾，对方在信用 证中出现偏差，或者由 于对方延误，需要延期 信用证	Owing to the late arrival of the L/C, we are unable to make the shipment according to the date specified in the S/C. 由于信用证的延误，我们无法按照销售确认书的规定进行装运。
	We regret to say that we have found some discrepancies in it. 我们遗憾地发现里面有一些不符之处。

续表

2. 指出不符之处，提出延期要求	The name of the beneficiary should read… 受益人应为……
	Please insert the word "about" before the quantity and amount in your L/C as it is impossible for us to ship the goods in the exact quantity as contracted. 请在信用证里的数量及金额前面插入"大约"，因为我们不可能完全按照合同规定的数量进行装运。
	To extend the time of shipment to the end of October, 20××. 将装运期延期至 20××年 10 月底。
	To extend the validity of the L/C to November 15, 20××. 将信用证的有效期延期至 20××年 11 月 15 日底。
3. 进一步确定修改和延期得到对方确认	We suppose that the above mistakes are clerical and hope you will make the necessary amendments immediately by fax so that we can ship the goods in time. 我们假定上述错误由笔误所致，希望您能尽快修改并传真以便我方及时装船交货。
	Please note that we require the amendment to L/C by October 30 as otherwise we shall be unable to effect shipment at the time mentioned above. 请注意上述信用证的修改我们希望能在 10 月 30 日之前完成，否则我们将无法按上述规定来装运。

Exercises

I. Put the following English phrases into Chinese or Chinese phrases into English.

1. in receipt of   2. effect the shipment   3. clerical mistakes   4. conform to

5. general sales terms and conditions

6. 转船   7. 以……为受益人   8. 要求   9. 付款交单   10. 时限

II. Fill in the blanks of the following letter with the words given below, and change the form when necessary.

receive   sail   request   extend   deadline   available   book   return

Dear Sirs,

We have ___1___ your letter of July 7 and regret to learn that you are unable to ___2___ the subject L/C.

As is known to you, there is only one vessel ___3___ for your port each month and it usually leaves here in the first half of a month. So far as we know, the only vessel ___4___ in this month will leave here in a day or two and the ___5___ for ___6___ shipping space is long past. Therefore it is impossible for us to ship the goods this month, and we would ask you to do your best to extend the L/C as ___7___ in our letter of June 30.

Please act promptly and let us have your reply by ___8___ airmail.

Yours faithfully,

(Signature)

III. Translate the following English into Chinese or Chinese into English.

1. A 3% discount will be granted only on condition that your order exceeds USD12000.

2. We have made it clear that we would accept D/P terms for your present order.

3. We find your terms satisfactory and now send you our order for 2 sets of generators.

4. We hope you will make the necessary amendments immediately by telex so that we can ship the goods in time.

5. To our regret, however, this credit was found not properly amended on the following points despite our request.

6. 请注意，付款是以保兑的、不可撤销的、允许分船和转船、见票即付的信用证支付。

7. 我们通常的做法是凭即期付款交单而不是用信用证。因此，我们希望你对这笔交易和今后的交易也接受付款交单方式。

8. 对你方 1156 号订单，我们可以接受你们所提的用远期汇票支付的建议。货物装运后，我们将向你方开出 60 天期汇票，请到期即付。

9. 请注意，信用证所规定的事项应该完全与合约条款一致。

10. 我方高兴地通知你方，以你方为受益人的信用证已由汇丰银行开出，估计不久可以到达你处。

IV. Translate the following letter into English.

尊敬的先生：

我们已收到你方 11 月 8 日来信，要求我们以承兑交单方式发运你方一批花生。众所周知，我们的货款必须用保兑的、不可撤销的即期信用证支付，因此我们难以接受这一要求。但鉴于你方推销我方产品的良好愿望，我们破例接受 60 天期的汇票信用证。我们相信我们的这一特别照顾一定能使你方做出肯定的决定。

等候你们的回信，以便进一步磋商。

谨上

(签名)

Unit 7 补充练习   Unit 7 补充练习答案   Unit 7 练习答案

Unit 8　Packing

【学习要点和目标】

通过本单元的学习，了解买卖双方在货物运输中对包装的具体要求与规定，掌握撰写此类信函的方法和写作词汇。

Lead-in

Packing is the necessary component part in the international trade. It is one of the most important business conditions to negotiate between the two trading parties. Therefore the seller should pay much attention to the features and appearance of packing.

As to packed cargo, there are usually two kinds of packing, outer packing (transportation packing) and inner packing (packing for sale).

The features of outer packing should be:

1. beautiful and durable.

2. easy to load and unload.

3. suited for long distance transportation.

4. proof against damage.

5. proof against pilferage.

6. waterproof/shakeproof.

7. standardized.

The features of inner packing should be:

1. novel and pleasing to the eye.

2. small and exquisite.

3. look appealing.

4. suitable for window display.

5. easy to publicize and sell goods.

After finishing packing according to the packing requirement from the buyers, packing marks should be done on the export packages, which mainly include:

1. Shipping marks.

It indicates the name of the importer, the port of destination, the country of origin of the goods, the order No., the weight and dimensions of the goods, etc.

2. Indicative and warning marks.

To ensure the benefit of both the owner and the carrier, indicative and warning marks regarding manner of handling, loading, unloading and lifting, etc. are to be stenciled on the package.

A packing letter will include the following:

1. The opening sentence: express thanks for the previous letter and introduce the matter of packing.

2. The middle part: state concretely the packing instruction of the goods. If necessary, the reasons are given.

3. The closing sentence: hope to get a response promptly.

Specimen Letter 1   Buyer's Requirement for Packing and Shipping Marks

Dear Sirs,

Referring to the shipment of our Order No.123 for 200 cases of glassware, we wish to draw your attention to the following:

As glassware are extremely fragile, the goods must be wrapped in a **polybag** and **packed** in a standard export wooden case **lined with foam** capable of **withstanding rough handling** during transit.

On the outer packing please mark our **initials** "ABC" in a triangle. Under which the **origin of the goods,** the port of destination and our order number should be **stenciled conspicuously.** In view of **precaution**, please mark **"FRAGILE"** and **"HANDLE WITH CARE"** on each package.

We state the above for your reference and look forward to your reply as to your opinion.

Yours faithfully,

(Signature)

Notes

1. referring to... 兹谈及……。常用于商务书信的开头，表示事由。

    类似的表达法还有：We refer to...；with reference to...；reference is made to...。

    With reference to the shipment of our Order No.124 for 120 cases of China Wares...

    兹谈及我方第 124 号订单下的 120 箱中国瓷器装船事宜……

2. polybag *n.* 塑料袋

    常用的包装容器名称如下：

bag 袋；sack or gunny bag 麻袋；carton 纸板箱；wooden case 木箱；crate 板条箱；cardboard；纸板盒；box 盒；bundle 捆；bale 包；keg 小圆桶；drum 铁皮圆桶；barrel 琵琶桶；hogshead 大桶；carboy 大玻璃瓶；can or tin 听。

3. pack *v.* 包装

部分常见的包装表示法如下：

(1) in… 用某种容器包装

Walnuts are packed in double gunny bags. 核桃用双层麻袋包装。

(2) in…of…each 用某种容器包装，每件若干

Cashmere sweaters are packed in wooden cases of 10 dozen each. 羊绒衫用木箱装，每箱 10 打。

(3) …to…and…to… 若干件装入某容器，若干此容器装另一种较大的容器

Pens are packed 10 pieces to a box and 100 boxes to a wooden case. 钢笔 10 支装一盒，100 盒装一木箱。

4. line with… 以……填塞

Each machine is wrapped in a standard export carton lined with foam. 每台机器装在标准的出口纸箱内，周围用泡沫填塞。

5. foam *n.* 泡沫，泡沫材料

6. withstand *v.* 抵挡，经受住

shoes that will withstand hard wear. 耐穿的鞋。

7. rough handling 粗鲁搬运，野蛮装卸

Please see to it that the packing is strong enough to withstand rough handling. 请务必做到包装牢固，经得住粗鲁搬运。

8. initial *n.* 姓名或组织名称的首字母

9. origin of the goods 货物的原产地

10. stencil *v.* 用模板印刷

Please stencil conspicuously the words: "FRAGILE, HANDLE WITH CARE" on both sides of the cases. 请在箱子的两侧用模板显著的印刷上"易碎，小心轻放"的字样。

11. conspicuously *v.* 显著的，惹人注目的

12. precaution *n.* 预防，预防措施

Please take necessary precautions that the packing can protect the goods from dampness or rain. 请采取必要的预防措施使包装能保证货物不受潮湿或雨淋。

13. FRAGILE, HANDLE WITH CARE 易碎物品，小心轻放

它们是刷在出口货物上的货物标记，称作"特别指示或警告"，通常需要大写。常用的特别指示或警告如下：

THIS SIDE UP 此面向上

KEEP UPRIGHT 保持直立

KEEP FLAT (STOW LEVEL) 注意平放

KEEP AWAY FROM HEAT 切勿受热

KEEP DRY 保持干燥

KEEP COOL 低温存放

USE NO HOOKS 切勿用钩

DO NOT DROP 切勿下扔

OPEN THIS END 此端开启

DO NOT STOW ON DECK 禁放甲板上

LIFT HERE 在此起吊

NO SMOKING 严禁烟火

GLASS—WITH CARE 玻璃制品——小心轻放

ACID—WITH CARE 酸——小心轻放

PERISHABLE 易腐物品

INFLAMMABLE 易燃物品

HAZARDOUS 危险品

POISON 有毒

TOP 顶端

Specimen Letter 2　Negotiation on Packing and Marking

Dear Sirs,

We thank you for your **packing instruction**, but regret to inform you that we can not **comply with** your request for packing.

In view of our long business relations and our **amicable** cooperation prospects, we suggest that you accept the following proposals:

1. The bed sheets will be packed 10 dozen to a packet, 4 **packets** to a carton and 6 cartons to a crate.

2. Your initials will be stenciled in a diamond instead of the full name.

3. In addition to the **gross and net weights**, the shipping marks outside the crate should stencil the words "MADE IN CHINA."

Your early reply will be highly appreciated.

Yours faithfully,

(Signature)

Notes

1. packing instruction 包装要求，包装须知

2. comply with 满足；依照

 We hope you will be able to comply with our request. 希望你方能按我方要求办理。

 in compliance with 依从，按照

 Please make us a firm offer in compliance with our requirement. 请按我们的要求报实盘。

3. in view of 鉴于，考虑到

 In view of the fragile nature of the goods, you need special packing precaution against breakage. 鉴于货物易碎的特点，你方需要采取特别的包装措施以预防破碎。

4. amicable *adj.* 友好的

 Especially when you've established a long-term good business relationship with us, it is usually much easier to handle the disputes through amicable negotiations. 尤其当我们双方之间建立了长期友好的贸易关系以后，通过友好协商来解决争议就更容易了。

5. packet *n.* 小包(= a small package)

 package *n.* 包件(指包、捆、束、箱等)

 The packages are intact. 包装完整无损。

 packaging *n.* 包装方法

 We have improved the packaging. 我们改进了包装方法。

6. weight gross weight 毛重

 net weight 净重

 tare weight 皮重

Specimen Letter 3　Reply to the Packing Instruction

Dear Sirs,

We thank you for your above order of October 15 and have pleasure in informing you that we can accept all the terms but the packing.

We would like to recommend you our latest package, which is **economical** and strong. The packing mentioned in your order was of the old method we **adopted** several years ago. From then on we have improved it with the result that our recent goods have all **turned out** to the complete satisfaction of our clients.

Our Men's Shirts are now packed in a polybag and then in a cardboard box, 5 dozen to a carton, with a gross weight about 25 kilograms. Each carton is lined with a **polythene sheet**, so that the content is **protected from moisture.**

We are awaiting your **prompt** reply and wondering if our proposal meets your requirement.

Yours faithfully,

(Signature)

Notes

1. economical *adj.* 经济的，节约的

   This is not an economical method of packing. 这不是一种经济的包装方式。

2. adopt *v.* 采用，采纳

   We adopt new techniques in manufacturing this kind of product. 我们采用新的技术来生产这种产品。

3. turn out 产生……的结果；结果成为；结果是

   Everything turned out to be well. 结果一切都很好。

   We hope everything will turn out (to be) satisfactory in the end. 我们希望最终一切都令人满意。

4. polythene sheet 塑料纸

5. protect from 使免受，保护

   Protect from direct sunlight to prevent drying-out. 避免阳光直射，以防干裂。

6. moisture *n.* 潮湿，湿气

   These cartons are well protected against moisture by plastic lining. 由于箱内铺有塑料衬里，防潮性能良好。

7. prompt *adj.* 立即的，迅速的，及时的

   We look forward to your prompt response. 我们盼望您及时的回复。

Specimen Letter 4　Packing Requirement

Dear Sirs,

　　We regret to inform you that the 100 cartons of Nails you shipped London on August 1, 15 were badly damaged, of course through no fault of yours.

　　We are now writing to you **in regard to** the packing of these nails, which we feel necessary to explain for our future business.

　　The packing for London is to be in double gunny box of 50kg each. For **Rotterdam**, we would like you to have the goods packed in wooden cases of 112 **lbs** net, each box **contains** 16 bag weight each 7 lbs of nail. As for the French market, our buyers prefer the goods packed in carton of 30kg each.

　　Kindly let us know whether these requirements could be met.

Yours faithfully,

(Signature)

Notes

1. in regard to　关于。与 with regard to，as regards，regarding 同义，一般可以换用。
   We have already written to you in regard to this matter. 关于此事我们已经给你方写过信。
2. Rotterdam　*n.* 鹿特丹
   鹿特丹位于荷兰西南部，是欧洲主要口岸(European Main Port，EMP)之一。按照国际航运公会统一规定，EMP 还包括意大利的 Genoa(热那亚)，法国的 Marseilles(马赛)，比利时的 Antwerp(安特卫普)，英国的 London(伦敦)，德国的 Hamburg(汉堡)，丹麦的 Copenhagen(哥本哈根)等港口。
3. lb=pound　磅(重量单位，合 0.454 千克)
4. contain　*v.* 包含，容纳
   This brochure contains all the information you need. 这本小册子包含你所需的一切资料。

Specimen Letter 5　Exporter's Advice of Packing, Shipping Marks and Shipment

Dear Sirs,

　　We are pleased to inform you that the **portable computers** have now been shipped to you as **specified** below.

Packing: In 20 cartons, 15 portable computers to a carton.

Shipping marks: BD123 in diamond, New York. Particulars of weight and **measurement** are given in the enclosed sheet.

Shipment: By **S.S.** "Fengqing" of **SINOTRANS**, which sailed from Shanghai on April 1, and is **scheduled** to arrive at New York on April 20.

We have given a complete set of **Bills of Lading**, together with **Invoice** and **Insurance Certificate,** both **in triplicate,** to Citibank with **a sight draft** for US$30,000 under the terms of the L/C, and we have received the sum from the said bank.

We shall appreciate your information on the arrival of the **consignment.**

Yours faithfully,

(Signature)

Notes

1. portable computer   手提电脑，笔记本电脑
2. specify   *v.* 明确说明，具体指定

   Please specify your packing instruction.   请明确说明你方的包装要求。
3. measurement   *n.* 尺寸，大小
4. S.S. =steam ship 汽船

   M.V.=motor vessel 机动船，两者通常译作"货轮"。
5. SINOTRANS=China National Foreign Trade Transportation Corporation 中国对外贸易运输总公司
6. scheduled   *adj.* 预定的

   The annual sales meeting will be held as scheduled. 年度销售会议将如期召开。
7. Bills of Lading   提单
8. invoice   *n.* 发票
9. Insurance Certificate   保险凭证(也称小保单)
10. in triplicate   一式三份
11. a sight draft   即期汇票
12. consignment   *n.* 装运的货物，运送物

Specimen Letter 6   Claim for Improper Packing

Dear Sirs,

We have **duly** received the machines you shipped to us but regret to draw your attention to the fact that the wooden case completely **collapsed** and a great part of the **components** of the machine were damaged when the goods arrived. It was obviously caused by **improper packing**. The wooden case used by you is not strong enough for packing so heavy a machine.

In such case, we have no alternative but to **make a claim on you**, which we hope will receive your prompt attention.

Yours faithfully,

(Signature)

Notes

1. duly *adv.* 按时地，准时地

We have duly sent the shipping advice. 我们已经按时发送了装船通知。

2. collapse

(1) *v.* 倒塌，使瘪掉

(2) *n.* 倒塌

Poor packing was the occasion of the case's collapse. 包装不当是箱子倒塌的起因。

3. component *n.* 零部件

4. improper packing(poor packing) 包装不当，包装不良

It was found, on examination that nearly 30% of the packages had been broken, obviously attributed to poor packing. 检验时发现，近30%的包件破损。很明显，这是包装不良所致。

5. make a claim on/against sb. (lodge/file/raise a claim on/against sb.) 向某人提出索赔

We hope you will understand that we are not willing to lodge a claim against you if we are not compelled to do so. 希望你们明白，如果我们不是不得已的话，实在不愿向你方提出索赔。

Useful Sentences

1. For the sake of precaution, the cartons must be secured with metal bands. 为预防起见，纸箱必须用金属带捆绑以确保安全。

2. Please line the containers with waterproof material so that the goods can be protected against moisture. 请用防水材料做容器里衬，以防货物受潮。

3. Each pair of socks is packed in a polybag and 12 pairs to a box. 每双袜子装入一个塑料

袋里，12 双袜子装入一个纸盒里。

4. The packing must be seaworthy and strong enough to stand rough handling. 包装必须适合海运，足够牢固，经得住野蛮装运。

5. Our way of packing has been widely accepted by other clients, and we have received no complaints what so ever so far. 我们的包装方式已经被其他客户广泛接受，到目前为止，还没有任何投诉。

6. In fact, this packing is both shockproof and waterproof. Nevertheless we have still marked the cartons with warnings like "FRAGILE", "USE NO HOOK" and "DO NOT DROP". 实际上，这种包装既防震又防潮。尽管如此，我们仍在箱子上刷上了诸如"易碎"、"切勿用钩"和"轻搬轻放"之类的标志。

7. In view of the fragile nature of the goods, they should be wrapped in soft material and firmly packed in cardboard boxes so as to reduce damage in transit to a minimum. 鉴于此货物为易碎品，故应以软材料包装，再牢牢放置于板条箱中，以尽量减少运输途中造成的损失。

8. The goods are to be marked with our initials in a diamond, and warning marks are to be clearly marked. 货物唛头为菱形，内印我公司名称缩写，警告标志应明显表示出来。

9. Cartons are comparatively light and compact, more convenient to handle in the course of loading and unloading, quite fit for ocean transportation. As a kind of packing container, they have been extensively used in international trade. 纸板箱比较轻巧，装卸搬运更为方便，很适合海洋运输。作为一种包装容器，纸板箱已在国际贸易中广泛使用。

10. The suppliers should be held responsible for short weight resulting from improper packing. 由于包装不当而引起的短重，供应商应该负责任。

Letter-writing Guide

The steps and expressions of a packing letter are as follows. (包装信函的写作步骤及常用表达方式如下。)

Writing steps (写作步骤)	Examples of expressions (表达方式举例)
1. 感谢先前的信件并提及商品的包装事宜	In reply to your letter of August 31st enquiring about the packing of our Color TV Sets, we wish to state as follows. 为答复你方 8 月 31 日询问我方彩色电视机包装之事的来函，今告知如下。
	Referring to the shipment of our Order No.123 for 200 cases of glassware, we wish to draw your attention to the following. 兹谈及我方 123 号订单中的 200 箱玻璃制品，我方请你们注意以下事项。

续表

2. 具体陈述包装的要求和方法，如果有必要，还应陈述理由	As glassware are extremely fragile, the goods must be wrapped in a polybag and packed in a standard export wooden case lined with foam capable of withstanding rough handling during transit. 由于玻璃制品极易破碎，因而货物必须包装在塑料袋里，然后装入标准出口木箱里，箱内四周填充泡沫材料，以能经受住运输途中的野蛮装运。
3. 希望对方及时做出回应	Please fax us your comments as soon as possible. 请尽快用传真告知我方贵方的意见。
	Kindly let us know whether these requirements could be met. 请贵方告知能否满足这些要求。

The steps and expressions of writing a reply to a packing letter are as follows. (回复包装信函的写作步骤及常用表达方式如下。)

Writing steps (写作步骤)	Examples of expressions (表达方式举例)
1. 包装信函已经收悉	Your fax of June 1st is greatly appreciated. 你方 6 月 1 日的传真收悉。
	We thank you for your packing instructions. 你方包装指示收悉，谢谢。
2. 告知是否同意对方的包装要求	We regret to inform you that we can not comply with your request for packing. 今歉告，我方难以满足你方的包装要求。
	We agree with your packing instruction. 我们同意贵方的包装要求。
3. 如果不同意对方的包装要求，要陈述理由，并提出修改建议。如同意对方的包装要求，可确认一下对方关于包装的细节	We would like to recommend you our latest package, which is economical and strong. Our Men's Shirts are now packed in a polybag and then in… 我方建议贵方采用我们最新的包装，它既经济又坚固。我们的男式衬衫现在是以塑料袋包装的，然后再装进……
	We are pleased to acknowledge them as follows: The walnut meats under the No.123 Order should be packed in… 我们谨对此作以下确认：123 号订单项下的核桃仁用……包装。
4. 希望得到对方的答复	We state the above for your information and shall fulfill your order accordingly if we do not hear from you to the contrary before the end of this month. 上述说明供你方参考。如在月底之前没有收到贵公司的不同意见，我们将照此执行。
	We are expecting a reply at your earliest convenience. 盼早日回复。

Exercises

I. Put the following English phrases into Chinese or Chinese phrases into English.

1. shipping mark   2. rough handling   3. for the sake of precaution   4. handle with care

5. poor packing   6. 包装要求   7. 切勿受热   8. 毛重   9. 外包装   10. 长途海运

II. Fill in the blanks of the following letter with the words given below, and change the form when necessary.

stencil   above   impossible   wrapped   reinforced   net   case   packing

Dear Sirs,

Referring to our Order No. BE135 covering 5 sets of Machine Tools with Model No. 234-2A, we wish to give you our comments on __1__ as follows:

1. A special crate with __2__ bottom will be needed for the transport of such a large machine, and both padding and bolting down will be necessary.

2. All parts and components are to be __3__ in soft material and firmly packed in cardboard boxes. These in turn are to be packed in wooden cases in such a manner that movement inside the cases is __4__.

3. Kindly __5__ our shipping marks in letter, 3 inches high, and give gross and __6__ weight on each __7__.

We trust the __8__ is clear to you. Looking forward to hearing from you.

Yours faithfully,

(Signatrue)

III. Translate the following English into Chinese or Chinese into English.

1. The new packaging of this commodity is exquisitely designed and we are confident that it will appeal to the most selective buyers.

2. Owing to poor packing, several of them arrived in such a bad order so that we were forced to dispose of them at lower prices.

3. Please take necessary precautions that the packing can protect the goods from dampness or rain, since these goods are liable to be spoiled by damp or water in transit.

4. This packing is both shockproof and moistureproof. Nevertheless we have still marked the cartons with warning like "FRAGILE", "USE NO HOOK" and "DO NOT DROP".

5. The packing must be seaworthy and strong enough to stand rough handling.

6. 我们女式内衣的包装为每件套一塑料袋，5 打装一纸箱，内衬防潮纸，外打铁箍两道。

7. 纸板箱比较轻巧坚固，装卸极为方便，很适合海洋运输。

8. 货物唛头为菱形，内印我公司名称缩写，警告标志应明显表示出来。

9. 请严格遵守包装及标记的细则。

10. 我们的包装方式已经被其他客户广泛接受，到目前为止，还没有收到任何投诉。

IV. Writing practice.

Draw a letter covering the following contents.

1. 感谢收到对方台式电脑的订单。

2. 每台电脑装入塑料袋里，然后装入标准的纸板箱里，四周用泡沫填塞，外有绳子加固。

3. 各箱上须注明"易碎"和"小心轻放"的字样。

4. 请回复，告知是否同意。

Unit 8 补充练习   Unit 8 补充练习答案   Unit 8 练习答案

Unit 9　Insurance

【学习要点和目标】

通过本单元的学习，了解货物运输中对保险的具体要求与规定以及常用的险别，掌握撰写此类信函的方法和写作词汇。

Lead-in

The international trade is subject to many risks. Ships may sink or goods may be damaged in transit; exchange rates may alter; buyers default or governments suddenly impose an embargo. Therefore, exporters and importers have to insure themselves against many of these risks.

As far as international trade is concerned, what mainly concerns us is still the marine insurance, for a large percentage of international trade goes by ship.

Exporters or importers arrange insurance cover for their goods according to the type of goods and circumstances. There is a wide range of standard types of coverage, the three basic ones being as follows:

1. Free of Particular Average (F.P.A.).
2. With Particular Average (W.P.A.) or With Average (W.A.).
3. All Risks.

General additional risks usually are: Theft, Pilferage and Non-Delivery (T.P.N.D.), Fresh Water and/or Rain Water Damage, Risks of Shortage, Risks of Hook Damage, Risk of Breakage of Packing, etc. It must be noted that, in China, all these general additional risks are included in "All Risks".

Special additional risks that are not included in All Risks and have to be taken separately are mainly: Failure to Delivery Risks, War Risk, and Strike, Riots and Civil Commotions (S.R.C.C.).

When an exporter under a CIF contract or an importer under an FOB contract wants to cover insurance, the first step it should take is to contact an insurance company whose agent, known as the "insurance broker", will bring along a printed proposal form, then the insured should complete it and submit to the insurance company. If the proposal is accepted, the insurer is required by law to issue an insurance policy, which lists the stipulations of the contract for the applicant to fill out, and which contains all the items including ownership, name of commodity, insured value, premium, insurance time span, risks and coverage, etc. The signed insurance policy is a binding contract, or a legal document that serves as certificate of the agreement between the insurer and the insured and forms part of the shipping documents.

Generally speaking, the value to be insured is based on the value of the commercial invoice. The recommended minimum amount is the total CIF value plus 10% for other expenses and normal margin of profit on the importer's part. A higher additional percentage of value can also be insured provided that an extra premium is paid.

An insurance letter is composed of three main parts as follows:

1. The opening sentence: express thanks for the previous letter of insuring the goods and confirming the insured goods.

2. The middle part can be divided into several paragraphs if necessary, and it states the details of insurance completely.

3. The closing sentence: hope to make a response promptly.

Specimen Letter 1   Asking for the Premium Rate

Dear Sirs,

We shall recently have a consignment of leather shoes, value at £5000 CIF **Xingang,** to be shipped from London by a vessel of London Liners Ltd.

We wish to **insure** the consignment against All Risks from our warehouse at the above-mentioned address to the port of Xingang. Will you please quote your **premium** rate?

Yours faithfully,

(Signature)

Notes

1. Xingang   *n.* 新港(天津附近的港口)

2. insure   *vt./vi.* 保险，投保

Please insure the goods against breakage. 请将此货物投保破碎险。

insurance   *n.* 保险

insurance agent 保险代理人

insurance amount 保险金额

insurance policy 保险单

insurance certificate 保险凭证

insurance company 保险公司

insurance coverage 保险范围

在表示"投保"，"办理保险"时，常与 insurance 搭配的动词或动词词组有

to cover insurance; to arrange insurance; to effect insurance; to take out insurance。在说明保险情况时，insurance 后接介词的一般用法。例如：

(1) 表示所保的货物，后接 on，如 insurance on the 200 metric tons of walnut meats。

(2) 表示投保的险别，后接 against，如 insurance against war risk。

(3) 表示保额，后接 for，如 insurance for 110% of the invoice value。

(4) 表示保险费或保险费率，后接 at，如 insurance at a slightly higher premium, insurance at the rate of 5%。

(5) 表示向保险公司投保，后接 with，如 insurance with the People's Insurance Company of China。

We have covered insurance on the 100 metric tons of walnut for 110% of the invoice value against all risks with the People's Insurance Company of China.

我们已将 100 公吨核桃按发票金额的 110%向中国人民保险公司投保一切险。

3. premium   *n.* 保险费

The insurance premium is for the buyer's account. 保险费由买方支付。

premium rate 保险费率，其他译法有 insurance rate；policy rate。

Specimen Letter 2   Reply to an Enquiry of Insurance

Dear Sirs,

We **acknowledge** with thanks the receipt of your letter of August 1st. We are pleased that you would like to insure with us the goods of 20 cases of Men's Shirts by the **International Shipping Line** from New York to Shanghai.

We will cover insurance **WPA** and **War Risks** according to usual practice in the absence of **definite** instructions from you. The premium is **at the rate of** 1.5% of the value **declared.** We enclose here the relevant file of our company for your reference. We are sure that you will find our rate is most **favorable.**

If our rate is acceptable for you, please let us know it so that our insurance policy can reach you timely.

We look forward to hearing from you promptly.

Yours faithfully,

(Signature)

Notes

1. acknowledge   *v.* 承认，告知收到(信件，礼物等)

It is universally acknowledged that the quality of our goods is of first-rate. 大家一致公认我方产品的质量是一流的。

We acknowledge the receipt of your letter of March 15. 我们收到你方3月15日的来信。

2. International Shipping Line 国际航运公司

3. WPA(With Particular Average.) 也写作 W.P.A，是中国人民保险公司制定的保险条款(China Insurance Clause，CIC 或 C.I.C.)中的海洋运输货物保险条款所包括的三个基本险别之一，其他两个险别为平安险(Free from Particular Average，FPA 或 F.P.A.)和一切险(All Risks，A.R.)。除以上三个基本险别外，还有附加险(Extraneous Risks)。常见的附加险如下：

Theft, Pilferage & Non-Delivery Risks (简称 T.P.N.D 或 TPND)偷窃、提货不着险

Fresh and/or Rain Water Damage Risks 淡水雨淋险

Shortage Risk 或 Risk of Shortage 短量险

Intermixture & Contamination Risks 混杂、玷污险

Leakage Risk 或 Risk of Leakage 渗漏险

Clash & Breakage Risks 碰损、破碎险

Taint of Odour Risk 串味险

Sweating & Heating Risks 受潮受热险

Hook Damage Risk 钩损险

Rust Risk 或 Risk of Rust 锈损险

Breakage of Packing Risk 包装破裂险

4. War Risk 战争险，它是特殊附加险之一，其他常见的特殊附加险有：

Strikes, Riots and Civil Commotions (简称 S.R.C.C.或 SRCC)罢工、暴动、民变险。注意这个险别没有 risk 这个词)

Failure to Delivery Risk 交货不到险

Import Duty Risk 进口关税险

Rejection Risk 拒收险

Aflatoxin Risk 黄曲霉素险

在函电中说各个险别时，除 all risks 和 war risk 外，其他保险中的 risk(s)这个词通常略去。

5. definite   *adj.* 明确的，确切的，肯定的

Is it definite that they will sign that contract? 他们肯定会签署这份合同吗？

6. at the rate of   按……比率，按……的速度

At the present rate of progress, we shall catch up with others soon. 按照目前的进步速度，我们会很快赶上别人。

7. declare   *v.* 宣布；申报

The customs officer asked if there is anything to declare. 海关人员询问是否有要申报交税的东西。

8. favorable   *adj.* 有利的；优惠的；赞成的

The market has so changed as to be favorable to the sellers.   市场变为对卖方有利。

We are favorable to your terms and conditions of this transaction.   我们同意你方的交易条件。

We are sure that you will find our price is most favorable. 我们确信您会发现我们的价格是最优惠的。

Specimen Letter 3   A Request for Insurance

Dear Sirs,

We would like to insure the following consignment against All Risks and SRCC for the **sum** of U.S. $ 50 000:

10 000 yards of **watered silk**.

These goods are to be loaded on to the S.S. Chang Feng which sail from Dalian on May 15 and is due in London on June 2.

As the matter is **urgent**, we would appreciate an early reply. Thank you.

Yours faithfully,

(Signature)

Notes

1. sum   *n.* 金额，款项

You will be fined the sum of U.S. $100.   你将被罚款 100 美元。

2. watered silk   水洗丝

3. urgent   *adj.* 紧急的，紧迫的

in urgent need of   急需

Our clients are in urgent need of these products.   我们的客户急需这些商品。

Specimen Letter 4   Reply to a Request for Insurance

Dear Sirs,

With reference to your letter of August 1 inquiring about the insurance on your order, we wish to inform you that for goods sold on CIF basis, our company will **cover** against All Risks and War Risks **for 110% of the invoice value**. If you want to insure broader coverage, the extra premium will **be borne by you**. The insurance shall **terminate** when the goods are delivered to the **consignee's warehouse** at the destination named in the policy. The cover is limited to 60 days upon **discharge** of the insured goods from sea-going vessel at the final **port of discharge** before the insured goods reach the consignee's warehouse.

Our **underwriter** — the People's Insurance Company of China — **enjoys high reputation** for **settling claims** promptly and **equitable**. Should any damage to the goods occur a claim may by lodged with the **insurance agent** at your end, who will undertake to compensate you for the loss **sustained**. For further particulars, please contact the People's Insurance Company of China or its agent **at your end**.

Yours faithfully,

(Signature)

Notes

1. with reference to 谈及

常用于商务书信的开头，表示事由。类似的表达法还有 We refer to…；referring to…；make reference to 或 reference is made to…。

With reference to your enquiry of 3 March for Model 790 machine, we regret to inform you that they can not be supplied from stock at present. 谈及你方3月3日关于790型号机器的询盘，我们很遗憾地通知您，目前没有现货供应。

2. cover…for 110% of the invoice value 按……发票金额110%投保

类似的表达还有 cover…for the invoice value plus 10%。

3. be borne by sb. 由某人负担

The re-inspection fee shall be borne by the buyers. 复验费由买方负担。

4. terminate *v.* 使终止，使结束

Your contract has been terminated. 你的合同已经被终止。

5. consignee *n.* 收货人

6. warehouse *n.* 仓库

7. discharge　*v.* 卸(货物等)

port of discharge　卸货港

8. underwriter　*n.* 保险人，承保人

9. enjoy high reputation　享有极高的声誉

类似的表达法还有 enjoy great popularity；enjoy high prestige。

10. settle claims　理赔

11. equitable　*adj.* 公平的，公正的

Extra efforts are needed to ensure that both parties can benefit from them in an equitable manner.　我们还需要做出额外努力，确保双方都能够以公平的方式从中受益。

12. insurance agent　保险代理人

13. sustain　*v.* 遭受

Every case has sustained some damage. 每个箱子都遭到了损坏。

14. at one's end　在某人处

in your place，on your side，at your end 均作"在你地区"或"在你处"解。

Specimen Letter 5　Importer Asks Exporter to Arrange Insurance

Dear Sirs,

We wish to refer you to our Order No.231 for 1000 cases Toys, from which you will see that this order was place on **CFR** basis.

As we now desire to have the shipment insured at your end, we shall appreciate it if you will kindly arrange to cover the same **on our behalf** against All Risks at invoice value plus 20%, i.e. US$100 000.

We shall of course refund the premium to you upon receipt of your **debit** note or, if you like, you may **draw on us at sight for** the same.

We sincerely hope that our request will meet with your **approval**.

Yours faithfully,

(Signature)

Notes

1. CFR　价格术语 cost and freight 的缩写，成本加运费价

2. on one's behalf　为……的利益代表。on behalf of sb. 代表或代替某人

On behalf of the department I would like to thank you all. 我谨代表全系感谢大家。

3. debit　*v.* 将……记入借方(会计用语)

　　debit US$500 against/to sb. 或 debit sb. with US$500　意思均为"把一笔 500 美元的账记入某人的借方"。

　　debit note　收款清单

4. draw (a draft) on sb. at sight for/against　向某人开即期汇票索取

5. approval　*n.* 赞成，同意

　　Do the plans meet with your approval? 这些计划你赞成吗？

Specimen Letter 6　The certification of Insurance Policy

Policy No.12345

This is to **certify** that this Company has insured on behalf of China National Textiles Import & Export Corp., Qingdao Branch.

The sum of US dollars Two Hundred Thousand only.

Upon Three Thousand cases "White Cat" Brand **Woolen Mixed Blanket**.

At & from Qingdao to **Hamburg**.

Ship or vessel: M.V. "East Wind".

Sailing on or about September 20th, 20×× .

Covering All Risks.

In the event of damage, to be surveyed by William Survey Co., and claims payable at Qingdao.

This policy is **issued in duplicate** at Qingdao on the 7th day of September in 20×× .

　　　　　　　　　　　　　　　　The People's Insurance Company of China

　　　　　　　　　　　　　　　　Qingdao Branch

　　　　　　　　　　　　　　　　 (Stamp)

Notes

1. certify　*v.* 证明

　　We certify that this is a true copy.　我们证明这是真副本。

2. Woolen Mixed Blanket　混纺毛毯

3. Hamburg　*n.* 汉堡(德国海港)

4. sailing on or about September 20th, 20××

　　在商务英语中，英译与时间有关的文字时，处理非常严格、慎重，常用双介词。

This credit calls for shipment on or before the 30th of December. 此信用证要求在 12 月 30 日或之前装运。

5. in the event of　如果发生，万一，倘若

In the event of an accident, call this number. 万一发生事故，请拨此号码。

6. issue　*v.* 开立，出具

We are very sorry for the delay in issuing the L/C, which was due to an oversight of our staff. 我们很抱歉延迟开立信用证，这是由于我们员工的疏忽造成的。

7. in duplicate　一式两份

in triplicate 一式三份

in quadruplicate　一式四份

一式四份及四份以上，常用 in four copies，in five copies，或 in four fold，in five fold 表述。

Useful Sentences

1. We shall cover the insurance ourselves. 我们将亲自投保。

2. According to our usual practice, we have insured the goods with PICC. 按照我们的惯例，我们将货物在中国人民保险公司投保。

3. According to the international practice, we do not insure against such risks unless they are called for by the buyers. 按照国际惯例，我们不投保此类险别，除非买方有此要求。

4. For transactions concluded on CIF basis, we usually cover the insurance against All Risks for 110% of the invoice value. If you wish to cover insurance for 130% instead, the extra premium should be for your account. 凡以 CIF 条件成交的业务，我们通常按照发票金额的 110%投保一切险。如果你方想按发票金额的 130%投保，额外的保险费由你方负担。

5. In the absence of your definite instructions, we usually cover the insurance against WPA and War Risks. If you want to cover FPA, please let us know in advance. 在你方没有具体要求时，我们通常投保水渍险和战争险。如果你方想要投保平安险，请事先告知。

6. We can arrange insurance on your behalf. 我们可以为你方代办保险。

7. The cover is to be from warehouse to warehouse and comes to effect from May 20th. 这项保险为仓至仓保险，从 5 月 20 日起生效。

8. We have concluded the business on FOB basis, so the insurance should be effected by you. 我们在 FOB 的条件下达成这笔交易，因此由你方办理保险。

9. Breakage is a special risk, for which an extra premium will have to be charged. 破碎险是一种特殊险别，须额外收费。

10. We are willing to take out FPA and WPA covers for the shipment. Would you please give us the policy rates for FPA coverage and for WPA coverage? 我们要为这批货物投保平安险和水渍险。请告知上述两种险别的保险费率。

Letter-writing Guide

The steps and expressions of writing an insurance letter are as follows. (保险信函的写作步骤及常用表达方式如下。)

Writing steps (写作步骤)	Examples of expressions (表达方式举例)
1. 提出想要将何种货物保险的意向	We would like to insure the following consignment against All Risks and SRCC for the sum of U.S.$ 50 000. 我方想对如下 50 000 美元的货物投保一切险和罢工、暴动、民变险。
	We shall recently have a consignment of leather shoes, value at £5000 CIF Xingang, to be shipped from London by a vessel of London Liners Ltd. 我们最近将有一批价值 5000 英镑的皮鞋货物，成本加保险、运费到新港，预备由伦敦班轮有限公司的船只从伦敦起运。
2. 陈述保险的具体细节，例如，询问保险费率，说明想要投保的险别，货物的运输方式，起航日期及抵达日期	These goods are to be loaded on to the S.S. Chang Feng which sail from Dalian on May 15 and is due in London on June 2. 这批货物由"长风"号货轮运载，预计 5 月 15 日从大连启航，6 月 2 日抵达伦敦。
	We wish to insure the consignment against All Risks from our warehouse at the above-mentioned address to the port of Xingang. Will you please quote your premium rate . 我们希望将这批货物从我方上述地址至新港投保一切险，请报来保险费率。
3. 表达早日收到保单的愿望或请贵方尽快办理保险	We look forward to the insurance policy, and the earlier the better. 请将保单寄给我们，越快越好。
	Kindly give this matter your prompt attention. 请尽快办理此事。
	We look forward to hearing from you soon. 盼佳音。

The steps and expressions of writing a reply to an insurance letter are as follows. (回复保险信函的写作步骤及常用表达方式如下。)

Writing steps (写作步骤)	Examples of expressions (表达方式举例)
1. 感谢对方关于投保的来信，同时对投保的货物予以确认	We acknowledge with thanks the receipt of your letter of August 1st. We are pleased that you would like to insure with us the goods of 20 cases of Men's Shirts by the International Shipping Line from New York to Shanghai. 兹确认收悉贵方 8 月 1 日来函，特此感谢。很高兴贵公司选择我公司为这批由国际航运公司运输、从纽约至上海的 20 箱男式衬衫的货物承保。
	Thank you for your letter of July 25th. With regard to your inquiry about insurance, we wish to give the following in reply. 感谢贵方 7 月 25 日来函询问保险事宜。对此，我们答复如下。
2. 如果需要可分成不同的段落，就投保的细节问题逐一陈述。例如，按惯例，应投保什么类型的险别，保险费率是多少，由哪一家保险公司承保	We will cover insurance WPA and War Risks according to usual practice in the absence of definite instructions from you. The premium is at the rate of 1.5% of the value declared. 根据惯例，在没有得到你方明确指示的情况下，我们为货物投保水渍险和战争险。保险费率是申请投保金额的 1.5%。
	Our underwriter—the People's Insurance Company of China—enjoys high reputation for… 我们的承保人——中国人民保险公司——享有极高的声望……
3. 希望得知对方是否同意保险条件并要求早日回复	If our rate is acceptable for you, please let us know it so that our insurance policy can reach you timely. 如贵方认为我方的费率可以接受，请及时通知我们，以便我们可以尽快给你们寄去我公司的保险单。
	We wonder whether the above information will serve your purpose and we look forward hearing further news from you. 我们不知道上述信息是否满足了贵方的要求，希望尽快获悉贵公司的情况。

Exercises

I. Put the following English phrases into Chinese or Chinese phrases into English.

1. insurance coverage　　2. insurance amount　　3. cover insurance　　4. invoice value

5. all risks

6. 保险单　　7. 保险费　　8. 中国人民保险公司　　9. 国际惯例　　10. 中国保险条款

II. Fill in the blanks of the following letter with the words given below, and change the form when necessary.

| agreement underwriter basis end benefits |

Dear Sirs,

Thank you for your fax of July 7.

The quotation you faxed us is on CIF ___1___. As we are in open cover ___2___ with our ___3___ we prefer that you send us CFR quotation.

However, we will also be interested to know what ___4___ we are likely to get if consignments are to be covered at your ___5___.

We are looking forward to your early reply.

              Yours faithfully,

              (Signature)

III. Translate the following English into Chinese or Chinese into English.

1. For the sake of safety, we recommend you to cover insurance for the shipment against All Risks and War Risks.

2. Since the premium varies with the extent of insurance, extra premium is for buyer's account, should additional risks be covered.

3. We shall take out insurance at this end under open policy.

4. If you wish to cover the goods against TPND, it can be easily done on payment of an additional premium.

5. We wish to know whether you can issue a special rate for shipment.

6. 保险须按发票金额的130%投保一切险。我们知道你方惯例是只按发票价格加10%投保，因此额外保费由我方负担。

7. 我方客户要求对其货物投保钩损险和渗漏险。请按此要求投保。

8. 我们的出口商品通常向中国人民保险公司投保。

9. 破碎险的保险费率为5%，如果贵方愿意投保破碎险，我们可以代为办理。

10. 在我方客户没有具体要求时，我们通常投保水渍险和战争险。如果贵方想要投保平安险，则请事先告知。

IV. Writing practice.

Draw a letter covering the following contents.

1. 请安排为100台"苹果"电脑投保一切险，包括破碎险。

2. 此批货物由"风庆"号货轮从纽约运至上海，8 月 1 日启航。

3. 按高出发票价值的 20%投保。

4. 要求速寄保单和保险证明书副本。

Unit 9　补充练习　　　　Unit 9　补充练习答案　　　　Unit 9　练习答案

Unit 10　Shipment

【学习要点和目标】

通过本单元的学习，了解装运相关程序和单证，掌握装运函电的基本写作技巧，学会通过商业函电处理装运问题。

Lead-in

Transport is a very important means in international trade because goods sold by the seller have to be delivered to the buyer abroad, and the delivery of goods is made possible by transport services. In order to fulfill an export transaction and effective transport in a safe, speedy, accurate, and economical way, a global businessman will find it useful to have a fairly good knowledge of transport. Such knowledge includes modes of transport, clauses of shipment, shipping procedure, and major shipping documents, etc. This unit will pay attention to the shipping procedure.

International trade, shipping is made according to the shipping instructions of the buyers (take ocean carriage for example). At first, ships are chosen based on the shipping schedule, and an application is made to book ship's space. After packed and marked, the goods are to be moved to the warehouse of the shipping company two or three days before sailing. At the same time, the seller should issue the commercial invoice, get export permit, and put forward shipping order made by the shipping company to the shipmaster in order to load the goods into that ship. Shipping advice should be sent to the buyer after loading in a timely manner, whose purpose is not only to inform the buyer of accomplishment of shipping, but also to notice the counterpart to early prepare the money. Lastly but not least importantly, shipping must be in total accordance with the instruction of the L/C to clearly make sure of the date of shipment, transshipment and partial shipment, otherwise the buyer can refuse to pay for the goods.

Letters regarding shipment mainly include the followings:

1. Discussing terms of shipment or asking for amendment to terms of shipment.

2. Giving shipping instructions to the seller.

3. Urging an early, immediate or punctual shipment.

4. Sending shipping advice and/or shipping documents.

Specimen Letter 1 Asking for Amendment to the Terms of Shipment

Dear Sirs,

We have received your letter of January 10, 20×× and also your **L/C** No.DC-125 covering our Contract No.406 for Shirts, Article No.01 in our **illustrated catalogue**.

In regard to the **port of loading**, we wish to point out we cannot ship the shirts from Qingdao, China, because our manufacturer is in Shenyang, China, close to Dalian port, China. In order to reduce the domestic transportation cost, it is better to choose a port of loading that is close to the origin of the goods, which is a generally accepted principle. Besides, the facilities at Dalian port are advanced and loading efficiency is very high. Therefore, we request that you change the port of loading from Qingdao Port, China to Dalian Port, China.

As to the latest **date for shipment**, we regret to inform you that February 5 is too tight, as there is a seven-day holiday in-between during the Spring Festival of China in the end of January, it is impossible for us to get the goods ready before February 5.

We shall appreciate it if you will amend the latest date for shipment to read "February 20, 20××", which is the same as the contract terms.

Meanwhile, please also have the **expiry date** of the L/C **extended** until March 5, 20×× to leave us enough time for presenting the documents to the bank for **negotiation**.

Thank you for your cooperation in advance and look forward to your amendment advice.

Yours sincerely,

(Signature)

Notes

1. L/C Letter of Credit 信用证。the written promise of a bank that acts at the request and on the instructions of the applicant and undertakes to pay the beneficiary the amount specified in the credit, provided that the terms and conditions of the credit are observed by the beneficiary.

2. illustrated catalogue 图解目录

3. port of loading 装运港

4. date for shipment 装运期

5. expiry date 有效期

6. extend   *v.* 延长

The company's activities are extended. 公司的业务在扩大。

7. negotiation   *n.* 议付

negotiation L/C 议付信用证 (指开证行在信用证中，邀请其他银行买入汇票及/或单据的信用证)

Specimen Letter 2   Giving Shipping Instructions to the Seller

Dear Mr. Wang,

We are pleased to receive your Sales Contract No.666 in duplicate against our Order No.888 for 50 000 bottles of Tsingtao beer.

Although the price is quoted on **FCA** basis, we wish to request that you sign the contract of **carriage** with the **carrier** on usual terms **at our risk and expense**.

When you have booked the shipping space, please advise us of the name and **voyage number** of the vessel, **B/L** No., **estimated time of departure (ETD)**, **estimated time of arrival (ETA)**, and any other information necessary for us to **procure** insurance **at our end**.

As the bottles of the beer are **vulnerable**, please pack them in specially made cases capable of withstanding **rough handling**.

Your close cooperation in the above respects is highly appreciated.

Yours faithfully,

(Signature)

Notes

1. FCA   货交承运人

2. carriage   *n.* 运输

They do not charge much for carriage. 他们只收一点儿运费。

3. carrier   *n.* 承运人

4. at our risk and expense   费用和风险由我方承担

5. voyage number   航次

6. B/L= bill of lading   海运提单

7. estimated time of departure (ETD)   预计离港时间

8. estimated time of arrival (ETA)   预计到达时间

9. procure   *v.* 获得，办理

She managed to procure a ticket for the concert. 她好不容易弄到一张演唱会的门票。

10. at our end 在我地

11. vulnerable   *adj.* 易受损的，脆弱的

12. rough handling 野蛮装卸，粗暴搬运

Specimen Letter 3   Urging an Immediate or Punctual Shipment

Dear Miss Wang,

With reference to Sales Contract No.102 covering 1000 cartons of Christmas Candles, we wish to invite your attention to the fact that shipment should be **effected** in October.

However, up to now, we have not received any information about it. As Christmas season is drawing near and our customers are **in urgent need of** these candles during the Christmas holidays, you are requested to effect punctual shipment so that we can catch the **busy season**. In case you fail to ship the goods according to the stipulations of the Contract No.102 and the covering L/C No.A436, we will have to **lodge a claim against you** for the losses **sustained** by us. In that case, repeat orders will be impossible.

Please inform us immediately whether you have shipped the goods or not so that we can make some arrangements in advance.

Yours sincerely,

(Signature)

Notes

1. effect   *v.* 产生，实现

Weight memo is made out by a seller when a sale is effected in foreign trade. 重量单是对外贸易中卖方售货时出具的单据。

2. in urgent need of 急需

3. busy season 旺季

4. lodge a claim against/with/on sb. 就我方遭受的损失向某人提出(索赔)

5. sustain   *v.* 蒙受，经受

The sea wall sustained the shock of waves. 海堤经得起海浪的冲击。

Specimen Letter 4　Sending a Shipping Advice
(Reply to Letter 3)

Dear Robinson,

Thank you for your letter of November 1, 20×× urging immediate and punctual shipment of Christmas Candles. I am awfully sorry for the delay in sending you the shipping advice because of my seven-day absence for taking care of my mother ill in bed. I hope that this delay has not put you into too much inconvenience.

Referring to Contract No.102, we are pleased to tell you that the goods were shipped on October 25, 20××. The details are as follows:

Your L/C No.A436.

Name of Commodity: Christmas Candles.

Quantity: **Art. No.**201, 500 CTN; Art. No.301, 500 CTN; totaling 1000 CTN.

Packing: Art. No.201, 200 PCS/CTN; Art. No.301, 100 PCS/CTN.

Gross weight: 19 810kg.

Net weight: 18 810kg.

Measurement: 55 234m^3.

Name of vessel: "East Wind" V. 085.

Sailing date: October 25, 20××.

Port of shipment: Shanghai, China.

Port of destination/discharge: Vancouver, Canada.

ETA: November 15, 20××.

Shipping Marks:

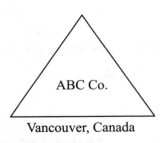

Vancouver, Canada

No. 1-1000

Made in China

We are also enclosing a full set **non-negotiable** shipping documents for your reference. We hope that the above-mentioned goods will arrive at your port **safe and sound**.

Awaiting your further orders the same time next year.

Truly yours,

(Signature)

Notes

1. Art. No. 货号

2. gross weight 毛重

3. net weight 净重

4. sailing date 起航日期

5. port of shipment 装运港

6. port of destination/discharge 目的港

7. shipping mark 运输标志

8. non-negotiable *adj*. unable to be transferred and negotiated 不可议付的，不可转让的

9. safe and sound   without any damage or injury 安全地、完好无损地

Specimen Letter 5   Apologizing for the Delay of Shipment (Reply to Letter 3)

Dear Sirs,

We regret very much your letter of November 1, 20×× urging immediate and punctual shipment of Christmas Candles. We are, of course, aware that your goods are long **overdue**, but the work at the plant was **suspended** for several weeks because of earthquakes.

However, we have been doing everything in our power to deliver the goods within a week, and now are arranging for shipment. In the meantime we offer you our apologies for the inconvenience the delay has caused.

Yours faithfully,

(Signature)

Notes

1. overdue *adj*. 过期的

2. suspend *v*. 中止

Trade with that country has been suspended for ten years. 和那个国家的贸易中断了十年。

Specimen Letter 6　Notifying the Goods Received

Dear Sirs,

The case of chinaware which you **dispatched** on November 1, 20×× was delivered yesterday. We unpacked the case immediately and found no breakages. The contents were in fact in perfect condition.

We are arranging for the case to be returned to you by road carriers, **carriage forward** and shall be glad if you will **credit** us with the amount charged for it on your invoice.

Yours faithfully,

(Signature)

Notes

1. dispatch　*v.* 发运

   We have to ask you to dispatch the consignment immediately. 我们要求你方立即发送该批货物。

2. carriage forward　运费到付

3. credit　*n.* 赊销

   He bought the furniture on credit. 他赊账买了这家具。

Specimen Letter 7　Enquiry for Freight Rate and Time of Voyage

Dear Sirs,

We shall shortly have ready for shipment from London to Sydney 10 cases of **crockery**. The cases measure 1.25 m×1.25 m×1 m, each weighing about 80 kg.

Will you please quote your rate for freight and send us details of your sailings and the time usually taken for the voyage. We understand that vessel Western Star is due to sail on June 25, but we should like an earlier sailing if possible.

Yours faithfully,

(Signature)

Notes

crockery　*n.* 陶器

Specimen Letter 8   Reply to Letter 7

Dear Sirs,

Thank you for your enquiry of May 3.

The vessel "Princess Victoria" will be loading at No. 4 Dock from June 10 to 15 **inclusive**. Following her is the vessel "Western Star", loading at No. 7 Dock from June 20 to 25 inclusive. The voyage to Sydney normally takes 14 days. The freight rate for crockery packed in wooden cases is ￡60 per **tonne**.

We shall be glad to book you 10 cases for either of these vessels and **enclose** our shipping form. Please complete and return it as soon as you can.

Your faithfully,

(Signature)

Notes

1. inclusive   *adj.* 包括在内的

   an inclusive tour 包括一切费用在内的旅游

2. tonne   *n.* [法]公吨

3. enclose   *v.* 附寄

   Enclosed herein you will find the bill. 内附账单。

Specimen Letter 9   Enquiry for the Container Service

Dear Sirs,

I understand that your company is now operating a container service on **the Southampton-Cape Town route** and should be glad if you would send me **particulars** of it, including your charges for using the service. I am a manufacturer of leather shoes.

Yours faithfully,

(Signature)

Notes

1. the Southampton-Cape Town route   南安普敦—开普敦航线

2. particulars   *n.* 详情

I suppose the secretary knows the particulars of the plan. 我想那位秘书知道这一计划的详细情况。

Specimen Letter 10 Reply to Letter 9

Dear Sirs,

Thank you for your enquiry of October 6. The shipping containers we provide are of two sizes, namely 3 m and 6 m long and built to take **loads** up to two and four tonnes respectively. They can be opened **at both ends**, thus making it possible to load and unload at the same time. For carrying goods **liable to** be spoiled by damp or water they have the great advantage of being both **water-tight** and **air-tight**. Containers can be loaded and locked at the factory, if necessary. **Pilfering** is therefore impossible.

There is also a saving in freight charges when separate **consignments** intended for the same port of destination are carried in one container and an additional saving on insurance because of the lower **premiums** charged for container-shipped goods.

We enclose a copy of our tariff and look forward to receiving your instructions.

Yours faithfully,

(Signature)

Notes

1. load   *v./n.* 负荷

   a heavily loaded truck 负载沉重的卡车

2. at both ends 两端

3. liable to 易于

   Children are liable to catch cold. 小孩子易患感冒。

4. water-tight   *adj.* 不透水的

5. air-tight   *adj.* 不透气的

6. pilfer   *v.* 偷窃

7. consignment   *n.* 装运的货物，托运的货物；托运，运送

   consignment invoice   发货单

   consignment note 发货通知书

   consignment out 寄销品

   Their consignment of bananas was bad. 他们托运的一批香蕉质量不好。

8. premium   *n.* 保险费

Useful Sentences

1. Please make/arrange for shipment in three equal installments beginning from May. 请从 5 月开始安排三次数量相同的分批装运。

2. We require shipment by the next available steamer. 我们要求于下一艘轮船进行装运。

3. Please make your best efforts to get the goods dispatched with the least possible delay. 请你方尽力毫无拖延地发送货物。

4. We trust that you will make all necessary arrangements to deliver/forward the goods in time. 我们相信你方会做好一切必要安排及时发货。

5. Your failure to deliver the goods within the stipulated time has greatly inconvenienced us/caused us a lot of trouble. 你方无法在约定的时间运送货物已经给我方带来了极大的不便。

6. It is stipulated that the goods are to be shipped in October. However, we shall appreciate it if you will manage to advance the shipment to September to enable us to catch the busy season. 按规定，货物应于 10 月装运。但是，如蒙你方设法提前于 9 月份发货以使我方赶上旺季，则不胜感激。

7. As the goods are ready for shipment, please designate a vessel and let us know its name as early as possible. 由于货物已备好待运，请选派船只，并尽快将船名告知我方。

8. Please let us know immediately the name of the transshipping vessel and its sailing date from Hong Kong, so that we may inquire about its whereabouts. 请立即把转运船的船名及其在香港的开航日期告诉我们，以使我方打听其去向。

9. The goods will be shipped by…Voyage, which is due to arrive at…(place) on…(date). Please book the shipping space immediately and confirm that the goods will be ready in time. 货物将由……轮……航次装运，该轮预定于……月……日抵达……港，请速订舱。请确认货物将按时备妥。

10. Something unexpected compels us to seek your cooperation by advancing shipment of the goods under Contract No.×× from August to July. 意外的情况迫使我们寻求你方配合，请将……号合同项下的货物装期由 8 月提前到 7 月。

11. We understand your position, but we are sorry to tell you that we can not advance. 我们理解你方的处境，但很遗憾，我们无法提前发货。

12. We have the pleasure to inform/advice/notify you that goods under S/C No.×× have been dispatched by M/V "Greenwood" sailing on May 14, 20×× for Hong Kong. 我们很高兴地通知你方……号合同项下的货物已于 20××年 5 月 14 日装 "格林伍德"

轮发往香港。

13. For the goods under S/C No.××, we have booked space/freight on S.S. "Daqing" due to arrive in London around May 19. Please approach/contact/communicate with Lombar Bros. Co., London, our shipping agent, for loading arrangements/for delivery instructions/for further information. 我方已经为……号合同项下的货物在"大庆"轮定好舱位，该轮预计于5月19日前后抵达伦敦。请联系我方在伦敦的装运代理人Lombar Bros.公司，以做好卸货准备/做好运货准备/了解详细信息。

Letter-writing Guide

The steps and expressions of writing letters of giving shipment advice are as follows. (装运通知的写作步骤及常用表达方式如下。)

Writing steps (写作步骤)	Examples of expressions (表达方式举例)
1. 开门见山，表明用意	This is to inform/advice/notify you that… 兹通知……
	I am pleased to inform/advice/notify you that… 我们很高兴地通知贵方……
2. 对装运具体事宜进行描述(合同号、品名、数量、包装、船名、航次、净重、毛重、预计到达时间等)	…the goods under S/C No.123 went forward per M/V "Washington" V.002 of the Pacific Line on October 20, and the relevant shipping samples had been dispatched to you by air before the ship sailed. ……123号销售确认书项下货物已于10月20日装太平洋航运公司的"华盛顿"号货轮：002航次，有关货样已于该轮启程前航空邮寄你方。
3. 表达早日收到回复的愿望	We look forward to receiving… 希望早日收到……
	Hope to receive… 希望收到……
	Your early reply is appreciated. 盼早回复。
	We are anticipating your answer. 盼早回复。

Exercises

I. Put the following English phrases into Chinese or Chinese phrases into English.

1. non-negotiable B/L   2. voyage charter   3. ETD   4. dispatch money   5. shipping space
6. 运输合同   7. 班轮提单   8. 滞期费   9. 指示提单   10. 运费

II. Translate the following English into Chinese or Chinese into English.

1. We are also enclosing a full set non-negotiable shipping documents for your reference.

2. Our shipment terms are shipment within two months after receipt of L/C.

3. The earliest shipment possible is December. We hope this will be acceptable to your

customers.

4. Owing to the delayed arrival of the scheduled vessel, we have failed to effect shipment within the L/C validity.

5. We hope that the goods will arrive at your port safe and sound.

6. 请告诉我方你方何时能发运 123 号合同项下的玻璃器皿。

7. 我方库存越来越少，所以要求你方根据合同规定按时发运 500 箱茶叶。

8. 关于 5000 千克中国东北大豆，我方很高兴地通知你方我们已订上"华胜"号货轮093 航次的舱位。

9. 根据你方要求，我们已经将全套副本装运单据航空邮寄你方，供你方办理进口报关之用。

10. 我们很遗憾地通知你方，由于此地工人的罢工，我方不能按时发运货物。

III. Translate the following letters.

1. From English to Chinese.

Dear Sirs,

Re: Our Order No.168

With reference to the shipment of our Order No.168 for 100 cases of China Wares, we wish to draw your attention to the followings:

As the goods are susceptible to be broken, the wares must be packed in wooden cases capable of withstanding rough handling.

Please mark the cases with our initials in a diamond, under which comes the destination with contract number and stencil conspicuously the words: "FRAGILE, HANDLE WITH CARE" on both sides of the cases.

We trust that the above instructions are clear to you and that the shipment will give the users entire satisfaction.

Yours faithfully,

(Signature)

2. From Chinese to English.

敬启者：

很抱歉不得不通知贵方，延迟履行您 10 月 23 日的 DA－283 号订单。

如您所知，当地政府最近禁止各种药品出口到美国。本公司要履行贵方订单，必须取得特殊许可证。我方认为此种延迟将不超过 3 周，一旦收到装运许可，必定特别优先处理贵公司的订单。

无论如何，致使您感受到不便，请接受我方致歉。

谨上

(签名)

IV. Fill in the blanks of the following letter with the words and expressions given. Change the form where necessary.

punctual shipment   against   place an order   overdue   do one's utmost   by return

Dear Sirs,

Concerning our order No. 251 for 50 units of Hi-Fi stereo, you have so far delivered only 30 units ___1___ the shipment during May; 20 units on May 20 and 10 units on June 18; 20 units are much ___2___ .

When we ___3___ we pointed out that ___4___ was of special importance, because we have given our customers a definite assurance that we could supply by the end of July.

Your delay causes us considerable difficulties and we must ask you to ___5___ to dispatch the overdue goods as soon as possible. Please inform us ___6___ when you can ship them with certainty so that we can promise the responsible time of delivery to our customers who are proposing to cancel this order.

Yours faithfully,

(Signature)

V. Write a letter according to the information given in the following situations, applying the writing principles discussed in this chapter.

1. 通知进口商，300 吨低碳扁钢装上定于明日启航驶往对方港口的"无锡"轮。

2. 随附此批货物的装船单据副本一套，包括：

(1) 不可转让的提单副本一份。

(2) 商业发票一式两份。

(3) 品质检验证书一份。

(4) 重量检验证书一份。

(5) 保险单一份。

(6) 重量单一式两份。

Unit 10 补充练习

Unit 10 补充练习答案

Unit 10 练习答案

Unit 11　Complaints, Claims and Adjustments

【学习要点和目标】

通过本单元的学习，了解投诉和处理方法的常识，掌握解决问题的常用技巧，以及书写投诉函电和相关处理函电的写作技巧。

Lead-in

On execution of a sales contract, both the seller and the buyer must abide by the terms and conditions of the contract and strictly perform their respective obligations. If one of the parties breaches the contract, the other may run into trouble, or suffer great losses. In this case, the affected party can either request the defaulter to make sure that such things will not happen again, which is known as a "complaint", or request him to make up his losses according to the relevant provisions under the contract, which is called a "claim". When the other party gets a complaint or claim, he may either grant an adjustment or reject it depending on the circumstances.

Claims should be adjusted fairly and amicably between the parties concerned. It is better not to submit/render a claim for arbitration or (to a) court of law, so long as the claim is likely to be settled through friendly negotiations. When making a claim, it is important that the claimant should lodge his claim within the time stipulated in the contract. Otherwise, the claim will be ineffective. And the claim should, in most cases, be supported by sufficient documents (e.g. a survey report) so that it is persuasive.

When drafting correspondence of this sort, the writer should be polite as well as reasonable. The wording he uses should be firm and persuasive. The phrases like "According to contract stipulations, (you should...)", "We apologize for our mistakes which caused you a lot of trouble and will (do sth. to rectify the errors)" often appear in this kind of letters. To enforce his arguments, the writer often quotes the statements in the relative contract or documents. But when quoting, the statements written in the following letter should not be contradictory to those in previous ones. And the Ref. Numbers, dates, sentences or specific requests quoted from either party's correspondence should be completely correct. Otherwise, the writer will easily find himself in an awkward, unfavourable situation which will probably bring about harm to his own business.

Specimen Letter 1   Complaining about the Inferior Materials

Dear Mr. Wang,

The consignment of the clothing materials we ordered on August 10 is not the quality as shown in the samples.

The consignment arrived yesterday, but on checking the materials with the samples you sent us, we are surprised to find that they do not match each other. Their quality seems inferior to the samples, so they do not **meet our customers' requirement**.

We have arranged for the production of the customized suits and planned to start as soon as the materials arrive. However, we will have to postpone the original orders from our customers **owing to** the poor quality of the clothing material you sent us. This is bringing us much inconvenience.

Would you take them back and replace them with the one as we ordered? We allow you another 10 days to prepare them. If you cannot guarantee delivery for whatever reason before October 1, we should ask for a complete **refund** of the money and full compensation for all our costs.

Your prompt cooperation will be beneficial to both of us.

Sincerely yours,

(Signature)

Notes

1. inferior   *adj.* (质量等)劣等的，差的

   inferior goods 低档货

2. to meet our customers' requirement 符合我们客户的需要

3. owing to   由于

   They could not cross the river owing to the flood. 由于洪水，他们不能过河。

   Owing to the immediate danger of war, there will be an extraordinary meeting of Parliament tonight. 由于即将发生的战争危险，今晚议会将召开特别会议。

4. refund   *n. & vt.* 偿(归，退)还；偿付

   To cancel an order after payment is not refunded all the money. 付款后取消订单一律不退回款项。

Specimen Letter 2   Adjustment for the Wrong Materials (Reply to Letter 1)

Dear Clean Presley,

The correct consignment of the clothing material will reach you within 20 days.

I'm grateful for your letter dated September 1. We're sorry to learn that the clothing materials don't match the sample. After careful examination, we found that we had **mishandled** your order and another order that was different from yours with only one letter. We have arranged for the correct consignment and it would arrive at your place by September 24.

As **compensation** for the wrong delivery, I would like to provide you a 5% **discount** on this consignment, and I hope such an arrangement is satisfactory to you.

Yours sincerely,

(Signature)

Notes

1. mishandle   *v.* 错误处理，未按订单交货

   We mishandled your order owing to the carelessness on the part of our warehouse worker.
   由于我方仓库工人的疏忽，致使未按订单交货。

2. compensation   *n.* 赔偿

3. discount   *n.* 折扣；贴现；贴现率

   at a discount   折价，减价发行

   with some discount   打折扣，以保留态度

Specimen Letter 3   Claim on the Damaged or Blemished Goods

Dear Mr. Ji,

Defective Grade 'A' **USB flash disk** (Order No. 254334522)

We received our consignment of 2000 Grade 'A' USB flash disks this afternoon.

However, on checking the flash disks we have discovered that they do not function properly. They appear to be incapable of storing data for some reason. Therefore, I am afraid they are completely unusable.

We had planned to start a **promotion** of these flash disks from Monday. In fact, we already have many advanced orders which we shall now have to postpone because of your poor quality control. This will cause us a great deal of inconvenience.

I should like you to replace these **faulty** disks with fully-functioning Grade 'A' flash disks within the next week. If you are unable to guarantee delivery for whatever reason, I should be prepared to accept a complete refund of the money which was paid for the order.

Yours sincerely,

(Signature)

Notes

1. defective   *adj*. 有缺陷(缺点)的，不完美的，故障的(in)；变化不全的；智力或行为不健全的

    He is defective in moral sense. 他不能分辨邪正。

2. USB flash disk   U 盘

3. promotion   *n*. (商品的)宣传，推销；(推销中的)产品

    a promotion worker 推销员

4. faulty   *adj*. 有过失的；有缺点(毛病)的；有错误的；不完善的；不合格的

    a faulty reasoning 错误的推理

    a faulty design 不完善的设计方案

Specimen Letter 4   Adjustment for the Damaged or Blemished Goods (Reply to Letter 3)

Dear Mr. Tsai,

I refer to your letter of 10 October **regarding** the standard of the USB flash disks we supplied to you recently. Thank you very much for bringing this matter to our attention. We agree with you that strict quality control is very important.

Having checked with our suppliers, it is clear that they mistakenly sent us a consignment of faulty disks. **Apparently**, the damage was caused during the production process, and the suppliers are currently recalling all of batch 76lbs.

I really must apologize for the inconvenience you have been caused. I can assure you that in future we shall do all we can to avoid this error occurring again.

We take all our customer' comments seriously. **With this in mind**, we are more than happy to replace the faulty flash disks. I shall arrange for a replacement consignment to be sent to you immediately, and would be grateful if you could return the faulty disks to us. We shall, of course, **reinforce** freight charges.

Please accept my apologies once again for the inconvenience.

Yours sincerely,

(Signature)

Notes

1. regarding　*prep.* 关于，有关

   I wrote a letter regarding my daughter's school examination. 我写了一封信，谈及我女儿考试的情况。

2. apparently　*adv.* 显然；似乎

   Apparently, you have done a lot of work. 很明显你们已经做了很多工作。

3. with this in mind　记在心里

   bear…in mind　把……记在心里，记住

4. reinforce　*vt.* 加强，加固；补充增援，支援

   reinforce a fleet　增加一个舰队

Specimen Letter 5　Complaining about the Wrong Invoice

Dear Mr. Mark,

Subject: Invoice No.P5643/9

We have just received the above invoice for a consignment of books which was delivered on 4 May,　20×× as part of our exhibition of contemporary Chinese photographers' work.

However, your invoice states that the consignment containing 240 copies of *China on the Move* by Shui Wen-xing, whereas, in fact, it contained only 200 copies. If you check our **original order** (No. 4378528-copy attached) you will see this was all we ordered.

We trust you will arrange for a new invoice to be **issued** in the near future, as we shall be happy to **settle** this account as soon as possible.

Yours sincerely,

(Signature)

Notes

1. original order 正本订单

2. issue *v.* 开具，发行

   They issued a fixed number of shares that trade publicly. 他们发行了一定数量的可公开交易的股票。

3. settle *vt.* 解决

   Settle this matter immediately. 尽快解决这件事情。

Specimen Letter 6   Apologizing for the Wrong Invoice (Reply to Letter 5)

Dear Mr. Wan,

Reference is made to your letter of 27 May 20×× regarding our invoice (P5643/9). I **appreciate** your bringing this matter to my attention.

Having checked with our suppliers, it appears that a mistake has been made on this occasion, and that you have been sent an invoice with incorrect details. The reason for this is that we have recently introduced **a computerized stock control system**, and there have been a number of "teething problems". revised and correct invoice is attached for your convenience.

I hope you have not been too inconvenienced by our mistake, and that you will continue to **honour** us with your custom.

Yours sincerely,

(Signature)

Notes

1. appreciate *vt.* 赏识，感谢，感激；意识到，懂得；提高(价值)，抬高……的价格

   appreciate sb.'s friendship 珍视某人的友谊

   We all appreciate the holiday after a year of hard work. 经过一年的辛苦工作之后，我们都十分珍惜这个假期。

   We shall appreciate hearing from you again.   我们恭候佳音。

2. a computerized stock control system 电脑库存管理系统

3. honour = honor *v.* 给予……荣誉

   He has honored us with his presence. 他的到来是我们的光荣。

Specimen Letter 7   Refusal to Claim on Replacement

Dear Mr. Mitchell,

We understand your concern about the software Model 4050 you mentioned in you letter of May 6. We are willing to do as much as we reasonably can to make things right.

From your description and our staff's careful research, we found that there was something wrong in the computer networks you adopted.

As it is stated in the operating instruction, this software is solely **compatible** with Windows XP, which is different from Windows 98. And before you use this software, you should have to install the **starting system at the bottom** of the box first. But you haven't installed it.

Therefore, please install the starting system first and then try it with Windows XP. **For other procedures**, please follow the procedures strictly with our instruction **brochure**.

We hope the software will bring much convenience and profit to you.

> Frankly yours,
> (Signature)

Notes

1. compatible   *adj.* 兼容的

   The two systems are not compatible. 这两种系统不兼容。

2. starting system 驱动系统

   The new starting system proves much faster than the older ones. 新驱动系统的运行速度比旧系统的快得多。

3. at the bottom of   *prep.* 在……的底部

4. for other procedures 关于其他的步骤

5. brochure   *n.* 小册子，说明书，简介材料，背景资料，手册

   sales brochure 推广小册子，宣传品

   manufacturer's brochure 制造厂样本(小册子)

Specimen Letter 8　Refusal to Request for Compensating for the Damaged Material

Dear Mr. Wilson,

　　Every customer **has a right to** expect the best product and service from Caring Plastic Material. Every caring material is the result of years of experimentation.

　　I have **routed** your letter of August 10th **attached with** photos to our production department. After careful inspection in our laboratory, we find that the materials Series 0150 you intended for refund were apparently exposed to a long-time sunlight. As we have noted from the beginning as well as mentioned in our advertising, Series 0150 cannot be shined for a long time.

　　However, Series 2115 can withstand exposure to all sunlight. They share all the merits of Series 0150 and are **sunlight-proof** and **waterproof**. They are also **economical**. If you need further details and any help we can offer on your selection, please call us at 01-45-4318188 or send us an e-mail at *caringmaterial@yahoo.com*.

　　　　　　　　　　　　　　　　　Frankly yours,

　　　　　　　　　　　　　　　　　(Signature)

Notes

1. to have a right to 有权利做······

2. route　*v.* 按特定路线发送

　　We will route the information to the headquarters by tomorrow. 我们明天将把该情况转给总部。

3. attached with 附加的，附上的

4. sunlight-proof　*adj*. 防晒的

5. waterproof　*adj*. 防水的

6. economical　*adj*. 节俭的，节省的；经济的；经济学的

　　be economical of one's time 节省时间

　　My new car is economical of fuel. 我的新汽车节省燃料(不费油)。

Useful Sentences

1. On examination, we found that the goods do not agree with/correspond to/conform to/tally

with the original patterns/samples. 经过检查，我们发现货物与原样并不相符。

2. Upon examination, we found that many of the goods were severely damaged, though the cases themselves show no trace of damage. 经过检查，我们发现许多货物已严重损坏，但是包装箱却没有损坏的痕迹。

3. The bulk of the goods delivered is not up to sample/does not conform to the sample. 运送的整批货物都与样品不符。

4. We have to/are compelled to/regret to complain about the serious/grave defects in the…(goods) dispatched to us on July 7. 我们不得不提出投诉，你方于 7 月 7 日发往我方的……(货物)有严重的瑕疵。

5. We are sorry/regret to say that the cargo has not turned out to our satisfaction. 我们很遗憾地说，我们并不满意该货物。

6. A thorough examination showed that the broken bags were due to insecure/improper/negligent packing for which the suppliers are definitely responsible. 经过全面的检查发现，包装袋的破损是由于不恰当的包装导致的，供应商对此肯定有责任。

7. This delay is causing us serious inconvenience because we, in our turn, promised delivery on the strength of your assurance. 该拖延给我们带来了极大的不便，因为我们是在你方的保证之下承诺发货的。

8. We reserve the right to claim compensation from you for any damage. 对于你方造成的损害我方保留索赔的权利。

9. On the basis of Clause 18 of the Contract, we hereby place our claims before you as follows. 根据合同第 18 款规定，我们因此向你方提出以下索赔。

10. We believe this is a fair adjustment, and trust that it will be acceptable to you. 我们认为这样赔偿比较公平，希望你方能够接受。

11. The document/evidence produced by you to support your claim are/is insufficient. Therefore, we cannot take your claim for compensation into consideration. 你方提供的文件/证据无法支持你方的索赔，因此，我们无法考虑你方的索赔要求。

12. We cannot agree with you that responsibility for such losses rests with us. 我们不认为该损失是我们的责任。

13. Since the goods were in perfect condition when they were shipped as was evidenced by their Bill of Lading, it is quite obvious that they were damaged en route. Accordingly we regret that we cannot admit/accept/assume any liability/responsibility for your claim. 海

运提单表明货物在装运的时候是完好的，很显然，损坏发生在运输途中。因此，我们很遗憾地告知你方，我们无法接受你方的索赔。

14. The shortage you alleged/claimed might have occurred in the course of transit, and that is a matter over which we can exercise no control. 你方提出的短缺索赔可能是由于转运造成的，这是我们无法控制的。

Letter-writing Guide

The steps and expressions of writing complaints and claims are as follows. (投诉和索赔信函的写作步骤及常用表达方式如下。)

Writing steps (写作步骤)	Examples of expressions (表达方式举例)
1. 开门见山，摆明事实	We have just received a consignment of personal computers from your company (details attached). 我们刚收到贵公司发出的一批个人电脑(随函附清单)。
	Our consignment to Fujita overhead projector pens was delivered this afternoon. 兹于今天下午收到一批富士通高射投影机笔。
	The above shipment of components was delivered today, and was checked on delivery. 上述这批零部件已于今天收到，并已收验。
2. 投诉	On checking the camera I discovered that it did not function. 经检查我发现照相机不能正常使用。
	I really must complain about the quality of the goods that you recently sent us. 对于贵方最近发送的货物存在的质量问题，我不得不向您提起投诉。
	You have sent us goods which we did not order. 贵方运送之货物，我方并未订购。
	We are not happy about the inconvenience that this situation is causing us. 这种状况给我方带来不便，我们深表不满。
	We already have many advanced orders which we shall now have to postpone because of your inefficiency/slowness/poor quality control. 我们已经收到许多预订单，但由于贵方效率欠佳/办事拖拉/质量控制不严，现不得不延期执行。
3. 提出解决办法	We should be obliged/grateful if you would replace the goods you delivered with the correct ones. 贵方若能更换发错的货物，我们将不胜感激。
	We trust you will arrange for a new invoice to be issued in the near future. 我们相信贵方能很快做出安排，开具新发票。
	We should appreciate your looking into this matter and arranging for delivery within the next three days. 谨希望您对此进行调查，三天之内安排发货，我们将不胜感激。

续表

4. 表明立场	I regret that unless you can comply with my request within three days, I shall be forced to/compelled to/obliged to consider canceling my order. 贵方如三天之内不能满足我们的要求，我们只能遗憾地取消订单。
	Further delays in delivery will/may/might/could result in our canceling our order. 如果贵方再次延误交货，我们将可能取消订单。
	If you do not refund all of the money we have paid, we shall have no choice but to seek legal advice in the matter. 如果我方已付货款不能全数退还，我们别无选择，只能向律师征询法律意见。

The steps and expressions of writing letter of adjustments are as follows. (理赔信函的写作步骤及常用表达方式如下。)

Writing steps(写作步骤)	Examples of Expressions(表达方式举例)
1. 告知对方投诉信已收悉	I refer to your letter of...regarding delivery time/the standard of goods we supplied/our invoice... 现就您……关于运货日期/货物标准/发票的信件做出回复。
	Thank your for/We appreciate your bringing this matter to our attention. 感谢您提出此事使我们注意。
2. 采取的行动及调查结果	I have checked with the transporters/our suppliers, it is clear that... 我们向运输公司/供应商进行了核实，显然……
	The delay was due to/a result of the poor weather conditions. 发货延误是因为天气情况恶劣。
3. 决定	I really must apologize for the inconvenience which has been caused. 给贵方带来不便，对此我们深表歉意。
	We shall endeavor to assure you that in future we shall do all we can to avoid this error occurring again. 我们向您保证，我们将尽己所能，杜绝此类错误再次发生。
	I regret to inform you that sale goods cannot be returned to the shop. 我很遗憾地告诉您，本店货物一经售出，概不退货。
	Unfortunately I must inform you that we are not responsible for damage which takes place at sea. 我遗憾地向您表明，货物在海上受到损坏，我们对此不承担任何责任。
4. 给予补偿或提出折衷方案	We take all our customers' comments seriously. With this in mind, we are more than happy to cover the cost of replacing the defective goods. 我们素来重视客户意见。本着这一原则，我们非常乐意承担更换缺损货品而带来的一切费用。
	If you would like us to call by and take a look at the vehicle, please let me know and I shall be happy to give you a free quote for its repair. 如果您愿意让我们前来检查车辆，请告知我们，我们很乐意为您提供免费维修。

Exercises

I. Put the following English phrases into Chinese Phrases into English.

1. breach of the contract   2. legal action   3. invoice   4. shoddy goods   5. force majeure

6. 理赔   7. 商检局   8. 有毛病的货物   9. 磨损   10. 索赔申请表

II. Translate these sentences into Chinese or English.

1. It contained articles different from what we have ordered.

2. The goods we ordered from you on June 6 haven't arrived yet.

3. We regret that only 20 sets have been received to date whereas our order indicates 25.

4. All the packages appeared to be in perfect condition, whereas most of the contents were found damaged.

5. The wheat you shipped to us on vessel "Golden Horse" was found short in weight by CCIB, for which we regret we must lodge a claim on you.

6. 货物没有达到标准。

7. 你们的错误给我们带来了巨大的麻烦。

8. 你们运来的鞋我们已及时收到了，但遗憾地提请你们注意这种情况：货物到达时发现短少 300 双。

9. 你方使用的木箱不够坚固，不适于包装这么重的机器。因此，货物抵达时，我们发现木箱完全压扁了，大部分机器的零件已损坏。

10. 那些仪器的损坏主要是由于它们在木箱内装得太松又未做适当的填充。因此，我们别无选择，只好把这个问题交给你方处理。

III. Translate the following letters.

1. From English to Chinese.

Dear Sirs,

　　We regret to learn from your letter of September 8 that your Order No.C426 of 20 cartons of Wool Carpet arrived in poor condition.

　　If we were at fault we would be responsible to agree to your proposal. But in view of the fact that our goods were carefully packed by experienced workman and sent out in perfect condition as shown by a copy of the clean B/L which we enclose herewith. We are certain they were damaged through careless handling while in transit.

We therefore suggest you had better lodge a claim immediately against the Shipping Company. If you send us the papers which show exactly the condition the goods reached you, we will take up the matter for you with the view of recovering damages from the Shipping Company.

We are awaiting your reply.

Yours faithfully,

(Signature)

2. From Chinese to English.

敬启者：

感谢你方如此迅速地交付我方 3 月 15 日订购的煤气焦炭，但发现对我们订购的以每袋 50 千克装的 5 吨货，你方的运输行只交来 80 袋。他无法对此次短量做出解释，我们也没有接到你方的任何解释。

我方仍需要所订购的全部数量的货物。若你方能尽快地将剩下的 20 袋交来，我们将甚为高兴。

谨上

(签名)

IV. Fill in the blanks of the following letter with the words and expressions given. Change the form where necessary.

compensation　packing　consignment　profit margin　examination　expense

Dear Sirs,

We refer to our order CW5210 for 1,000 dozen towels. The goods were delivered. On ___1___, we found the cartons were in a damaged condition. 21 of 100 cartons had burst open due to poor ___2___. The rest were in a damaged condition too.

We have repacked the whole ___3___ in new cartons. The ___4___ involved amounted to $150. As you know, the ___5___ on this consignment is tight. Therefore, we have no choice but to ask you to make ___6___ to us.

You will be aware that poorly packing will lead to false impression of the quality of goods. We suggest that, in future, you make sure that the goods are properly packed.

We look forward to your cooperation.

Yours sincerely,

(Signature)

V. Write a letter according to the information given in the following situations, applying the writing principles discussed in this chapter.

Suppose your company has just received 35 sets of machines, which you ordered for 40 sets. Make a claim against the supplier, ABC Machine Works, on the shortage of the machines.

Unit 11 补充练习   Unit 11 补充练习答案   Unit 11 练习答案

Unit 12　Agency

【学习要点和目标】

通过本单元的学习，了解不同的代理方式，掌握要求跟对方进行代理、同意代理请求以及拒绝代理请求等信函的写作方法和写作词汇。

Lead-in

A vast amount of international trade is handled not only by **direct negotiation** between buyers and sellers but also **by means of** agencies. An important reason for **appointing** a foreign agent is his knowledge of **local conditions** and of the market in which he operates. He may have better knowledge about what goods are best suited to his area and what prices the market will bear. In developing foreign trade, agents and intermediaries often **play a very important role**.

The exporter who has an agent is called principal. The relationship between a principal and an agent is based on commissions. Before he makes his decision of an agent, the exporter should carefully verify the aspects as follows:

1. Business standing and financial status.

2. Sales experience in the relevant field.

3. Technical capability of handling the goods to be distributed.

4. Personal qualities.

There are three types of agents according to the **scope of the authority** granted by the principal:

1. General Agent: This type of agent has a full authority from the principal and can not only sign contract directly with the customer on his principal's behalf but also deal with other commercial activities in a certain region.

2. Sole Agent (Exclusive Agent): This type of agent can only enjoy the full privilege of exclusive sales for some kind of goods in certain district within a certain period.

3. Commission Agent: This type of agent does not enjoy the full privilege of exclusive sales for some goods. A principal may have several commission agents to push his sales in the same district within the same period.

Our import and export corporations usually appoint some firms in foreign countries to act as their agents to sell the goods produced or manufactured in our country. The **terms of agency** are sometimes set out in correspondence between the parties. However, when there are large-scale transactions between the parties, a formal agreement will be necessary. Matters to be covered in the agreement may include all or some of the followings:

1. The nature and duration of the agency.

2. The territory to be covered.

3. The duties of agent and principal.

4. The method of purchase and sale (e.g. whether the agent is to buy for his own account or "on consignment").

Notes

1. direct negotiation 直接磋商

2. by means of   through/by way of/by/via 以……方式

   By means of communication, many misunderstanding could be avoided. 通过沟通，可以避免许多误会。

3. appoint   *v.* 指定，任命，委派

4. local conditions 当地情况

5. to play a very important role 起一个很重要的作用

6. scope of the authority 权利范围

   business scope 营业范围

   production scope 生产 范围

7. terms of agency 代理条款

   terms of payment 付款方式

Specimen Letter 1   Offering to Act as the Sole Agent

Dear Sirs,

We have a **well-developed** sales organization in China and **are represented by** a large staff in various parts of the country. From their reports, it seems clear that there is a good demand for your tools and as we believe you are not directly represented in China, we are writing to offer our service as your sole agent.

There are good **prospects** of a very profitable market for your manufactures. **Provided** detailed terms could be arranged, we think our 20 years' experience in these goods should enable us to establish a **mutually beneficial** business relationship with you.

In view of the network we own for distribution and rich experiences in this field, we think that you will agree that a 5 percent commission on net sales is quite reasonable.

It is natural that you would like to know more information about us. Please kindly **refer to** Bank of China in your city, where we are sure that they will provide you with all necessary information about us.

We hope to **hear favorably from** you and feel sure that we could **come to an agreement** as to terms.

Yours truly,

(Signature)

Notes

1. well-developed　发展良好的

   well-educated　受到良好教育的

   well-organized　组织良好的

   well-constructed　构造精良的

2. be represented by　由……所代表

   We are represented by a committee.　我们由一个委员会所代表。

3. prospect　*n.* 景色；前景；期望

   The prospect to win the election is small.　竞选胜出的机会不大。

4. provided　*conj.* if/on the condition that/in case　倘若

   Provided the weather is OK, we will have a picnic.　天气好我们就出去野餐。

5. mutually beneficial　对双方都有益的

6. in view of　鉴于

7. refer to　打听，参考，提到

   You may refer to Mr. Johnson for my academic performance.　您可以向约翰逊先生询问我的学习情况。

8. hear favorably from　得到肯定的答复

9. come to an agreement　达成一致

Specimen Letter 2　Favorable Reply to Offering to Act as Sole Agent

Dear Sirs,

Thank you for your letter asking to be our **sole agent**. After careful **consultations with** the **references** you provided, we are **convinced** that you are the right **partner** we can **entrust**.

We have **drafted** an agency agreement **as enclosed** to this letter. Please have a look of the **prices and terms** to see whether they are **acceptable**.

We sincerely hope that we could be able to **establish** a business relationship between our two parties which is pleasant and **mutually beneficial**.

　　　　　　　　　　　　　　　　　　　　　　　　　　Truly yours,

　　　　　　　　　　　　　　　　　　　　　　　　　　(Signature)

Notes

1. sole agent, exclusive agent　独家代理

2. consultation　*n.* 请教，咨询，会诊

   consultations with　同……磋商，咨询

   After consultation with other specialist, the doctor finalize the clinical plan. 经过同其他专家的会诊，大夫把治疗方案确定了下来。

3. reference　*n.* 证明人；提及，涉及；参考；证明，鉴定

   make references to the heroic deeds　提及英雄事迹

   reference book　参考书

   When I was looking for a job, I asked my teacher to give me a reference.　我找工作的时候问老师要一份证明。

4. convinced　*adj.* 确信的，深信的

   We are convinced that our team will achieve a good performance in the Olympics.　我们确信我们队将在奥运会上有上佳的表现。

   convincing　*adj.* 令人信服的，能说服人的

   a convincing speech　令人信服的发言

5. partner　*n.* 伙伴

   business partner　商业伙伴

   partnership　*n.* 合伙关系，合股

   strategic partnership　战略伙伴关系

6. entrust   *v.* 委托

   I entrust the child to your care. 我把孩子托给你照顾。

7. draft

   (1) *v.* 起草

   The plan is drafted by the newcomer. 计划由新人起草。

   (2) n. 草稿

   The draft plan was finished only yesterday. 计划的草稿昨天才完成。

   (3) n. 汇票

   sight draft 即期汇票

   (4) n. 挑选

   He did not make the first round draft. 他第一轮没被选中。

8. as enclosed 如所附

   Please find my resume as enclosed. 请您查阅我所附的简历。

9. prices and terms 价格和条款

10. acceptable *adj.* 可接受的，合意的

   His proposal is quite acceptable. 他的提议是可以接受的。

11. establish   *v.* 建立

   establish business relationship 建立业务关系

   establishment *n.* 建立，制定，商业机构

   These two companies are two excellent establishments. 这两个公司都是优秀的商业机构。

12. mutually beneficial 双方都受益

Specimen Letter 3   Declining a Request for Sole Agency

Dear Sirs,

We thank you for your inquiry **regarding** the sole agency for the sale of our products in your country.

After serious **consideration**, we think that it would be **premature** to **commit** ourselves **at this stage** when the record of transactions shows only a **moderate** volume of business.

Please do not **misinterpret** the above remark, which **in no way** implies dissatisfaction. As a matter of fact, we are quite satisfied with amount of business you have brought to us. However, we **are of the opinion** that a bigger turnover must be reached to **justify** establishing the agency.

In view of the above, we think it **advisable** to postpone this matter until your future sales **warrant** such a step. We hope that you will agree with us **on this point** and continue to give us your cooperation.

Yours faithfully,

(Signature)

Notes

1. regarding *prep*. 关于

   I make a proposal regarding the garbage disposal in our community. 我提了一个建议，是关于我们小区垃圾处理问题的。

2. consideration *n*. 考虑

   In consideration of the recent increase in the prices of raw materials, we have to adjust some of our own prices. 考虑到近期原材料价格的增长，我们必须调整我们自己的部分价格。

   considerable *adj*. 相当多的

   Considerable business has been down on L/C basis. 很多业务都是以信用证来进行的。

   considerably *adv*. 相当地

   The demand for private car has grown considerably in recent years. 对私人汽车的需求近年来有相当大的增长。

3. premature *adj*. 未成熟的，早熟的

   It is premature to talk about distribution of bonus. 现在讨论奖金有些太早。

4. commit *v*. 承诺

   commit oneself to 致力于

   Our manufacturers have committed themselves to substantial orders for a few months ahead. 我们的生产商几个月前就忙着赶很多订单。

   commitment *n*. 责任

   We have not made any commitment in this respect. 在这点上我们不负责任。

5. at this stage 眼下，暂时

6. moderate *adj*. 中等的，适度的

   The impact on the purchasing power is moderate. 对购买力的影响适度。

7. misinterpret *v*. 曲解

   The driver misinterpreted the policeman's signal. 司机错误地理解了警察的手势。

8. in no way 绝不

The result in no way suggests that you are a loser. 结果说明不了你是个失败者。

9. be of the opinion 认为，观点是

We are of the opinion that he is the right person for this position. 我们认为他是该职位的正确人选。

10. justify *v.* 证明……是正当的

This does not justify your rude reaction. 这并不能证明你的粗鲁反应是正当的。

11. advisable *adj.* 可取的，明智的

It is advisable to leave now. 现在走为上策。

12. warrant *v.* 保证，担保

We should warrant it against any risks. 我们应当担保不受任何风险。

13. on this point 在这一点上

Specimen Letter 4   Expecting a Personal Negotiation for an Agency Agreement

Dear Sirs,

We **duly** received your letter of November 25, and after careful consideration of the contents, we **are favorably impressed** with your proposal to act as our agent.

We have already been **in treaty with** several firms, but at present have **come to no decision** in the matter. However, if terms could be **arranged**, we think you would be just the people we should like to represent us. We believe you have a strong network of sales **in this line**, and it seems to us **a right timing** to further develop the business.

One thing is for sure that the decision **relies very much upon** the question of the amount of commission you could require on orders obtained and **executed**. Since Mr. Rodrigo will be in Shanghai in a week, we think we would prefer to discuss the detailed terms with him personally, instead of waiting and modifying through emails.

We shall, therefore, await Mr. Rodrigo's Call.

Yours sincerely,

(Signature)

Notes

1. duly   *adv.* 适时的，合适的，适度的

   Your suggestion has been duly noted. 您的建议得到了重视。

2. be favorably impressed 良好印象

3. in treaty with 跟······谈判

4. come to no decision 没有决定

5. arrange   *v.* 安排；准备；计划

   He arranged the books on the shelf. 他把书架上的书整理了一下。

   We have arranged a party. 我们准备了一个晚会。

   We have been trying every possible means to arrange peace. 我们想尽办法试图达成和解。

6. in this line 在这一行

7. a right timing 正确的时机

8. rely very much upon 完全依赖于

   The award of this prize relies very much upon the stage performance. 这个奖项的授予很大程度上取决于舞台表现。

9. execute   *v.* 执行

   You are supposed to execute the command coming from the boss. 你应该执行老板的命令。

Specimen Letter 5   Stating the Main Points for an Agency Agreement

Dear Sirs,

We are pleased to confirm the agreement reached during our discussion last month and look forward to a happy and **fruitful** working relationship with you. Before **finalizing** the formal agreement for signature, we would like to **reiterate** the main points upon which we have reached agreement as follows:

1. That you act as our sole agent for **a period of** two years **commencing on** January 1 this year.

2. That we pay you a commission of 3% on your sales of our products.

3. That you undertake not to sell the competing products of other manufacturers either **on**

your account or on that of other suppliers.

4. That you **render** monthly statements of sales and **honor** drafts we draw on you for the net amount **due**.

5. That you maintain **a full range of** our products in your showroom.

Upon receiving your letter confirming these above points we will arrange for the agreement to be drawn up and sent to you for your signature.

Yours faithfully,

(Signature)

Notes

1. fruitful　*adj.* 成功的，富有成效的

a fruitful meeting　一个富有成效的会议

2. finalize　*v.* 最后定稿，确定下来

3. reiterate　*v.* 重申，反复说，强调

We have reiterated the importance of this project. 我们已经重申了该项目的重要性。

4. a period of　一段时间

5. commence on　自……开始

The meeting commenced on the square in the afternoon. 会议下午在广场上开始。

6. on your account　你自己负责

Any consequences resulted from your conduct shall be on your own account. 你将为你的行为所造成的后果负责。

7. render　*v.* 提交

You are expected to render the report on a monthly basis. 你应当每月递交报告。

8. honor　*v.* 承兑

9. due

(1) *adj.* 应得的，应付的　due reward　应得的报酬

(2) *adj.* 欠的，应给的　Our thanks are due to him. 我们应感谢他。

(3) *adj.* 应到的，预期的　When is the steamer due? 船什么时候到？

10. a full range of　一整套

a full range of tools　一整套工具

Specimen Letter 6 Sole Agency Agreement

This agreement is entered into between the parties concerned on the basis of equality and mutual benefit to develop business on terms and conditions mutually agreed upon as follows:

1. The Parties Concerned

Supplier(Hereinafter called Party A):

Agent(Hereinafter called Party B):

Party A hereby appoints Party B to act as its Sole Agent to sell the commodity mentioned below.

2. Commodity and Quantity

Square Hinges

It is mutually agreed that Party B shall undertake the sales of the afore-said commodity for not less than 500 000 pairs in the duration of the agreement.

3. Territory

Canada

4. Validity of Agreement

This agreement when duly signed by the parties concerned shall remain in force for 12 calendar months to be effective from November 1, 20×× to October 31, 20××, and it will be extended for another 12 months upon its expiration unless notice is given to the contrary.

5. Confirmation of Orders

Party B shall submit offers to other parties completely in accordance with the specifications and trade terms given by Party A and is not allowed to make any alteration without Party A's permission. The commission on each transaction is to be fixed through mutual consultation and paid to Party B after full payment of the transaction has been received by Party A. Every transaction concluded is binding only after it is confirmed by Party A in writing.

6. Reports on Market Conditions

Party B shall have the obligation to forward once every three months to Party A detailed reports on current market conditions and of consumers' comments, and if there is any special change in the market, Party B shall also report timely to Party A its full particulars in writing.

7. Payment

Payment is to be made by confirmed, irrevocable letter of credit, without recourse, available by draft at sight upon presentation of shipping documents to the negotiation bank in Canada. The letter of credit for each order, whether opened by the agent or by the customer, shall reach Party A 21 days before the date of shipment.

8. Other Terms & Conditions

(1) During the validity of this agreement, Party A shall not make offers of the said goods to any party in the above-mentioned territory other than Party B, and Party B shall guarantee not to undertake the agency of, or to handle the sale of , the same kind of goods for any other countries.

(2) Party B must be responsible for placing orders and arranging L/C to be opened in favor of Party A for at least 250 000 pairs for the first six months and 250 000 pairs for the second six months of the duration of this agreement. Should Party B fail to pass on orders to Party A for a minimum quantity of 250 000 pairs for the first six months, Party A shall have the right to sell the same goods to any other buyers.

(3) It is understood that this sole agency agreement does not involve the transactions concluded in the following ways:

(a) Transactions concluded by Party A in the name of its government on one side with the government of Party B on the other.

(b) Transactions concluded between Party A and any other buyers in Canada for goods to be re-exported to other countries.

(4) When a transaction is confirmed by Party A, Party B is held responsible for its fulfillment.

(5) Party A has the right to revise or change the selling prices in accordance with the prevailing market conditions and shall notify Party B of the change in time.

(6) During the validity of this agreement, if either of the two parties is found to have infringed the stipulations of the agreement, the other party has the right to terminate this agreement by giving notice in writing to the infringing party.

Party A (Supplier)   Party B (Agent)
(Signature)   (Signature)

Useful Sentences

1. We have been in touch with your Chamber of Commerce, who recommend you as a possible agent for the sale of our products in your country. We are one of the largest toy manufacturers in China and wish to expand our sales to Southeast Asian countries. 我们已经联系您的商会，他们推荐您作为我们的产品在贵国的销售代理。我们是中国最大的玩具制造商之一，希望将我们的销售扩展到东南亚地区。

2. With your excellent connections, we believe it will be possible to promote the sale of our products in your territory, and we hope your acting as our agent will be to our mutual benefit. 鉴于你所拥有的广泛联系，我们相信您能够在您的地区促销我们的产品，我们也希望您作为我们的代理，使我们双方都受益。

3. Please consider appointing us as the exclusive representative responsible for selling your chemical fertilizers in our market. 请考虑将我们任命为您在我们市场进行化肥销售的独家代理。

4. We are experienced dealers in pumps, having been in the business for more than 20 years and enjoying good business relations with all the leading wholesalers and retailers in this line. With a view to expanding this business in our country, we should be glad if you could grant us sole agency for your pumps. 我们经营水泵多年，拥有 20 多年的经验，并同这一行所有的主要批发商和零售商保持着良好的业务关系。为了在我国扩展业务，我们希望您能让我们担任您的独家代理。

5. We have noted your request to act as our agent in your district, but before going further into the matter, we should like to know your plan for promoting sales and the annual turnover you may realize in your market. 我们收到您的请求，希望作为我们在您地区的代理，不过在更进一步讨论之前，我们想了解一下您的促销计划以及您打算在您市场实现的年销售额。

6. While appreciating your good intentions to act as our agents and your efforts in selling our products, we regret being unable to meet your request to act as our agents in your country as our record with you shows only a moderate volume of business. We therefore suggest postponement of the matter until a bigger turnover justifies establishing the agency. 虽然我们非常感谢您要求做我们代理以及您在销售我们产品方面付出的努力，我们很遗憾不能按照您的要求让您来做我们的代理，因为我们和您的交易记录显示的交易量并不大。所以我们建议将此事推迟到实现了更大的营业额之时再来谈代理一事。

7. We will provide you with our bank reference and information about our business integrity and financial standing. 我们将向您提供我们的银行资信证明人以及有关我们商业信誉以及财务状况的信息。

8. We feel it would be better to consider the matter of agency after you have done more business with us. 我们认为在您跟我方进行更多的业务后再考虑代理一事比较妥当。

9. Your past business record has shown your ability in handling our products. Bearing this in mind, we would like to offer you the sole agency if you are at all interested. 您过去的

商业记录已经显示了您在处理我们产品方面的能力。鉴于此，如果您感兴趣，我们愿意让您作为我们的独家代理。

10. We would be very honored to have your company act as our sole agent in the US. 如贵公司能作为我们在美国的独家代理，我们将不胜荣幸。

11. In view of the steady increase in the demand for our products, we have decided to appoint an agent to handle our export trade with your country. 鉴于我们的产品需求稳步地增长，我们已经决定指定代理来处理我们对贵国的出口业务。

12. We think it premature for us to discuss the question of agency at the present stage. 我们认为在目前的情况下讨论代理问题为时尚早。

13. We wish to inform you that this particular line has already been taken by A.B.C. Inc., who has acted as our sole agent for quite some time. 我们想通知您这个产品已经由A.B.C.公司经营，他们早已是我们的独家代理。

Letter-writing Guide

The steps and expressions of offering to act as sole agent are as follows. (有关要求做独家代理的写作步骤及常用表达方式如下。)

Writing steps (写作步骤)	Examples of expressions (表达方式举例)
1. 阐述自己在该产品行业已经积累多年经验	We have a well-developed sales network in our country. 我们在我国有一个发展良好的销售网络。
	For the past 10 years, we have been selling your products to wholesalers and large dealers in all parts of China and our clients are very much satisfied with your products. 过去10年里，我们一直在将你方产品销售给中国各地的批发商和大的经销商，我们的客户对你方产品很满意。
	We are experienced dealers in this product, having been in the business for more than 20 years and enjoying good business relations with all the leading wholesalers and retailers in this line. 我们在该产品上非常有经验，有20多年的业务经验，并同所有的批发商和经销商保持良好的业务关系。
2. 指出我方要求做独家代理	As we understand that you have no agent in China, we would like to offer our services. 我们了解到您在中国没有代理，我们愿意提供服务。
	We believe that you are not directly represented in China and we are writing to offer our service as your sole agent. 我们认为您在中国没有直接代表，我们写信的目的就是想提供独家代理的服务。
	We would like to act as agent on a sole agency commission basis and to serve you heart and soul. 我们愿意以独家代理的方式尽心为您服务。

续表

3. 提出佣金要求	In view of the wide connections we possess, we think you will agree that a 5 percent commission on net sales is quite reasonable. 鉴于我们所拥有的广泛的联系网络，我们认为你方应该会同意将净销售额的 5%作为佣金是非常公道的。
	On all sales, we are entitled to receive a commission of 15%. 对于所有的销售，我们有权享有 15%的佣金。
	We shall commit ourselves to the development of the market and sales of your products, in return, we require a 10% commission on all sales achieved. 我们将致力于开拓你方产品的市场，促进产品销售，作为回报，我们要求将所有完成的销售的 10%作为佣金。
4. 向对方提供资信证明人	You will naturally wish to have information about us. For that we refer you to the Bank of China. 您自然想了解关于我们的更多信息，我们请您咨询中国银行。
	For more information about us, please kindly refer to… 请咨询……以获得更多我方的信息。
	We believed that any questions left about us will be answered by… 我们相信所有有关我们的问题都会由……来给您答复。
	Any inquiries as to our financial standing or so on can be replied by… 所有有关我方的财务状况以及类似的咨询可以由……来回复。

The steps and expressions of declining a request for sole agency are as follows. (婉拒独家代理请求的写作步骤及常用表达方式如下。)

Writing steps (写作步骤)	Examples of expressions (表达方式举例)
1. 感谢对方的独家代理请求	We thank you for you inquiry regarding the sole agency for the sale of our products in your country. 我们感谢您的来信，要求做我们产品在你国的独家代理。
	Thank you for your letter of October 19 in connection with sole agency. 我们感谢您 10 月 19 日的有关独家代理的来信。
2. 感谢对方以往的努力，同时表示独家代理的机会还不成熟	In reply, we wish to state that we appreciate your efforts in pushing the sales of our products and we are satisfied with your work in the past. However, we do not think conditions are ripe to entrust you with the sole agency at the present stage. 作为回复，我们想说我们感谢您以往在推销我方产品方面做出的努力，而且我们对你过去的工作也非常满意。不过，我们认为目前情况下委托您作为我方的独家代理时机还不成熟。
	We are quite satisfied with the amount of business you have brought us. Nevertheless, after serious consideration, we think that it would be premature to commit ourselves at this stage. 我们对您曾经给我们带来的业务非常满意。不过，经过慎重考虑，我们认为在目前做出这样的委托时机尚未成熟。

Writing steps (写作步骤)	Examples of expressions (表达方式举例)
2. 感谢对方以往的努力，同时表示独家代理的机会还不成熟	To tell you frankly, the average annual quantity we sold to your country in the past few years is much larger than what you mentioned. In spite of this, please do not misinterpret our above remark, which in no way implies dissatisfaction. 坦率地告诉您，过去的几年里我们每年销售到你们国家的数量大大超过了你所提到的数量。尽管如此，请不要误解我们的这一说法，绝不表示我们对你不满意。
3. 提出等业务量达到一定程度再议合作	If a bigger turnover can be realized to justify establishing the agency we would like you to represent us. 如果能够实现更大的业务量，我们愿意你来做我们的代理。
	We think it advisable to postpone the matter until your future sales warrant such a step. We hope that you will agree with us on this point. 我们认为将这件事延期到你方今后的销售达到值得这样做时再讨论较为适当。希望你方同意我们的观点。

Exercises

I. Put the following English phrases into Chinese or Chinese phrases into English.

1. in no way　2. misinterpret　3. exclusive agency　4. moderate volume　5. well-established

6. 销售代理人　7. 担当　8. 批发商　9. 供您参考　10. 到期

II. Fill in the blanks with the words given below, and change the form when necessary.

refer　commission　taste　familiar　agent　assured　with　expiration

1. Having had experience in marketing chemicals, we are _____ with customer's needs.

2. We are confident that your products are to the _____ of our customers. They will surely like it.

3. Your are entitled to have a 5% _____ if you reach the turnover of on million US Dollars.

4. This is to inform you that we are acting as _____ on a sole agency commission basis.

5. For information concerning our credit standing and integrity in the trade we suggest that you _____ to ABC & Co.

6. The duration of this agreement is one year and can be automatically extended for a further year on _____.

7. After a discussion with your manager, we have decided to entrust you _____ the sole agency for our products.

8. Please rest _____ that for the duration of the agreement, we shall do our utmost to meet

your requirements.

III. Translate the following English into Chinese.

1. We need an agent in that country to help to market our products.

2. Our products are now being handled by ABC Co. in your city exclusively.

3. Thank you for your efforts in pushing the sales of our products.

4. In the past years, we have made efforts to develop business in this line.

5. As our sole distributor, please see that you will neither handle the same or similar products of other origins nor re-export our goods to any other areas outside your own.

6. 关于你方提出的代理协议，我方认为现在谈为时尚早。

7. 如果你方继续为促销我方产品做出努力，我方将乐意考虑贵方的独家代理事宜。

8. 目前本地对贵方产品需求稳步增长，如果你方佣金合适，我们会全力以赴为你方促销。

9. 我方提供的代理人佣金是所有产品售价的5%。

10. 为了使产品打入市场，必须开展系列促销活动。

IV. Writing practice.

You are not satisfied with the sales volume your agent in Sydney brought to you last year. Write a letter asking the agent for a full report on the matter and what measures the agent intends to take to improve sales. Point out tactfully that business cannot be continued unless a high level of sales is reached.

Unit 12 补充练习   Unit 12 补充练习答案   Unit 12 练习答案

Unit 13　Social Letters

【学习要点和目标】

通过本单元的学习，了解不同的社交信函的写作方法和写作词汇。

Lead-in

In everyday life, people **are engaged in** wide **social connections** to strength the relationship, communicate with each other and enhance connections. Social letters are one of the most important means by which people socialize with each other.

The **stereotyped** style of social letters is not difficult to **acquire** and comes automatically after a little practice, but to write an effective letter that suits the purpose needs skill. The present unit containing a few specimen letters for some **miscellaneous** purposes is designed to demonstrate how to deal with various kinds of correspondence **with assurance**.

The most common social letters are letter of thanks, letter of invitation, congratulation letter, letter of condolence, recommendation letter, letter of instruction, letter of apology, application letter, etc.

Moreover, the purpose of writing this unit is based on the understanding that international business is not only a matter of procedures and processes, but also a matter of business or even personal relationship among people. Therefore, in many **occasions**, the different types of social letters mentioned above play a very important role in enhancing the international trade as well as personal relationship.

Notes

1. engaged

   (1) *adj.* 忙着的

   The headmaster is engaged. 校长正忙呢。

   be engaged in sth. 从事于

   (2) *adj.* 占线

   The line is engaged. 电话占线。

   (3) *adj.* 订婚

   My son is engaged to a surgeon. 我儿子跟一个外科医生订婚了。

2. social connection 社交联系

3. stereotyped *adj.* 老套的

He plays a stereotyped role in this movie. 他在这个电影里饰演一个老套的角色。

4. acquire *v.* 获得，得到

You are supposed to acquire another degree within a year. 你一年内应再拿一个学位。

5. miscellaneous *adj.* 各种各样的，混杂的

6. with assurance 有把握，确定的

He achieved the first place with assurance. 他毫无悬念地获得第一。

7. occasion *n.* 场合，时刻，时候

special occasions 特殊场合

On another occasion, he scored 81 points. 还有一次，他拿了 81 分。

Specimen Letter 1   Letter of Thanks

Dear Mr. Smith,

I am writing to you just to tell you how very much I **appreciate** the warm welcome you **extended to** my wife when she visited your country last week.

The help and advice you gave to her, and the introductions you **arranged for** her, have **resulted in** a number of very useful meetings and I should like you to know how grateful I am for all you have done to make them possible.

Yours truly,

(Signature)

Notes

1. appreciate

(1) *v.* 感谢

I appreciate your help. 我感谢你的帮助。

(2) *v.* 鉴赏

Do you appreciate good wine? 你会鉴赏好酒吗？

(3) *v.* 察觉，意识到

We appreciate your danger. 我们察觉到你的危险。

(4) *v.* 增值

This land has appreciated in value. 这块土地增值了。

2. extend to 提供

The ceremony extended to her for her birthday is fantastic. 为她的生日举办的仪式非常隆重。

3. arrange

(1) *v.* 整理

He arranges the books on the shelf. 他把书架上的书整理了一下。

(2) *v.* 商定

We have been trying every means to arrange a peace but failed. 我们试图达成和解但没有成功。

(3) *v.* 安排

He tries to arrange a meeting between the rivals. 他给两个竞争对手安排了个会面。

arrange for 给……安排

4. result in 导致，结果是

This careless interpretation has resulted in a misunderstanding. 这个粗心的口译造成了一个误解。

Specimen Letter 2   Letter of Congratulations

Dear Mr. Black,

It was a **pleasure** to learn about your **promotion** to the position of sales manager of your company.

I really think that you **deserve** the position after years of service and experiences you have had **in this field** of business with your company.

My congratulations should also be **extended** to the general manager of your company. He has the good sense to recognize a good man in you. From what I know about people in the field **he couldn't have picked a better man**. Congratulations on a well-deserved promotion.

Yours truly,
(Signature)

Notes

1. pleasure   *n.* 愉快，快乐，乐趣

to have pleasure in doing sth. /have the pleasure of sth. 有兴趣做……

2. promotion

(1) *n.* 晋升

Our teacher has got a promotion. 我们的老师升职了。

(2) *n.* 促销

Advertising is often the most effective means of promotion. 广告往往是最有效的推销方法。

3. deserve   *v.* 应受(奖赏，特殊待遇等)，值得

She deserves a reward for her efforts. 她的努力应受奖赏。

4. in this field 在这个领域

He is an expert in this field. 他在这个领域是专家。

5. extend   *v.* 提供或给予某事物

extend hospitality/an invitation/a greeting to sb. 款待/邀请/问候某人

They extended a warm welcome to her. 他们向她表示热烈欢迎。

6. He couldn't have picked a better man. 您是最佳人选；他不能找到比你更合适的人了。

Specimen Letter 3   Letter of Apology

Dear Sirs,

Much to our regret, a delay in delivery has **caused you much inconvenience**, for which please accept my sincere apology.

As our business has increased rapidly, we are to make **a series of procedures** in our organization so as to **ensure** that such a mistake will never occur again.

Your understanding and patience in this matter would be greatly appreciated. We hope you **would give us the pleasure of** serving you again in the future.

Yours faithfully,

(Signature)

Notes

1. much to our regret… 令我们非常遗憾的是……

出现在道歉信中的类似表达还有：

I owe you an apology for…; I very regret that…/I offer my sincere apologies for…; Please forgive me for…; Here is my deepest apology for…

2. cause you much inconvenience 给您造成很大的麻烦

The rain caused a lot of trouble to the city. 雨给城市带来了很多麻烦。

3. a series of 一系列

A series of our products are displayed in the showroom. 我们的系列产品在陈列室展出。

4. procedure *n.* 程序

   legal procedure 法律程序

5. ensure *v.* 保证，担保

   We can ensure that the work will be done in the right way. 我们保证工作能正常完成。

6. give us the pleasure of 我们很高兴做……

   to have pleasure in doing sth. 很高兴做某事

   We have pleasure in offering superior services. 我们很高兴提供上佳的服务。

   have the pleasure of doing sth. 有做某事的乐趣

   We have the pleasure of informing you that the shipment has been effected in time. 我们高兴地通知您已经按时发货。

Specimen Letter 4 Letter of Invitation

Dear Sirs,

Our new factory is to **go into production** on December 28, and we would like to invite you to **be present at** the opening ceremony to make the **occasion**.

As you would **appreciate**, it is an important **milestone** for our organization and a result of our customers' continued demand for our products, both **at home and abroad**. Therefore, we invite all those who have **made their contributions**, and trust that you would pay us the **compliments** of accepting.

If you could confirm your **attendance**, would you advise us of your arrival time, so that we can **make arrangements for** you to be met **at our expense**.

We do hope that you would be able to spare the time sharing this occasion with us.

Yours sincerely,

(Signature)

Notes

1. go into production 开始生产

2. be present at 出席

   How many people were present at the meeting? 多少人出席了会议？

   at present 现在

   What is the situation at present? 现在什么局势？

   present an opportunity for 给……提供了一个机会

The new trend of globalization presents an opportunity for local enterprises. 全球化的新趋势给当地的企业提供了一个机会。

3. occasion   *n.* 场合，机会；时刻，时候

a great occasion 盛大场面

A birthday is no occasion for tears. 生日可不是掉泪的时候。

4. appreciate   *v.* 赏识；鉴赏；感激

5. milestone   *n.* 里程碑，重大事件

The invention of computer was a milestone in man's history. 计算机的发明是人类历史上的一个里程碑。

6. at home and abroad 国内外

7. make their contributions 做出他们的贡献

8. compliment   *n.* 称赞；恭维；致意；问候；道贺

They paid him a high compliments. 他们非常恭维他。

complimentary   *adj.* 赞美的，表示敬意的

complimentary word 敬意的措辞

9. attendance   *n.* 出席；出席人数；照料

attendance at school 上学，到校

She is in attendance on the sick man. 她在照料病人。

10. make arrangements for 做好……的准备，安排

We should make arrangements for the approaching season. 我们应该做好新赛季的准备。

11. at sb's expense 由……付款

Any consequences due to the discrepancies shall be at your expense. 由于差错造成的后果将由你方承担赔付责任。

Specimen Letter 5   Letter of Appointment

Dear Sirs,

Thank you for your fax of December 8. I would like to **extend a warm welcome** to you for your visit to our plant and your **inspection** of the **assembly lines**. The time you suggest for our meeting, i.e. 9:00 am on Monday, December 12 is fine with me. I would **be most delighted to** see you then.

Just as you wish to increase **mutual understanding** and **strengthen** cooperation between us, we are **in the earnest hope of** doing business with you **on the basis of** equality and mutual benefit. I assure you that our talk will be **constructive** and **lead up to** the conclusion of a business that will really benefit both of our companies.

I am looking forward to meeting you soon.

Yours faithfully,

(Signature)

Notes

1. extend a warm welcome 对某人表示欢迎

   extend/express greetings/thanks/congratulations to sb. 对某人表示问候/感谢/祝贺

2. inspection   *n.* 检查，视察

   He made an inspection of the school. 他视察了学校。

3. assembly line 装配线

4. be delighted to 高兴做……

   We are delighted to help those in need. 我们乐意去帮助那些需要帮助的人。

5. mutual understanding 相互理解

   mutual understanding and mutual accommodation 互谅互让

6. strengthen   *v.* 加强，巩固

   The enemy has strengthened during truce talks. 和谈期间，敌人的力量得以加强。

   The fence is strengthened with wires. 围墙用金属丝加固了。

7. in the earnest hope of 真诚地希望

   We are in the earnest hope of a strategic cooperative relationship. 我们真诚地希望建立一个战略合作关系。

8. on the basis of 在……的基础上

   On the basis of mutual trust, we establish our business relationship. 在相互信任的基础上，我们建立了业务关系。

9. constructive   *adj.* 建设性的

   Representative put forward many constructive proposals at the meeting. 会上代表们提出了很多建设性意见。

10. lead up to 渐渐引向，作为……的头一步

    Small transactions led up to a great business between them. 先是小来小往，后来他们做成了一笔大生意。

    His flattering words led up to a request for money. 他先是恭维奉承，接着开口要钱。

Specimen Letter 6 Letter of Complaint

Dear Sirs,

After carefully examining the mobile phones you sent to us in **execution** of our **Purchase Confirmation** No.237, we are compelled to express our surprise at their poor quality. The goods do not **correspond with** the samples which led to our **placing the order**. Enclosed are a photo and some pieces of the goods **for your examination**.

In view of the quality far from our customers' requirements, we would like to return the goods **at your expense** in accordance with your **guarantees**.

We look forward to your instructions on how it would be carried out.

Faithfully yours,

(Signature)

Notes

1. execution   *n.* 执行

execute   *v.* 执行

execute an order 执行一个订单

execute one's promise 履行某人的诺言

2. Purchase Confirmation 购货确认书

purchase contract 购货合同书

purchase agent 购货代理人

purchasing power 购买力

3. correspond with 与……相一致，相符合；与……通信

Your accounts of events correspond with hers. 你说的情况跟她说的相符。

4. place an order 下订单

place an order with sb. for sth. 下订单给……订购……

We have placed an order with you for tablecloth. 我们给您下了一个台布的订单。

5. for your examination 供您核对、检查

for your attention 请您注意

for your reference 供您参考

for your information 告知您

6. in view of 鉴于

7. at your expense   on your account 由你付款

The transportation fee shall be at your expense. 你方付运费。

8. guarantee   *v./n.* 保证，担保

The new TV has a guarantee with it. 新电视有保修单。

Letter-writing Guide

The steps and expressions of writing social letters are as follows. (有关撰写社交信函的写作步骤及常额头用表达方式如下。)

Writing steps (写作步骤)	Examples of expressions (表达方式举例)
1. 开门见山的表达感谢，祝贺，歉意之意。提出邀请和投诉。	I am writing to you to tell you how much we appreciated your efforts in this transaction. 我们致信给您表达我们对贵方在本次交易中所作努力的感激之情。
	It is our pleasure to learn that your company has achieved another sales record this year. 我们很高兴的获悉贵公司本年度销售业绩再次打破纪录。
	Much to our regret, we are unable to catch the final delivery date due to a communications error on our side. 令我们非常遗憾，由于我方的沟通出现问题，导致我方无法按时交货。
	We would like to invite you for a meeting in our booth during the Canton Fair next month in your convenience. 我们想在下个月广交会期间邀请您方便时在我们的展台会面。
	We are regretful that we have to make a formal complaint about the quality of your products for the last batch. 我们很遗憾必须对贵方上批货物的质量提出正式投诉。
2. 说明感谢，祝贺，抱歉，邀请和投诉内容。	The help offered by your side in this concern bring us back to our normal track. 我方在此事上得到贵方的帮助，使我们的业务重回正轨。
	We believe that you deserve the great financial success after some many years of efforts. 我们认为您多年的不懈努力使您配得上您财务上的巨大成功。
	We will upgrade our system to avoid such mistakes in the future. 我们将升级我们的系统以避免以后再发生此类错误。
	We would like to invite you to participate in our celebration of 30 Years' anniversary. 我们想邀请贵方参加我方的三十周年庆典。
	In view of the situation of the goods arrived, we would like to draw you a draft for the loss caused. 鉴于货物到达时的情况，我方将向贵方开具一个汇票以赔偿损失。
3. 期待对方回复的结尾。	Your understanding and cooperation in this concern will be highly appreciated. 贵方在这件事上如能理解并与我方合作，我方将不胜感激。
	We hope that you could spare the time to meet us in this occasion. 我方希望贵方能抽时间拨冗莅临与我方会面。
	We look forward to hearing from your side in terms of corrections carried out afterwards. 我们期待后续得到贵方整改的消息。

Exercises

I. Put the following English phrases into Chinese or Chinese phrases into English.

1. in compliance with   2. make an appointment   3. unforeseen event

4. correspond with   5. be of help

6. 投诉   7. 由······付款   8. 担保   9. 一系列   10. 晋升

II. Fill in the blanks with the words given below, and change the form when necessary.

execution   claim   support   compete   correspond with
at the expense of   in view of   in accordance with

1. _____ the friendly business relations between us, we would like to give you a 10% discount.

2. He built up a successful business but it was all done _____ his health.

3. Circumstances _____ a minor change in the plan.

4. Disputes arose in the _____ of the contract between the two parties.

5. Our contention is well _____ by facts.

6. We regret that we cannot entertain your _____ as it has nothing to do with us.

7. _____ what was stipulated in the contract, we have no choice but to return the defective goods.

8. The written record of our conversation doesn't _____ what was actually said.

III. Translate the following English into Chinese or Chinese into English.

1. I am writing to on behalf of my daughter, Alice, to enquire about the possibility of her being enrolled in Grade One of your school.

2. I should be appreciated if you could kindly let me know about the application procedures.

3. In general, the amount that a student spends on housing should be confined to one-fifth of the total living expenses available.

4. They consider it to be of great importance.

5. It is a great pleasure to have learnt that you have been engaged in leasing business for many years and have had rich experience in this line.

6. 我们能否在下周安排一次见面，讨论付款条件。

7. 我由衷地期待能够拜访您并参观贵公司研发部。

8. 如果没有什么特殊情况发生，我会按时赴约。

9. 此次取消约见，万望谅解。

10. 原本希望能与您会面。遗憾的是昨日公司发生意外，故明日不能前往。

IV. Writing practice.

根据以下材料写一封投诉信，投诉所订购的布料质量低劣。

布料的质量与样品不符，因此买方虽准备好人员和设备，现在却要等待原料，无法向顾客交代。提出解决问题的办法：换货。并指出为维系彼此之间的良好合作关系，再给予9 天的宽限期。但同时指出如到期仍不能将货送达，买方将收回全部货款并要求对造成的全部损失进行赔偿。

Unit 13 补充练习　　　Unit 13 补充练习答案　　　Unit 13 练习答案

Unit 14　Business Contract

【学习要点和目标】

通过本单元的学习，了解合同的结构、句式和用词三方面的特点，掌握撰写合同的要领和技巧。

Lead-in

A business contract is an agreement, enforceable by law. It may be formal or informal. The business contract which is generally adopted in international trade activities is the formal written one.

It is more difficult to write a contract or an agreement than to write a letter or a fax, but if you know the essentials and basic knowledge of the writing, you are surely able to write contracts and agreements well. Generally speaking, if you can write a contract in Chinese, and have a good grasp in English, you can write English contract and agreement versions according to the forms and stipulations. Also you can write a contract or an agreement in Chinese first then translate it into English. When writing, please pay attention to the following principles: writing completely, clearly, grammatically, and arranging properly and logically.

In international trade, there are a great variety of business contracts, which mainly include: Sales Contract, Sales Confirmation, Purchase Contract , Purchase Confirmation, Import Contract, Export Contract, Agency Agreement, Consignment Contract, Consignment Agreement and Compensation Trade Contract.

1. The Form of a Contract or an Agreement

Contracts or agreements don't have unified or fixed forms. In general, complete and valid contracts or agreements usually consist of three parts: Head, Body and End.

(1) The Head

The head covers the following contents:

(a) The title of the contract or agreement, e.g. Sales Contract, Purchase Confirmation, Import Contract, Sole Agency Agreement, etc. The title indicates the character of the contract or agreement.

(b) The number of the contract or agreement.

(c) The date and the place of signing the contract or agreement. (some contracts or agreements put the date and the place in the end.)

(d) The preamble of the contract or agreement. In the preamble, there are the parties names, stating clearly the Sellers and the Buyers or Party A and Party B, and explaining the principles and the purposes of signing the contract or agreement. e.g.:

ABC Company, New York, USA (hereinafter called Party A) and China National Textiles Import & Export Corporation Ltd, Harbin Branch (hereinafter called Party B) through amicable negotiation reached the following agreement on the basis of equality and mutual benefit.

(2) The Body

The body is the main part in the contract or agreement. We may use the style of clauses or the style of forms or we may combine the two styles together to state clearly the contents negotiated by the parties concerned. For example, the clauses in a sales contract or purchase contract are: the name and the specification of the commodity, quantity, unit price and total value, packing, shipment, payment, insurance, inspection, claim and arbitration, etc.. The contents of other contracts or agreements (Agency Agreement, Joint Venture Contract, Investment Agreement, and Agreement for Technology Transfer) are complex. The terms and conditions are different. But they have certain forms and formulas. When we write them we can consult example version.

(3) The End

The contents in this part are usually the followings: the copies and the conserves of the contract or agreement, the languages used, the full names of the parties, and the seals affixed by the parties, etc. If the contract or agreement is companied by some enclosures, we should state clearly the names of the enclosures as well as the number of the copies as the integral parts of the contract.

2. The Requirement of Writing a Contract or an Agreement

(a) The contents of contracts or agreements should conform to the principle of equality and mutual benefit and through common negotiation.

(b) The stipulations of contracts or agreements should be complete, concrete, clear and without careless omissions, in order to avoid unnecessary economic losses.

(c) Using words and expressions accurately, and arranging the contents properly, logically and without mistakes.

In order to let the readers have an intimate knowledge of different kinds of business contracts, some examples of them are illustrated as follows.

Specimen 1　Sales Confirmation

Sales Confirmation
销售确认书

Contract No.:NM2314

合同号：NM2314

Date: August 12, 20××

日期：20××年 8 月 12 日

Signed at: Beijing, China

签约地点：中国北京

The Seller: The China National Textiles Import & Export Corporation, Ltd., Beijing branch

　　　　　Building 12, Block 3, Anhuili, Chaoyang District, P.R. China.

　　　　　Zip Code: 100102

卖方：中国纺织品进出口有限公司，北京分公司

　　　中国北京朝阳区安慧里三区十二号楼

　　　邮政编码：100102

The Buyer: Black & White Inc.　P.O. Box: 6789-012-B, New York, USA

买方：布莱克-怀特公司　邮政信箱：6789-012-B　美国纽约

This contract is made by and between the Buyer and the Seller; whereby the Buyer agree to buy and the Seller agree to sell the undermentioned goods on the terms and conditions **stipulated** below:

兹经买卖双方同意，由买方购进、卖方售出下列商品，并订立条款如下：

Name of Commodity & Specification: Hand-embroidered Silk Scarves, Item 3

1. 品名及规格：手绣丝围巾，3 号货

Quantity: 2000 pieces

2. 数量：2000　条

Unit Price: CFR New York US$20.00 per piece

3. 单价：成本加运费抵纽约每条 20 美元

Total Amount: US$40000

4. 总金额：40 000 美元

Country of Origin and Manufacturers: Xi'an Red Star Company, China

5. 原产国及制造商：中国西安红星公司

Time of Shipment: September, 20××

6. 装运期：20××年 9 月

Port of Shipment: Qingdao, China

7. 装运港：中国青岛

Port of Destination: New York, USA

8. 目的港：美国纽约

Insurance: To be covered by the Buyer

9. 保险：由买方办理

Packing: Each piece packed in a plastic bag, 10 pieces in a carton

10. 包装：每件用塑料袋包装，10 条装一纸箱

Shipping Marks: at the Buyer's option

11. 装运标志：由买方决定

Terms of Payment: By confirmed, irrevocable, documentary L/C with transshipment is allowed, and with 5% more or less in quantity permissible, payable at sight and valid for negotiation in China till the 15th day after shipment. L/C should reach the Seller 30 days before the time of shipment.

12. 付款方式：以保兑的、不可撤销的即期跟单信用证支付，允许转船，允许 5%的溢短装，信用证须在装船前 30 天寄达卖方，装船后 15 天在中国议付有效。

It is mutually agreed that the Inspection Certificate of Quality and Quantity (Weight) issued by the **China Import and Export Commodity Inspection and Quarantine Bureau** at the port of shipment shall be part of the documents to be presented for negotiation under the relevant L/C. The Buyer shall have the right to reinspect the Quality and Quantity (Weight) of the cargo. The reinspection fee shall **be borne by the Buyer**. Should the Quality and/or Quantity (Weight) be found not in conformity with that of the contract, the Buyer is entitled to lodge with the Seller a claim which should be supported by survey reports issued by a recognized Surveyor approved by the Sellers.

13. 双方同意以装运港中国进出口商品检验检疫局签发的品质和数量(重量)检验检疫证书作为信用证下议付的所提示单据的一部分。买方有权对货物的品质和数量(重量)进行复验，复验费由买方负担。如发现品质或数量与合同不符，买方有权向卖方索赔。但须提供经卖方同意的公证机构出具之检验报告。

Remarks:

14. 备注：

The Buyer shall have the covering Letter of Credit reach the Seller (or notify the Import License Number) before _____ otherwise the Seller reserves the right to rescind without further notice or to accept whole or any part of this Sales Confirmation not fulfilled by the Buyer, or to lodge a claim for losses this sustained of any.

(1) 买方须于__年__月__日前开到本批交易的信用证(或通知卖方进口许可证号码)，否则，卖方有权不经通知取消本确认书，或接受买方对本约未执行的全部或部分，或对因此遭受的损失提出索赔。

Quality/Quantity Discrepancy: In case of quality **discrepancy**, claim should be lodged by the Buyers within 3 months after the arrival of the goods at port of destination, while of quantity discrepancy, claim should be filed by the Buyer within 15 days after the arrival of the goods at port of destination. It is understood that the Seller shall not be liable for any discrepancy of the goods shipped due to causes for which the Insurance Company, Shipping Company, other transportation organization/or Post Office are liable.

(2) 品质数量异议：如买方提出索赔，凡属品质异议须于货到目的港之日起 3 个月内提出，凡属数量异议须于货到目的港之日起 15 日内提出，对所装运物所提任何异议属于保险公司、轮船公司及其他有关运输机构或邮递机构所负责者，卖方不负任何责任。

The Seller shall not be held liable for failure or delay in delivery of the entire lot or a portion of the goods under this Sales Confirmation on consequence of any **Force Majeure** incidents.

(3) 本确认书所述全部或部分商品，如因人力不可抗拒的原因，以致不能履约或延迟交货，卖方概不负责。

The Buyer are requested always to quote The Number Of This Sales Confirmation in the Letter of Credit to be opened in favor of the Seller.

(4) 买方开给卖方的信用证上请填注本确认书号码。

Arbitration: Should any dispute arise between the contracting parties, it shall be settled through friendly negotiations. But if there is no agreement to be reached, the disputes arising out of the execution or performance of this contract shall be submitted by the parties for arbitration. Arbitration shall be conducted by China International Economic and Trade Arbitration Commission in Beijing in accordance with its **procedure** rules. The **award** given by the Arbitration Commission shall be **final and binding** upon both parties. The fees for arbitration shall be borne by the losing party.

(5) 仲裁：合同双方发生争议时，应由双方友好协商解决。达不成协议的，双方可将本确认书执行当中发生的争议提交仲裁解决。仲裁应由中国国际经济贸易仲裁委员会在北京依照其仲裁规则进行。仲裁委员会的裁决为终局性的，对双方生效。仲裁费用由败诉方承担。

The Buyer is requested to sign and return one copy of this Sales Confirmation immediately after receipt of the same. Objection, if any, should be raised by the Buyer within five days after the receipt of this Sales Confirmation, in the absence of which it is understood that the Buyer has accepted the terms and conditions of the Sales Confirmation.

(6) 买方受到本确认书后立即签回一份，如买方对本确认书有异议，应于收到后 5 天内提出，否则认为买方已同意本确认书所规定的各项条款。

The Seller: The Buyer:

卖方：   买方：

(singnature)   (singnature)

Notes

1. Sales Confirmation 销售确认书，可缩写为 S/C

2. stipulate *vt*. 规定，约定

   The contract stipulated that the goods should be delivered in March. 合同规定必须在 3 月份交货。

   stipulation *n*. 规定，约定；(条约，契约等的)条款，项目

   All the stipulations in your L/C should be in conformity with that in the contract. 你方信用证的所有条款都必须与合同条款相一致。

3. Country of Origin 原产国，生产国别

   Certificate of Origin 原产地证明书

   Certificate of Quality/Quantity/Weight 质量/数量/重量证明书

4. China Import and Export Commodity Inspection and Quarantine Bureau 中国进出口商品检验检疫局

5. be borne by sb. 由某人负担

   The insurance premium should be borne by the Buyers. 保险费应由买方负担。

6. discrepancy *n*. 差异，不一致，不符

   Wide discrepancies in prices quoted for the work. 这项工作的报价出入很大。

7. force majeure 人力不可抗力

8. procedure *n*. 程序

9. award *n*. 裁决，裁定

10. final *adj*. 最后的，最终的，决定性的

11. binding   *adj.* 有约束力的，负有义务的

final and binding 决定性的并具有效力的

The treaty is binding on (upon) all parties.   本条约对缔约各方都具有约束力。

Specimen 2   Sales Contract

Sales Contract
销售合同

Contract No.:
合同编号：

Signed at:
签约地点：

Date:
签约日期：

The Buyer:
买方：

The Seller:
卖方：

The Buyer agrees to buy and the Seller agrees to sell the following goods on terms and conditions as set forth below:

双方同意按下列条款由卖方向买方售出下列商品：

1. 货物名称及规格 Name of Commodity and Specification	2. 数量 Quantity	3. 单价 Unit Price	4. 总值 Total Value

With ＿＿ % more or less both in amount and quantity allowed at the Seller's option.
数量及总值均得有＿＿＿%的增减，由卖方决定。

Packing:
5. 包装：

Time of Shipment:
6. 装运期限：

Port of Loading:

7. 装运口岸：

Port of Destination:

8. 目的口岸：

Insurance: To be covered by the _____ for 110% of the invoice value against _____.

9. 保险：由____方负责，按发票总值 110%投保____险。

Terms of Payment: By 100% Confirmed, Irrevocable, Transferable and Divisible Letter of Credit to be available by sight draft and to remain valid for negotiation in China until the 15th day after the aforesaid Time of Shipment.

10. 付款条件：开给我方 100%不可撤销的即期付款及可转让可分割之信用证，并须注明可在上述装运日期后 15 天内在中国议付有效。

Inspection: The Inspection Certificate of Quality/Quantity/Weight/Packing/**Sanitation** issued by _____ of China shall be regarded as evidence of the Seller's delivery.

11. 商品检验：以中国 _____ 所签发的品质/数量/重量/包装/卫生检验合格证书作为卖方的交货依据。

Shipping Marks:

12. 装运唛头：

Other Terms.

13. 其他条款。

Discrepancy: In case of quality discrepancy, claims should be lodged by the Buyer within 30 days after the arrival of the goods at the port of destination; while for quantity discrepancy, claim should be lodged by the Buyer within 15 days after the arrival of the goods at the port of destination. In all cases, claims must be accompanied by Survey Report of Recognized Public Surveyors agreed to by the Seller. Should the responsibility of the subject under claim be found to rest on the part of the Seller, the Seller shall, within 20 days after receipt of the claim, send their reply to the Buyer together with suggestion for settlement.

(1) 异议：品质异议须于货到目的口岸之日起 30 天内提出，数量异议须于货到目的口岸之日起 15 天内提出，但均须提供经卖方同意的公证机构的检验证明。如责任属于卖方，卖方须于收到异议 20 天内答复买方并提供处理意见。

The covering Letter of Credit shall stipulate the Seller's option of shipping the indicated percentage more or less than the quantity hereby contracted and be negotiated for the amount covering the value of quantity actually shipped. (The Buyer is requested to establish the L/C in amount with the indicated percentage over the total value of the order as per this Sales Contract.)

(2) 信用证内应明确规定卖方有权可多装或少装所注明的百分数，并按实际装运数量议付。(信用证之金额按本销售合同金额增加相应的百分数。)

The contents of the covering Letter of Credit shall be in strict conformity with the stipulations of the Sales Contract. In case of any variation thereof necessitating amendment of the L/C, the Buyer shall bear the expense for effecting the amendment. The Seller shall not be held responsible for possible delay of shipment resulting from awaiting the amendment of the L/C and reserve the right to claim from the Buyer for the losses resulting **therefrom**.

(3) 信用证内容须严格符合本销售合同的规定，否则修改信用证的费用由买方负担，卖方并不负因修改信用证而延误装运的责任，并保留因此而发生的一切损失的索赔权。

Except in cases where the insurance is covered by the Buyer as arranged, insurance is to be covered by the Seller with a Chinese insurance company. If insurance for additional amount and/or for other insurance terms is required by the Buyer, prior notice to this effect must reach the Seller before shipment and is subject to the Seller's agreement, and the extra insurance premium shall be for the Buyer's account.

(4) 除经约定保险归买方投保者外，由卖方向中国的保险公司投保。如买方需增加保险额及/或需加保其他险，可于装船前提出，经卖方同意后代为投保，其费用由买方负担。

The Seller shall not be held responsible if they fail, owing to Force Majeure cause or causes, to make delivery within the time stipulated in this Sales Contract or cannot deliver the goods. However, the Seller shall inform immediately the Buyer by Facsimile. The Seller shall deliver to the Buyer by registered letter, if it is requested by the Buyer, a certificate issued by the China Council for the Promotion of International Trade or by any relevant authorities, attesting the existence of the said cause or causes. The Buyer's failure to obtain the relative Import License is not to be treated as Force Majeure.

(5) 因人力不可抗拒事故使卖方不能在本销售合约规定期限内交货或不能交货，卖方不负责任，但是卖方必须立即以传真通知买方。如果买方提出要求，卖方应以挂号函向买方提供由中国国际贸易促进委员会或有关机构出具的证明，证明事故的存在。买方不能领到进口许可证，不能被认为系属人力不可抗拒范围。

Arbitration: Should any dispute arise between the contracting parties, it shall be settled through friendly negotiations. But if there is no agreement to be reached, the disputes arising out of the execution or performance of this contract shall be submitted by the parties for arbitration. Arbitration shall be conducted by China International Economic and Trade Arbitration Commission in Beijing in accordance with its procedure rule. The award given by the Arbitration Commission shall be final and binding upon both parties. The fees for arbitration shall be borne by the losing party.

(6) 仲裁：合同双方发生争议时，应由双方友好协商解决。达不成协议的，双方可将本确认书执行当中发生的争议提交仲裁解决。仲裁应由中国国际经济贸易仲裁委员会在北京依照其仲裁规则进行。仲裁委员会的裁决为终局性的，对双方生效。仲裁费用由败诉方承担。

The Seller: The Buyer:

  卖方：   买方：

Notes

1. sanitation   *n.* 公共卫生，卫生设备，卫生设施体系

   disease resulting from poor sanitation 卫生条件差导致的疾病

2. therefrom   *adj.* 从那里，从那一点

   We believe that big profits will result therefrom.

   我们相信从那里将会产生很大利润。

Specimen 3　Purchase Confirmation

Purchase Confirmation
购货确认书

No.: PC-140811

编号：PC-140811

Date: August 11, 20××

日期：20××年 8 月 11 日

Buyer: America Cool-Play Trade Company.

      5th Avenue, New York, USA

买方：美国酷玩贸易公司

      美国纽约市第五大道

Seller: Chengde Children Dream Imp. & Exp. Co., Ltd.

      118 College Road, Development Zone, Chengde City, Hebei Province, China

卖方：承德童梦进出口有限公司，

      中国河北省承德市开发区学院路 118 号

The Buyer agrees to buy and the Seller agrees to sell the following goods on terms and conditions as set forth below:

双方同意按下列条款由卖方向买方售出下列商品：

1. Name of Commodity and Specification 货物名称及规格	2. Quantity 数量	3. Unit Price 单价	4. Total Value 总值
Teddy Bear NO.96857 40×50 cm G.W.:0.11kg	1500pcs	US$5.52 CIFC5 New York	US$8280.00
Teddy Bear NO.96858 80×100 cm G.W.:0.22kg	1500pcs	US$5.52 CIFC5 New York	US$8280.00
		Total	US$16560.00

5. Time of shipment: Not later than September 15, 20××

装运期限：不迟于20××年9月15日

6. Port of loading: Tianjin, China

装运港：中国天津

7. Port of destination: New York, USA

目的港：美国纽约

8. Terms of payment: Irrevocable L/C at sight

付款方式：即期不可撤销信用证

9. Insurance: The seller shall cover insurance against ALL RISK for 110% of the total invoice value as per the relevant ocean marine cargo clause of PICC dated Jan. 1, 1981.

保险：卖方按发票金额的110%投保一切险，按照1981年1月1日执行的中国人民保险公司的海洋运输货物保险条款。

10. Inspection: It is mutually agreed that the Inspection Certificate of Quality and Quantity (Weight) issued by the China Import and Export Commodity Inspection and Quarantine Bureau at the port of shipment shall be part of the documents to be presented for negotiation under the relevant L/C. The Buyer shall have the right to re-inspect the Quality and Quantity (Weight) of the cargo. Should the Quality and/or Quantity (Weight) be found not in conformity with that of the contract, the Buyer shall return the goods to or lodge a claim with the Seller which should be supported by the Inspection Certificate issued by a recognized Surveyor, with the exception of those claims for which the insurers or owners of the carrying vessel are liable. All expense (including inspection fees) and losses arising from the return of the goods or claims should be borne by the Seller.

检验：双方同意以装运港中国进出口商品检验检疫局签发的品质和数量(重量)检验检

疫证书作为信用证下议付的所提示单据的一部分。买方有权对货物的品质和数量(重量)进行复验。如发现品质或数量(重量)与合同不符，除属于保险公司或船公司的责任之外，买方可凭检验机构出具的检验证明向卖方提出索赔或退货。所有因退货索赔的一切费用(包括检验费)及损失均由卖方负担。

11. Arbitration: All disputes in connection with this contract or the execution thereof shall be settled by way of amicable negotiation. In case no settlement can be reached, it shall be submitted for arbitration to the arbitration commission of China Council for the Promotion of International Trade in Beijing in accordance with the **Provisional Rules** and Procedures of the said commission. The award by the said commission shall be accepted as final and binding upon both parties. The fees for arbitration shall be borne by the losing party.

仲裁：合同双方发生争议时，应由双方友好协商解决。达不成协议的，双方可将本确认书执行当中发生的争议提交仲裁解决。仲裁应由中国国际经济贸易仲裁委员会在北京依照其仲裁规则进行。仲裁委员会的裁决为终局性的，对双方生效。仲裁费用由败诉方承担。

12. Force Majeure: The Seller shall not be responsible for late delivery or non-delivery of the goods owing to "Force Majeure" causes, such as war, flood, fire, storm, heavy snow, earthquake, seaquake, etc. However, in such cases, the Seller shall immediately notify the Buyer by e-mail or fax about the accident and furnish the Buyer with a certificate attesting such event or events.

不可抗力：由于发生不可抗力的原因，例如战争、洪水、火灾、风暴、大雪、地震、海啸等，可免除卖方延迟交货或没有交货的责任。在这种情况下，卖方必须立即以电子邮件或传真通知买方此事故，并向买方提供该事件的证明。

12. Remark:

备注：

(1) Partial shipments and transshipment are not allowed.

不允许分批装运和转船。

(2) All documents must be presented within 15 days after B/L issued but within the validity of L/C.

所有的单据必须在提单签发的 15 天后被提交，但须保证在信用证的有效期之内。

The contract is signed in duplicate for each party. The contract in both languages is of equal validity. In case of any dispute, the English version shall **prevail**.

本合同一式两份，买卖双方各执一份。本合同以中英文两种文字书写，两个版本具有同等效力，如有争议，以英文版本为准。

Confirmed by:

确认方：

The Buyer: The Seller:

买方：   卖方：

(Signature)   (Signature)

Notes

1. Purchase Confirmation   购货确认书，可缩写为 P/C

2. provisional rules   暂行条例，暂行规则

3. prevail   *vi.* 占上风，占优势

In case of any discrepancy, the arrival inspections shall prevail. 如果异议，以到货检验为准。

Specimen 4   Sales Agency Agreement

Sales Agency Agreement
销售代理协议

Contract No:

合同编号：

Date:

签订日期：

This agreement is entered into between the parties concerned on the basis of equality and mutual benefit to develop business on terms and conditions mutually agreed upon as follows:

为在平等互利的基础上发展贸易，有关方按下列条件签订本协议：

Contract Parties:

1. 订约人：

Supplier (hereinafter called "Party A") :

供货人(以下简称甲方)：

Agent (hereinafter called "Party B") :

销售代理人(以下称乙方)：

Party A **hereby** appoints Party B to act as his selling agent to sell the commodity mentioned below.

甲方委托乙方为销售代理人，推销下列商品。

Commodity and Quantity

2. 商品名称及数量

It is mutually agreed that Party B shall undertake to sell not less than _____ of the aforesaid commodity in the duration of this agreement.

双方约定，乙方在协议有效期内，销售不少于_____的商品。

Territory

3. 经销地区

In _____ only.

只限在_____。

Confirmation of Orders

4. 订单的确认

The quantities, prices and shipments of the commodities stated in this agreement shall be confirmed in each transaction. The particulars of which are to be specified in the Sales Confirmation signed by the two parties **hereto**.

本协议所规定商品的数量、价格及装运条件等，应在每笔交易中确认，其细目应在双方签订的销售确认书中做出规定。

Payment

5. 付款

After confirmation of the order, Party B shall arrange to open a confirmed, irrevocable L/C available by draft at sight in favor of Party A within the time stipulated in the relevant S/C. Party B shall also notify Party A immediately after L/C is open so that Party A can get prepared for delivery.

订单确认后，乙方须按照有关确认书所规定的时间开立以甲方为受益人的保兑的、不可撤销的即期信用证。乙方开出信用证后，应立即通知甲方，以便甲方准备交货。

Commission

6. 佣金

Upon the expiration of the Agreement and Party B's fulfillment of the total turnover mentioned in Article 2, Party A shall pay to Party B _____ % commission on the basis of the agreement amount of the invoice value against the shipments effected.

在本协议期满时，若乙方完成了第二款所规定的数额，甲方应按装运货物所收到的发票累计总金额付给乙方 _____ %的佣金。

Reports on Market Conditions

7. 市场情况报告

Party B shall forward once every three months to Party A detailed reports on current market conditions and of consumers' comments. Meanwhile, Party B shall from time to time, send to Party A samples of similar commodities offered by other suppliers, together with their prices, sales information and advertising materials.

乙方每三个月向甲方提供一次有关当时市场情况和用户意见的详细报告。同时，乙方应随时向甲方提供其他供应商的类似商品样品及其价格、销售情况和广告材料。

Advertising & Publicity Expense

8. 宣传广告费用

Party B shall bear all expenses for advertising and publicity within the aforementioned territory in the duration of this agreement and submit to Party A all patterns and/or drawings and description for prior approval.

在本协议有效期内，乙方在上述经销地区所做广告宣传的一切费用，由乙方自理。乙方须事先向甲方提供宣传广告的图案及文字说明，由甲方审阅同意。

Validity of Agreement

9. 协议有效期

This agreement, after its being signed by the parties concerned, shall remain in force for _____ days from _____ (Date) to _____ (Date). If either Party wishes to extend this agreement, he shall notice, in writing, the other party one month prior to its expiration. The matter shall be decided by the agreement and by consent of the parties hereto. Should either party fail to **implement** the terms and conditions **herein**, the other party is **entitled** to terminate this agreement.

本协议经双方签字后生效，有效期为____天，自____(日期)至____(日期)。若一方希望延长本协议，则须在本协议期满前 1 个月书面通知另一方，经双方协商决定。若协议一方未履行协议条款，另一方有权终止协议。

Arbitration

10. 仲裁

All disputes arising from the execution of this agreement shall be settled through negotiation between both parties. In the event that no settlement can be reached, the case in dispute shall then be submitted for arbitration to the Foreign Trade Arbitration Commission of the China Council for the Promotion of International Trade, Beijing, in accordance with the Provisional Rules of

Procedure of the said commission. The decision made by this Commission shall be regarded as final and is binding on both parties. Arbitration fees shall be borne by the losing party, unless otherwise awarded.

由执行本协议所引起的所有争议都应由双方协商解决。如果不能解决，争议应提交北京中国国际贸易促进委员会对外贸易仲裁委员会，依据上述委员会的仲裁程序暂行条例进行仲裁，该委员会做出的裁决将被视为最终裁决，对双方均具有约束力。仲裁费用，除另有规定外，由败诉方负担。

Other Terms & Conditions

11. 其他条款

Party A shall not supply the contracted commodity to any other buyers in the above mentioned territory. Direct enquiries, if any, will be referred to Party B. However, should any other buyers wish to deal with Party A directly, Party A may do so. But Party A shall send to Party B a copy of Sales Confirmation and give Party B _____ % commission on the basis of the net invoice value of the transactions concluded.

(1) 甲方不得向经销地区其他买主供应本协议所规定的商品。如有询价，当转达给乙方洽办。若有买主希望从甲方直接订购，甲方可以供货，但甲方须将有关销售确认书副本寄给乙方，并按所达成交易的发票金额给予乙方 _____ %的佣金。

Should Party B fail to pass on his orders to Party A in a period of _____ months for a minimum of _____ , Party A shall not bind himself to this agreement.

(2) 若乙方在 ___ 月内未能向甲方提供至少 _____ 订货，甲方不承担本协议的义务。

For any transaction between governments of both parties, Party A may handle such direct dealings as authorized by Party's government without binding himself to this agreement. Party B shall not interfere in such direct dealings nor shall Party B bring forward any demand for compensation/commission thereof.

(3) 对双方政府间的交易，甲方有权按其政府授权进行有关的直接贸易，而不受本协议的约束。乙方不得干涉此种直接贸易，也无权向甲方提出任何补偿或佣金要求。

This agreement shall be subject to the terms and conditions in the Sales Confirmation signed by both parties hereto.

(4) 本协议受签约双方所签订的销售确认条款的制约。

This agreement is signed on (D) ___ (M) ___ (Y) _____ at ____ (Place) and is in two originals; each Party holds one.

本协议于 ____ 年 ____ 月 ____ 日在 ____ 签订，正本两份，甲乙双方各执一份。

Party A Signature: Party B Signature:

甲方签字：   乙方签字：

Notes

1. hereby   *adv.* 特此，因此，据此，由此

   We hereby revoke the agreement of May 8, 2022. 我们特此宣告 2022 年 5 月 8 日的协议无效。

2. hereto   *adv.* 到此为止，对此

   We attach hereto two extra copy of invoice covering our shipment. 关于所装运货物，兹附寄发票副本两份。

3. implement   *v.* 执行，实施，使生效，贯彻

   to implement changes/decisions/policies/reforms   实行变革；执行决议/政策；实施改革

4. herein   *adv.* 在此处，此中，鉴于

   The price quoted herein is based on CIF London with 3% commission. 此报价均是 CIF 伦敦，包括 3%佣金。

5. entitle   *vt.* 给……权利(或资格)

   entitle sb. to do sth.   给某人做某事的权利

   Party B is not entitled to change the price quoted by Party A, but a proposal in connection with the price is acceptable. 乙方无权更改甲方所报价格，但是有关价格的建议是可以接受的。

Exercises

Ⅰ. Translate the following contract stipulations into Chinese.

1. Packing: To be packed in strong new wooden cases, suitable for long distance ocean/parcel post/air freight transportation and to change of climate, well protected against moisture and shocks. The Seller shall be liable for any damage of the commodity and expenses incurred on account of improper packing and for any rust attributable to inadequate or improper protective measures taken by the Seller in regard to the packing. One full set of service and operation instructions concerned shall be enclosed in the cases.

2. Terms of Shipment

(1) In case of FOB terms

(a) Booking of shipping space shall be attended to by the buyer. The Seller shall, 45 days before the date of shipment stipulated in this contract, advise the Buyer by fax or e-mail of the contract number, commodity, quantity, value, number of package, gross weight and measurement and date of readiness at the port of shipment.

(b) The Buyer or his shipping agent shall, 12 days before the estimated date of arrival of the vessel at the port of shipment, advise the Seller of the name of the vessel, contract number, the name of the shipping agent. The Seller shall come into contact with the shipping agent and arrange for the goods to be ready for loading. When it becomes necessary to change the carrying vessel or in the event of her arrival having to be advanced or delayed, the Buyer or the shipping agent shall advise the Seller in time.

(c) The Seller bear all costs and risks before it passes over the vessel's rail and is released from the tackle.

(2) In case of CFR terms

The Seller shall ship the goods within delivery time as per this contract from the port of shipment to the port of destination and advise shipment as stipulated in clause 8 of this contract for the Buyer to arrange insurance in time.

3. Inspection and Claim

The Buyer shall have the right to apply to the Shanghai Commodity Inspection and Quarantine Bureau (SCIQB) for reinspection after discharge of the goods at the port of destination. Should the quality, specification and/or quantity/weight be found not in conformity with the Contract, Letter of Credit or Invoice, the Buyer shall be entitled to lodge claims (including reinspection fee) with the Seller on the basis of SCIQB's Inspection and Quarantine Certificate, within 90 days after discharge of the goods at the port of destination, with the exception, however, of those claims for which the shipping company and/or the insurance company are to be held responsible.

4. Neither party will be liable to the other for any default hereunder if such default is caused by an event beyond such party's control, including without limitation acts or failure to act of the other party, strikes or labor disputes, component shortages, unavailability of transportation, flood, fires, governmental requirements and acts of God (a Force Majeure Event).

5. Miscellaneous/Supplementary Provisions: Should the articles stipulated in this contract be in conflict with the following supplementary provisions, the supplementary provisions shall prevail (shall be taken as valid and binding).

II. Translate the following terms into English.

1. 品质、数量和重量的异议与索赔：货到目的港后，买方如发现货物品质及/或数量/重量与合同规定不符，除属于保险公司及/或船公司的责任外，买方可以凭双方同意的检验机构出具的检验证明向卖方提出异议，品质异议须于货到目的港之日起 30 天内提出，数量/重量异议须于货到目的港之日起 15 天内提出。卖方须在接到索赔后 30 天内答复买方。

2. 仲裁：由执行本协议所引起的所有争议都应由双方协商解决。如果不能解决，争议应提交北京中国国际贸易促进委员会对外贸易仲裁委员会，依据上述委员会的仲裁程序暂行条例进行仲裁，该委员会做出的裁决将被视为最终裁决，对双方均具有约束力。仲裁费用，除另有规定外，由败诉方负担。

3. 卖方须向议付行提供如下单据：清洁装船提单、发票，由中国进出口商品检验检疫局签发的质量检验证明书、数量/重量检验证明书，以及由中国人民保险公司开具的保险单/证明。

4. 付款条件：凭以 ABC 公司为受益人的、保兑的、不可撤销的、可转让的、可分割的即期信用证支付。该信用证必须在 20××年 9 月 30 日之前到达卖方，该信用证的有效期至上述装船日期后第 15 天，议付地为中国北京，否则卖方有权不经通知取消本销售合同，并有权因此而发生的损失向买方索赔。

5. 即使有与本合同相悖的规定，保险范围和责任限制应以合同各方同意为准。

III. Writing pratice.

Draft a Sales Contract according to knowledge you learn from this chapter. And figure out the difference between the Purchase Contract and Sales Contract.

Unit 14 补充练习

Unit 14 补充练习答案

Unit 14 练习答案

第一单元　商务信函写作的基本知识

导　　读

在今天的商业社会，更加强调良好沟通技巧的重要性，因为这是必要的，员工可以利用不断发展的信息技术工具来进行清楚、准确和有效的沟通。

商务信函的关键是要使买卖双方的货物或者服务的交流得以成功地完成。商务信函的用途十分广泛，可以用于征询信息、订购货物、商议调整、出售货物、推销、索赔等。在国际贸易中，交易的磋商和合同的签订大多是通过信函的方式进行的。商务信函是具有法律效力的文件。因此，从形式到内容都必须加以重视。

因此对于商务专业的学生来说，掌握阅读和书写一份能够使读者易于理解的商务信函的技能，是非常重要的。

一、商务信函的写作原则

一封得体的信函在贸易中可以起到非常重要的作用，包括增进与对方的友谊和获得对方的理解。写商务信函是一项必要的商务工作。一般地说，商务信函的作用有：①索取或传递信息；②报盘或接受报盘；③处理业务磋商的各种问题。此外，有些信的目的仅仅是提醒收信人知道写信人的存在。

撰写信函与其他形式的创作没有区别。良好的英语是写好商务信函的重要基础之一。信函应该在语法上没有缺点，也没有丝毫会使人误解的地方。商务信函有它的一些特点，可归纳为 6 个 C，也就是：①清楚(Clearness)；②简要(Conciseness)；③礼貌(Courtesy)；④体谅(Consideration)；⑤正确(Correctness)；⑥完整(Completeness)。

1. 清楚

首先，要确保你的信十分清楚，不会使人误解。信中即使有一处模棱两可的地方也会给双方带来麻烦。为了进行解释，难免要来回写信，从而浪费时间。

其次，当已确定要写些什么，就用普通、简单的词句来写。商务信函所需要的是直接、简明而正确的语言表达。

2. 简要

清楚和简要经常是相辅而行的。摒弃信中的陈词滥调可使信更清楚、更简要。

一封简要的信不一定很短。有时候一封信涉及许多问题，难免要长一些。如果简要和礼貌发生矛盾时，那么就要在简要性方面做出一些牺牲。一般来说，短句要比长句更能达到清楚和简要的效果。

适当分段可使信更清楚易读和更有吸引力。一事一段是个好章法。

3. 礼貌

在通信中，不必过于客套，最重要的是"及时"。及时处理来信会使不喜欢等待多天才收到回复的客户感到高兴。

怀疑或甚至反驳对方坦诚的陈述是不适当的。在业务中肯定会发生意见分歧。但圆通和外交策略可以克服并解决分歧而不损及双方的友好关系。

4. 体谅

体谅是书写得体的商务信函的重要原则。信函必须给阅读者一个好印象。尽量处在对方的立场考虑其愿望、需求、兴趣及难处。关注"你"的态度，而不是"我"或"我们"的态度。我们在写信时应该时刻牢记读信人是谁，以他的观点来看问题，考虑他的处境，了解他的问题和困难，并依据他的感受来表达我们的意见。找出一种最佳的方式来表达自己的高见且使对方能够接受。

比较下面的两组句子：

(1) "你"立场

为你的成功而祝贺。

你得到了 2%现金付款折扣。

(2) "我"或"我们"立场

我/我们向你表达热烈的祝贺。

我/我们给你 2%的现金付款折扣。

很显然，"你"立场优于"我"或"我们"立场。

5. 正确

正确意味着不仅语法、标点符号和拼写要正确，而且，还要用适合的语气来表达目的。要用一定的语气表达和传递正确的信息，即使书写投诉或回应投诉的信函，也不要造成对对方的伤害和冒犯而引起冲突。商务信函必须表达真实的信息，使用准确的数字和正确的术语，因为每个不同的术语所代表的买卖双方的权利和义务都不一样，而且这些信函通常是各种票据往来的基础。所以，保守或夸大事实都可能使自己处于不利的地位。

6. 完整

商务信函必须包含所应具备的全部信息才能顺利达成其目的。列出要点会使信的内容完整而充实，需要表达的信息都要涵盖在内，需要解答的问题也一一回复。不完整的信件不仅不礼貌，而且会让读信人误认为你的公司不好。

他可能会因为别的公司提供了完整的信息，或者怕麻烦，不想再向你询问而放弃与你公司的这桩生意。

因此，写信时要牢记内容的完整性：为什么写信？支持陈述的具体数据有哪些？是否回答了所有的问题？

二、商务信函的布局

混合式(见样函 1)是长期使用的习惯格式。许多人认为这是所有格式中最有吸引力的一种。因为齐头式信函紧凑和整洁，所以受人喜爱，大多数读者欢迎这种格式。有人喜欢首行缩进式的分段，声称该格式阅读方便，也有人不喜欢缩进式，他们说首行缩进浪费打字员的时间。因此，齐头式(见样函 2)现在比以前更为被广泛使用。

现代书信格式中的行名、地址常用免标点法，但这一点并不重要，如喜欢也可用加标点法。

三、商务信函的主要内容

商务信函包括 7 个主要部分：①信头；②日期；③信内公司名称、地址；④称呼；⑤信的正文；⑥表示敬意的结尾；⑦写信人的职位和签名。

1. 信头

信头可以展示公司的个性，有助于建立公司形象。信头格式是多样化的，但所介绍的情况相似。除了公司名称、地址以外，信头还可以包括电话号码、电报挂号、使用的电报码、传真号码以及经营的业务。

2. 日期

日期按日、月、年的顺序全文缮打。例如：

12th October，20××或 12 October 20××。

日可用基数(1、2、3、4 等)或序数(1st、2nd、3rd、4th 等)。例如：

1st March 20××或 1 March 20××；

3rd April 20××或 3 April 20××；

29th October 20××或 29 October 20××。

日也可放在月份后。例如：

March 1st，20××。

October 29，20××。

在这种形式下，日和年之间必须用一个逗号隔开。

用诸如 12/10/20×× 的形式表示日期是不得体的，容易引起误解。因为在英国这种形式的日期是指 20××年 10 月 12 日，而在美国和一些其他国家，这种形式的日期又指 20××年 12 月 10 日。

3. 信内姓名和地址

惯常的方式是把收信人的姓名和地址放在信首(如样函 1 和样函 2)，但在公函中有时放在信末的左下端。

如果知道某部门的主管人员，那就用他的头衔把信写给他。例如：

The Sales Manager

当按收信人的名字写信给他时，要确保名字拼写正确。

英文信函的地址有下列几个部分(但不是所有地址都如此)：

(1) 商行名称。

(2) 门牌号码和街名。

(3) 城市或镇名。

(4) 州/县名及其邮政编码。

(5) 国名。

当写信给别的国家时，即使所写的城市是该国的首都，也应把国名写上，以免误解。例如：

Birmingham，Alabama，USA

Birmingham，England，UK

(注：美国亚拉巴马州北部一个城市叫 Birmingham；英格兰中部也有一个城市叫 Birmingham)。

在商务信函中，先生(Mr.)和先生们(Messrs.)作为礼节上的尊称是很普遍的。然而，Messrs. (法文 Messieurs 的缩写)是 Mr.的复数，它仅用于公司行号，而该公司行号的名称中包含人的姓名，例如：

Messrs. J. Harvey & Co.

Messr. J. MacDonald & Evous.

4. 称呼

称呼是每封信开头所表示的致敬。商务信函惯用的表示敬意的词是"亲爱的先生"或"亲爱的先生们"(若信是写给公司的)。但美国人通常用 Gentlemen 而不用 Dear Sirs。注意，不能单用 Sirs，而且 Gentlemen 不能用单数。美国人写的信在称呼之后总是放上一个冒号，例如：

Dear Mr. White:

现在由女性开设或经营公司已经很常见。因此，倘若写信人不能确定阅信者将是男士还是女士，可用 Dear Madam or Sir 表示敬意。

5. 信的正文

信的正文是信函的主体，是最重要的部分。在开始写信之前，必须考虑下列两点：

(1) 写这封信的目的何在？

(2) 如何下笔最佳？

由于信函的主要目的是传递信息，因此应该用易懂的语言来撰写，以下几点可作为提示。

(1) 书信要简单、清楚、有礼貌，符合语法规则，并有针对性。

(2) 分段要正确，每段限于一个主题。

(3) 避免那些陈规套语以及难懂的商业行话。

6. 表示敬意的结尾

像称呼一样，表示敬意的结尾纯粹是一个习惯问题，是有礼貌地结束一封信的一种方式。措辞要恰当，同时也要与称呼相称。下列称呼和与之匹配的敬意结尾，都是现代商务信函中的常用语句。

7. 写信人的职位和签名

签名部分包括写信人手签的名字(紧随表示敬意的结尾之后)和打印的名字。签名要用墨水笔写在表示敬意的结尾下面。用橡皮图章盖印的形式是不礼貌的。

四、商务信函的其他内容

1. "请某人注意"行

"请某人注意"行用于写信人在发信给一个单位时表明希望把信递交给某个具体成员或部门。该短语要在称呼之上空两行缮打，或置于信的中央，并加下划线。

2. 主题语

主题语被认为是商务信函主体的一部分。主题语中的字母通常首字母大写，或其字母全部大写，或在其下加下划线。主题语一般位于信的中央位置，除非信是齐头式的(从左边写起)，并且放在敬语称呼的下面两行处，为引起对信内容的注意。

3. 信函编号

给出信函编号是为了便于查找过去的往来信函，并且确保没有延误地到达所要接受信函的人或部门。很多信头提供了编号的位置。信函编号包括档案号、部门代码或者写信人名字的缩写(后接打字员名字缩写)。当提到本次写信是针对过去的某一封信时，应当给出原来的信的日期。

4. 附件

假如信封内除信纸外，还附有其他文件，如产品目录、价目表、销售合同条款等，可以在信中说明附件份数和内容。附件的说明在签名下面两行处，标注 Enclosure 或缩写 Enc. 或 Encl.。附件为一件以上时，要加上编号或属性，以便收信人识别。例如：

> 附件-2
> 1. 价目表
> 2. 销售确认书

5. 抄送

发信人若需把此信抄送给有关人员，可在附件下方(即信左下端)两行处打上 CC 或 cc，然后打上被抄送人员的名称。

6. 附笔

在封信之前，如果发现还有某些项目没有写，就需要补充。这时需要增加一个附笔。增加附笔意味着写信没有做好充分的安排。有时并不是真的忘记了事情，而是为了故意引起对方的注意。如果真的忘记了重要的事情，应当重新写信，而不是用附笔。

如果不可避免地要写附笔，应写在其他注语的下方两行，靠左面写。

五、信封的写法

信封的书写要求正确、字迹清楚和美观。用于信封的纸与用于信笺和便条的纸，其质地应该相同。撰写商务信函选用的文具、布局和格式反映出一家公司的个性。

信封上的地址及标志和信内的地址及标志应格式相同，可用缩行式或齐头式。齐头式是写信封常用的格式。同时在打字时一般不加标点符号。很多公司的信封的左上角已印刷好邮信人的地址。收信人的名字和地址打印在距离信封的左侧和顶部三分之一或二分之一的位置，上面留出邮票和邮戳的位置。"航空"之类的注明邮寄方式的标识位于左下方。

信封上面可以附注下列各项。

(1) 可在信封的左下角注明信的类别，标明邮递方式等。

① 航空。

② 航空挂号。

③ 挂号邮件。

④ 快递邮件。

⑤ 包裹邮件。

⑥ 印刷品。

⑦ 样品邮件。

(2) 私人信件或密件，可在信封的左下角标明下列字样。

① 私人信件。

② 个人信件。

③ 机密信件。

(3) 下列用法和含义应予注意。

① Attention，Attention of 或 For the attention of 用以表明属于谁的事情，交由谁办理。如 attention(ATTN): Hardware Dept.意为"请交五金部办理"。

② c/o 意为 Care of，"由……转交"。

③ "Kind of…""Per Kindness of…""By Kindness of…""Through the Courtesy of…"均用于表明带信人的姓名。托人带信，不写地址，只注明带信人的名称。如：

Mr. Charles Wood

Kindness of Mr. Wang Ming

意为托 Wang Ming 先生把信带给 Charles Wood 先生。

样函 1　混合式

(样函函头略，具体格式见英文部分)

先生/女士：

收到你方 1 月 15 日询价殊为欣慰。今附上你方要求的具有详细内容的附图目录及价格单。另邮寄上一些样品，我们相信在你方细查这些样品后，你方将会同意，这些货物是价廉物美的。

对于定期购买单项商品数量不少于 100 打：我方可给予 2%的折扣。用不可撤销的即期信用证付款。

由于品质柔软而耐用，我们的全棉床单及枕套很快成了畅销商品。你方在研究我方价格之后，对我们为什么甚难满足市场需求这一事实就不难知道了。但你方如能在本月底前向我们订货，我们将保证迅速发货。

同时我们也请你方注意我们的其他产品，如台布及台巾，其详细情况也可以从目录中找到。等候你方的首次订单。

谨上

中国进出口有限公司

经理

20××年1月24日

附件2

附图目录

价格单

样函2　齐头式

(样函函头略，具体格式见英文部分)

先生/女士：

信用证3179号

兹复你方6月18日来信，我们已经通知我们的密特兰银行修改上述信用证，加注下列条款：

"发票一式五份由中国国际贸易促进会证明"，以代替上述信用证中原来规定的"发票一式五份由你处的英国领事证明"。

我们是用电报修改信用证的，想必在此信到达前你方已经收到修改书了。

相信现在一切都已就绪，在下月的上半月内你方能装运订货。

如果货物到达时证明是令人满意的话，我们确信将会进一步大量订购。

盼得悉你方有关装运的情况。

谨上

Brownson，Clarke & Co.

经理

20××年6月26日

第二单元　建立业务关系

导　读

为了开拓与其他公司的买卖市场，或者继续巩固或扩大业务往来，建立业务关系是国际商务往来中的第一步。

写信给新的客户请求建立业务关系是商业交流的常见做法。首先必须知道将要与谁做生意。与有潜力的客户建立业务关系是非常重要的，尤其是一些新的公司。所以，在与对方联系之前，最好对对方的金融状况、商业活动以及信誉度等资信情况做调查。

同时，对于原来的老客户应当给予更多的关照。记住不要遗忘老客户。

获得希望合作的公司的名称和地址，可以通过以下途径。

(1) 银行。

(2) 在国外的商会。

(3) 贸易行行名录。

(4) 中国驻国外商务处。

(5) 同业商行等。

(6) 广告。

(7) 展销会或贸易交易会。

在从上述任何途径获得需要的信息之后，就可以向有关方面发"首函"或"通函"了。

总体说来，这样的信函开场白可以告诉收信人你是如何获得对方的名称和地址的，然后表达想与对方建立业务关系的愿望，同时告诉对方你的目的、你公司的经营范围和金融状况、地位等。在信的结尾，你要表达希望能合作，并等待对方早日回复。

如果想购买某种产品，应该索要样品、价格单、产品目录或者其他可以参考的资料。不论想买卖什么东西，信函都应该写得有礼貌、简单、清晰和简洁。

给人的第一印象是很重要的。一定要按照标准的格式，尽量避免出错。在收到这种信函后，一定要及时地回复信中提到的所有信息。这样可以给人留下一个好的印象。

样函 1　请求建立业务关系

(样函函头略，具体格式见英文部分)

尊敬的先生们：

从我使馆商务处得悉贵方的名称和地址，我司借此机会致函贵方以探讨合作之可能。

我公司是国有进出口公司，专门经营台布等棉制品，并且可以依据客户的来样来图，及规格和包装的要求接受订单。另外，我们还可以接受以客户的商标、品牌供货的订单。

为了让贵方对我们的各种棉制台布有大概的了解，我们另寄出我们最新的产品目录以供参考。如贵方对某种产品有兴趣，请即告。在接到贵方的询盘后，我方将报盘并提供样品。

盼早回复。

您忠实的

刘云

刘云经理

中国纺织进出口有限公司

样函2 请求建立业务关系

(样函函头略，具体格式见英文部分)

尊敬的先生们：

我们从中国驻加纳使馆商务处得悉贵公司的名称和地址。兹告知我公司专营工业和药物化工原料，并想同你们建立业务联系。

为了使你们对我方产品有个全面的了解，现附上有关我公司经营的各种产品的一整套小册子，内有详细规格和包装情况。一收到你们的具体询价，我们将马上寄样报价。

我们将以货物在装运时的质量和重量为准达成交易，而货物在出运前将由上海商检局进行检验。有关货物质量和数量等的证明将由上海商检局提供。

盼早日收到你们的回信。

中国化工产品进出口有限公司

(签名)

20××年11月15日

样函3 请求建立业务关系

敬启者：

经我方澳大利亚渣打银行的介绍，今写信给你们。我们冒昧向你方介绍，我们经营牛皮，向欧洲和日本出口。

我们专营上述业务，许多年前，我们同你们国家就上述产品做过大笔的生意。既然我们两国已建立了外交关系，我们愿同你方建立直接的业务关系，因为你们是澳大利亚牛皮的进口商。

贵方如能告诉我们你方是否对上述牛皮生意抱有兴趣，我们将深表感谢。若有兴趣，请通知我们你方所需数量。

您忠实的

(签名)

样函4 某建立业务关系请求的回复函

(样函函头略，具体格式见英文部分)

敬启者：

关于你方20××年12月2日的来信，我们很高兴获知贵公司想在罐头食品业务方面同我们建立业务关系。

按照你方要求，我们通过航空邮递寄上目录一本，并附一套小册子，供你方参考。

如果目录中所列的任何商品符合贵方要求，请具体询价，我方将立即提供报价单。

同时，在第一笔生意做成之前，请将你们银行的行名告诉我们。

中国进出口公司

(签名)

20××年12月9日

样函5 某建立业务关系请求的回复函

敬启者：

谢谢你方4月1日的来信，我们从信中注意到你方愿同我方建立业务关系。我们始终愿意在平等互利的基础上与愿同我们做生意的人们从事贸易，也欢迎你们来做生意。

我们另函寄去一套小册子，以便你方了解我们的产品。请告知你方具体需求，我们将立即报价。

谨上

(签名)

样函6 主动要求提供销售代理服务

敬启者：

我们知道贵公司在中国并没有代理商，我们愿意提供这项服务。

过去十年来，我们一直向中国各主要城市的批发商和大的零售商销售各种不同的耐用商品，并已建立起为数可观的、显示出良好业务效果的、相当确定的关系网。

一直到最近，本公司尚未销售过额外的产品，因为我们只致力于原来销售的产品。然而，我们现在已有足够的能力扩大销售。若贵公司同意我们成为你方的独家代理，我们将竭力为贵公司产品在我方建立起市场。

如果贵公司对我们的建议感兴趣，我们将乐意提供我方的银行及贸易资料。

谨上
(签名)

样函7　尝试恢复中断的业务关系

敬启者：

回顾过去一年来我们双方的业务往来记录，我方发现已有好长时间没有得到贵方的任何订单了。

若你方仍在经销我方的商品，恳请告知最近贵方推销意图和目标。若你方对向我们订货有什么意见和建议，请不吝向我方提出，以便我方慎重研究。

贵方一定乐意获悉我方的产品已在工艺和包装方面做了一系列的改进。现另函寄去贵公司过去常订购产品的新式样品。当你们见到这些样品之后，将会发现它们很符合贵方的要求，可促进你我之间的友好业务往来的恢复和发展。

希望得到贵方的积极响应。

谨上
(签名)

第三单元　询盘和回复

导　　读

当商务人士打算购买某种商品或获得所需的服务时，他总会首先发询价函。换句话说就是通常由买方向卖方发出询价函邀请报价，因此询价函对买卖双方都意味着潜在的商机。

按内容划分，询价函可分为一般询价和具体询价。一般询价内容包括询问商品的总体情况、索要商品目录本、价格单或样品手册。具体询价涉及特定商品或服务的细节信息。一封询价函应包括以下内容：

(1) 如何得知这家公司的名称，并要求对方寄来商品目录及价目表。

(2) 介绍本公司的情况和经营范围，说明感兴趣的产品。

(3) 询问可以给予的折扣及要求的支付条件(如 FOB 或 CIF 等)。

(4) 询问对方能够提供的发货服务。

(5) 希望得到对方的答复。

收到询价函就有了做生意的机会，因此回复函应及时，语气应得体，回信的内容应完整涵盖询价函中的所有问题。回复询价函时，特别是初次询价函，需要格外重视，以便给对方留下好的印象。若被询问的产品没有库存，卖方需要告知买方缺货原因及何时能有现货。如果被询问的产品不再生产，或是特殊的要求不能被满足，卖方需要注意措辞，避免直接拒绝对方导致冒犯买方。此外，卖方应确保询价函中所有问题在回复函中都做了答复。若问题很多，推荐使用圆点或数字来区分答复。一封回复信函应包含以下内容：

(1) 询价函已经收悉。

(2) 提及已将所索要的商品目录及价目表附于信中或另函寄送，并清楚地介绍有关商品的种种优点。

(3) 强调所报价格具有竞争性，并明确地说明对方可得到的折扣。

(4) 说明要求的支付条件及能提供的发货服务。

(5) 希望得到对方的答复。

样函 1　读到广告后进行的询盘

尊敬的先生：

我们从《21世纪》高兴地得知你公司是中国棉花生产与出口的主要公司之一。我们热切盼望与你方建立直接的贸易关系。我们相信这也符合你方的愿望。

目前，我方对棉麻印花衬衫感兴趣。希望你方能航空邮寄该商品的目录册、样品和所有所需要的信息，以便我方了解所供产品的质量和工艺。同时，请报该商品的 CIF 温哥华价，包含 5%佣金，并告知最早的装船日期。

如果你方价格很有竞争力且装船日期范围适当，我们打算向你方大量订货。

相信你方能尽早给我们答复。

谨上

（签名）

样函 2　客户对展示的产品感兴趣

敬启者：

作为巴基斯坦最大的纺织品公司之一，我方对你方在春季商品交易会上展示的机械设备很感兴趣。我方急需这批货物以便淘汰陈旧设备。请报最新 CFR 卡拉奇港价，并告知所需支付方式及最早的装船日期。对您的密切关注预祝谢意。

谨上

（签名）

样函 3　请求索要产品目录和价目表

敬启者：

从《美国贸易指南》中看到贵公司的广告。请贵公司尽快寄送男式大衣和合成纤维产品的最低报价单、折扣、支付条件以及带有图片的商品目录。

同时，我们也希望获知贵公司的财务状况和商业信誉。我们的资信证明人是香港的美国花旗银行。

盼早回复。

谨上

（签名）

样函4　寄送产品目录和价目表

敬启者：

　　欢迎你公司 12 月 26 日来函询价手工制人造革手套，谨表谢意。按照要求，现附上图解目录及价目表，以供你公司了解详细情况。此外，另封寄样品一批。深信只要你公司审视一下这批样品，并且比较一下我们的报价，定会同意这批货质优且价格合理。

　　如单种货品订购量不少于五件，我公司可给予七折优惠。

　　我公司还出口各类手工制皮鞋，质量与手套一样好，在商品目录中有详尽说明，相信你公司也会感兴趣。

　　愿样品及时送到你公司，并盼早来订单。

谨上
(签名)

样函5　索要报价单

白砂糖

敬启者：

　　我们刚刚从日本一客户处收到询盘，他需要 1 万公吨的白砂糖，我们将感谢您在最快的时间里给我们报最惠盘。

　　顺告你方，所需的是优质白砂糖，新麻袋包装，每袋装 100 千克。与此同时，将由公众检验机构检验货物的质量和重量。关于询购的货物，买主将安排装运和保险。因此，你方应以大连港船边交货价为基础报价。

　　由于日本奇缺这种白砂糖，因此，货物应尽早地备妥待运。请相信，如果你方价格是可以接受的，我们将立即向你方订货。

　　请尽快对此询盘予以答复。

谨上
(签名)

样函6　对询函的回复

敬启者：

　　我国驻贵国商务参赞处已转来你方对笔的询盘。

我厂专门生产各种型号的"英雄"牌笔，已有 64 年的历史，所附寄的目录将使你方了解我们的一些产品。

我们特别推荐如下型号产品并作报价，这些产品在中东市场很畅销，我们相信你方会感兴趣。

货　号	商品名称	规　格	价格/打
200 型	礼品对笔	14K 金笔尖，与圆珠笔配对	89 美元
13 型	高级金笔	12K 金笔尖，不锈钢笔套	52 美元
251 型	高级铱金笔	明尖型，铝套塑杆	36 美元

上面所报价格按 FOB 上海作价，无约束力，需以我方最后确认为准。我方要求以保兑的、不可撤销的即期信用证付款。在收到你方书面订单后一个月货可备妥待运。

期望得到你方试购订单。

谨上

(签名)

第四单元　发盘和还盘

导　　读

  根据《联合国国际货物销售合同公约》，向一个或一个以上特定的人提出的订立合同的建议，如果十分确定并且表明发价人在得到接受时承受约束的意旨，即构成发盘(也称发价)。一个建议如果写明货物并且明示或暗示地规定数量和价格或规定如何确定数量和价格，即为十分确定。

  发盘函应包括以下内容：

(1) 如果有来自对方的询盘，对此表示感谢。

(2) 商品的名称、质量和规格。

(3) 详细的关于价格、贸易术语、折扣、付款方式的规定。

(4) 包装和交货日期。

(5) 发盘的有效期。

(6) 希望得到对方的答复。

  对发盘表示接受，但如果载有添加、限制或其他更改的答复，即为拒绝该项发盘并构成还盘。

  但是，对发盘表示接受但载有添加或不同条件的答复，如所载的添加或不同条件在实质上并不变更该项发盘的条件，除发盘人在不过分迟延的期间内以口头或书面通知反对其间的差异外，仍构成接受。如果发盘人不反对，那么合同的条件就以该项发盘的条件以及接受通知内所载的更改为准。

  有关货物价格、付款，货物质量和数量，交货地点和时间，一方当事人对另一方当事人的赔偿责任范围或解决争端的办法等内容的添加或不同条件，均视为在实质上变更发盘的条件。

  还盘信函应包含以下内容：

(1) 对对方发盘表示感谢。

(2) 对不能接受对方发盘表示抱歉并说明理由。

(3) 做出还盘或建议其他的贸易机会。

(4) 希望对方早日答复。

样函 1　根据询盘报盘：实盘

尊敬的先生：

感谢贵方 7 月 5 日的询盘，要求我方向你方发出 5000 公吨大米的报盘。贵方对我方产品的兴趣，我方深表感谢。按贵方要求，我方报出如下实盘，以你方的答复在 7 月 30 日或此日期之前到达我方为有效。

1. 商品名称：优质大米，产地为黑龙江。

2. 数量：5000 公吨。

3. 价格：每公吨……美元，FOB 大连。

4. 包装：新麻袋包装，每袋装 100 千克。

5. 装运时间：20××年 10 月。

6. 付款方式：用不可撤销、保兑的即期信用证付款，信用证金额为发票全额，装运前 30 天开出。

请注意我方报出的价格为最优惠的价格，我方不能接受任何的还盘。

盼早复。

谨上
(签名)

样函 2　根据询盘报盘：虚盘

尊敬的先生：

我方收到贵方 10 月 20 日的来函，对我方 456 号男鞋询盘。贵方对此产品感兴趣，我方深表感谢。

按照贵方要求，我方向贵方报出 500 双 456 号牛皮男鞋的价格，每双 50 美元 FOB 上海，以我方最终确认为准。装运在收到你方通过一流银行开出的以我方为受益人的相关信用证的 30 天之内进行。

我公司生产各种型号的男女鞋用于出口，我方另邮寄一份我方产品的小册子供你方参考。希望其中一些产品能够满足贵方顾客的要求。

盼早复。

您忠实的
(签名)

样函 3　还盘：要求减价

尊敬的先生：

我方已经收到贵方 6 月 4 日的发盘以及棉布衬衫的样品，非常感谢。

此复，我方很遗憾地告知贵方，尽管我方非常欣赏衬衫的优良品质，但我方的客户认为你方价格过高，不符合现行市场的价格水平。

事实既然如此，我方不能说服我方客户接受此价，因为同样质量的产品可以以一个低得多的价格买到。如果贵方能把价格降低，比方说 10%，我们就能达成交易。

我方相信贵方会认为此还盘是合理的，希望早日得到贵方的答复。

谨上

（签名）

样函 4　还盘：要求降低数量

尊敬的先生：

感谢贵方 10 月 10 日的发盘以及牛皮鞋的样品。

我方认为，贵方皮鞋是符合标准的，贵方报出的价格也是令人满意的。但是关于贵方在信中提到的 10000 双的最低订货量，我方必须指出，在你方 9 月 20 日的信中要求的最低订货量是 5000 双。请你方接受这个最低订货量。

请尽早确认。

谨上

（签名）

样函 5　还盘：要求改变付款方式

尊敬的先生：

我方感谢贵方 6 月 5 日对女鞋的发盘。我方认为贵方所报的价格以及产品的质量都很令人满意，但是我方建议对付款方式进行修改。

一般说来，按惯例，我方同贵国的所有客户进行交易均采用即期付款交单方式，因此，我方不能破例。

鉴于我们长期的业务关系，我方建议贵方接受即期付款交单方式。

盼早回复。

谨上
(签名)

样函6　拒　绝　减　价

尊敬的先生：

从贵方10月15日的传真得知，贵方认为我方男衬衫的价格偏高。

尽管我方乐于与贵方合作以扩大销售，但是我方很遗憾不能接受贵方还盘，因为如果把产品质量考虑在内的话，我方报出的价格是最优惠的。

尽管不能降低价格，我方仍希望能够接到你方的订单。由于目前供货量有限，我方希望贵方尽快订货。

盼早回复。

谨上
(签名)

样函7　做　出　让　步

尊敬的先生：

感谢贵方3月30日的来函。贵方对我方衬衫的还盘已经引起了我方极大的注意。

尽管我方十分希望满足你方的要求，但是很遗憾我方难以按贵方的要求降价，因为我方的价格是经过精确计算的。即使我方和其他供应商的价格存在差异，但是贵方订购我方货物仍然是有利润的，因为我方产品的质量要优于贵国的其他制造商的产品。

然而，为了发展我们双方的业务关系，如果贵方的最低订货量达到5000件的话，我方准备给你方5%的折扣。

如果贵方接受我方的建议，请尽早向我方下订单。

谨上
(签名)

样函8　接　受　还　盘

尊敬的先生：

我方收悉贵方5月17日的来函，要求我方男衬衫降价10%。

兹答复，很遗憾，我方认为很难满足贵方要求，我方所报价格仅包含很少的利润，如果不是因为我们的一些买主定期向我们订货，我们不可能按这样的价格供货。

　　然而，为了在贵地开发市场，我方决定破例接受贵方还盘。

　　希望我们能够达成交易，盼望早日收到贵方的答复。

谨上

(签名)

第五单元　订单和订单的履行

导　读

订货信是买方对卖方提供一定量货物的要求。订货信要求准确、清楚。订货信应包括以下内容：

(1) 商品的名称和规格。

(2) 订购的数量。

(3) 商品的单价和总值。

(4) 包装方式。

(5) 装运日期和方式。

(6) 付款方式。

当卖方同意买方订单中的条款时，卖方应该向买方发一封确认信函。当卖方由于缺货或商品的价格和规格有所变动而不能接受买方的发价时，一定要小心谨慎地写一封拒绝订单的信函。最好可以提供适合的替代品，然后说服买方接受这种替代品。

样函 1　试 订 货

尊敬的先生：

感谢贵方 6 月 23 日的来函。在仔细研究了你方的图解目录及价目表之后，我方从中选择了 5 个型号的产品，并随函附上了我方订单。

我方要强调的是此次订货是一次试订货。如果我方对产品质量以及装运满意的话，我方会定期地重复订购。为避免在我方处通关过程中产生麻烦，请严格遵照我方的装运须知行事。

关于我方的财务和资信状况，请向贵国的商会查证。

谨上

(签名)

样函 2　随函附寄订货单

尊敬的先生：

感谢贵方 7 月 6 日的来函。我方很高兴地告知贵方，我方对贵方产品的价格及质量都十分满意，特随函附寄针对这些产品的 1234 号订单一份。

我方很高兴与贵公司达成首次交易，希望能够为我们双方的利益进一步扩展贸易。

谨上
(签名)

订 货 单

编号：1234
日期：20××.7.20

尊敬的先生：

我方很荣幸地按照如下条件向你方订购下列货物：

商品名称	数量	单价(CIF 纽约)	总价
121 号男鞋	500 双	35 美元	17 500 美元
223 号女鞋	400 双	30 美元	12 000 美元
312 号童鞋	500 双	20 美元	10 000 美元
		扣除折扣 5%	37 525 美元

包装：用适合长途海运的、新的、结实的纸箱包装。

装运：20××年 9 月。

付款：即期的、不可撤销的信用证。

我方会指示我方银行开出此订单金额的信用证。贵方会很快得到银行通知。

谨上
(签名)

样函 3 订 购 货 物

尊敬的先生：

收到贵方 1 月 3 日的发盘以及皮鞋的样品，十分感谢。在检验样品后，我方认为质量和工艺都符合我方的要求，因此很高兴地向贵方订购以下货品：

商品名称	数量	单价(CIF 纽约)	总价
121 号男鞋	500 双	35 美元	17 500 美元
223 号女鞋	400 双	30 美元	12 000 美元
312 号童鞋	500 双	20 美元	10 000 美元
			共计 39 500 美元

请在 6 周内交货。付款方式为 30 天远期付款交单。如果这次订货令我方满意，我方

会再次订购。

谨上

(签名)

样函4 拒 绝 订 购

尊敬的先生：

感谢贵方8月19日向我方订购5000双黑皮鞋。然而，很遗憾我方不得不谢绝贵方订单，因为目前我方没有所需颜色的皮鞋存货，而且至少一个月之内也不会有货。

但是目前我方可供棕色和白色皮鞋，它们与黑皮鞋质量相同而且同样流行。如果贵方对此感兴趣，可以考虑以此作为替代产品。

再次感谢贵方订单，希望我们可供黑色皮鞋的时候，贵方可以给我们履行订单的机会。同时，希望收到贵方的其他询盘。

谨上

(签名)

样函5 确 认 订 单

尊敬的先生：

很高兴收到贵方4月5日男鞋的订单。我方确认按照贵方123号订单中的价格供1000双鞋。我方很荣幸为您服务，相信贵方会对我方产品的质量感到满意。

我方销售确认书 ABC111 号正本一式两份已经航寄你方。请会签并寄回一份供我方存档。

关于这批货物的以我方为受益人的信用证应立即开立。我方要指出的是，相关信用证条款必须严格遵照合同条款开立以避免日后的修改。贵方可放心，一收到信用证，我方立刻安排装运。

感谢贵方的合作，期望再次收到贵方的订单。

谨上

(签名)

样函 6 确认重复订单

尊敬的先生:

感谢贵方来函重复贵方 12 月 12 日 5000 双皮鞋的订单。

尽管现行价格稍高于此价格，但是为了促进我们双方的业务往来，我方将像以前一样按照同样条件接受订单。

按照贵方以前信中的要求，我们缮制第 123 号销售确认书一式两份，如蒙会签后及时寄回一份，我们将不胜感激。

我们很高兴得知以我方为受益人的信用证将立即开出。然而我们想提请你方注意，为了避免随后的传真修改，有关信用证的规定应该同我方的销售确认书严格一致。

感谢你们的合作，相信一收到信用证马上发运货物会让你们完全满意。

谨上

(签名)

样函 7 推荐替代品

尊敬的先生:

很高兴收到贵方 12 月 15 日来函，订购 200 台 113 号电暖气。然而，很遗憾地告知贵方，您所订购的货物目前无货可供，因为对这种产品的需求下降，我方已经停止生产。

为满足贵方要求，我方推荐一种非常好的替代产品。它在质量上优于贵方订购的产品，但是价格几乎相同。这种产品在欧洲已经有了市场，我方确信它在贵国也会受到热烈的欢迎。

随函附上该产品的图解说明及文字材料，由此贵方可以了解产品细节。

期望收到贵方订单。

谨上

(签名)

第六单元　促　销　信

导　读

促销信的主要目的是说服读者购买要销售的商品，因此写信时要尽量从买方的立场出发，而不是从卖方的立场出发，这样才能将商品推销出去。为了做到这一点，就需要了解潜在的客户。他们需要哪些产品或服务？他们感兴趣的是什么？他们对你的产品最关心的是什么？动笔之前应对这些问题做细致的分析，并在促销信中给出读者想要的答案。通常来讲，一封好的促销信要包括下列几点：

(1) 引起买方兴趣。

(2) 激起买方购买欲望。

(3) 说服。

(4) 行动。

为了让所推销的商品给客户留下一个好的印象，在写促销信时需要注意以下几点：

(1) 尽可能简短。

(2) 在开头一段就要引起读者的兴趣。

(3) 信的外观要有吸引力，并尽力使其具有人情味。

样函 1　介 绍 商 品

敬启者：

承日升贸易有限公司相告，贵公司正寻购销往伦敦的高级羊毛衫。我们愿意供售我公司的"舒适"牌商品，该商品品质好，足以增加贵公司的信誉。

"舒适"牌羊毛衫完全采用澳大利亚高品质新羊毛制成。这种羊毛衫弹力适中，手感柔软，以其独特的品质给人以自然的温暖和舒适感。该产品也是风湿症、关节炎和脊背病痛者的理想用品，已畅销 25 个国家和地区。

由于该商品在上述国家成功的销售使得经销商都获利甚丰，这使我们相信贵公司也能分享这一成果。

现附上该商品的目录本一册，供你方参考。盼早回复。

谨上

（签名）

样函2　提供折扣

尊敬的先生：

　　我公司是组织完善的出口商之一，公司还拥有大量经验丰富、市场销售知识广博的销售人员。为了向你方说明商品的优越性，我方另寄免费样品，并附上价目表及目录册以作参考。

　　所附价目表显示我方能够提供比其他竞争者低 5%～10%价格的商品。我方价格虽然低，但质量却很好。

　　这些优势可使你方顺利开拓市场而不必担心竞争对手，因此我方相信会很快收到订单。

谨上

（签名）

样函3　促　销　信

您的窗框出现裂缝了吗？

　　迄今为止，窗框出现严重裂缝，唯一的解决办法就是拆下这个窗框，把破损的地方换掉。

　　现在有了一种省时、省钱的好办法，那就是使用热结合绝缘材料。

　　有了热结合绝缘材料，就不必搭脚手架了，所以费用远低于传统的处理方法。此外，热结合绝缘材料能大大加强家居的绝缘效果和安全性，保养期为 10 年。热结合绝缘材料用优质铝合金制成，在马来西亚由熟练技工进行装配。

　　所以，如果您受够了漏雨漏风的窗户，不想再受冬季的寒风之苦，请寄出随函所附邮资已付的索取资料卡，我们便会给您寄上一本彩色的产品介绍手册，以向您详细介绍热结合绝缘材料的性能。

　　尽早来函索取，以便能早日享受舒适生活！

样函4　比较商品函

先生们：

　　我们很高兴地从中国国际贸易促进会获悉你方欲购蜂蜜。兹奉告，我们专门经营此商品的出口。中国蜂蜜以其独特风味而受到欧洲顾客喜爱。按你方要求，现附寄报价单，样品和目录将另邮寄出。我们相信所报价格是你方可以接受的,它要比印度的同类产品低10%。公正地比较我方产品和其他供应商的产品质量会使你方相信我方报价的合理性。由于此商品需求甚殷,特建议你方尽快惠赐试订单。

谨上

(签名)

样函5　推荐替代产品

尊敬的先生:

很高兴地收到你方10月18日来函,询问我方可否供应型号为210的计算机。但是,很遗憾地告知,由于订单接踵而至,所说商品无货供应。为满足你方需要,现推荐一种优良的代用品。

我方有剩余库存330型号商品并可提供给贵方。该商品使用起来效率高,实用性强且耐用,价格便宜,对中学生尤为实用。在质量上,它和所询购的商品一样好。我方打算给予贵方折扣以售清库存。在目前每台总价CIF香港280港元基础上:

若购买100~199台,减9%;

若购买200~299台,减12%;

若购买300台(含)以上,减15%。

你方在6月20日或之前回复我方,此报价有效。

我方希望你方能接受这次绝无仅有的报价。

谨上

(签名)

样函6　给老顾客的促销信

尊敬的先生:

回顾记录,我方不无遗憾地发现自从去年8月起我方就没再接到贵方订单。由于贵方是我方老主顾之一,我方非常关心贵方不满意之处是在于我方商品还是服务。如果贵方遇到任何问题,可否填写所附回执卡?对于您的回函,我们将立刻给予密切关注。

对于我方被指定为美国四大计算机厂商的全国代理商这件事,我想贵方一定很感兴趣。现我方仓库存有各式高品质个人电脑,价格极具竞争力。从所附目录册中可以看出我方价格比其他进口商要低。另外我方还可采用对你方有利的支付条件。热切盼望你方再次订购。

谨上

(签名)

第七单元　付款条件

导　读

国际贸易中的货款支付比国内贸易中的更为复杂。付款方式有很多种。其中有三种使用最为广泛，即汇付、托收和信用证(缩写为 L/C)。

汇付是进口商通过银行将货款汇给出口商。主要有三种汇付方式，分别是信汇(M/T)、电汇(T/T)和票汇(D/D)。

支付也可以通过银行以付款交单(D/P)和承兑交单(D/A)的方式来进行。付款交单要求付完货款才能收到货运单据。它又分为即期付款交单和远期付款交单。承兑交单要求对出口商开出的汇票进行承兑才能得到货运单据。

信用证(L/C)是国际贸易中最常用的一种付款方法。它可靠、安全并且灵活。信用证可以定义为银行根据买方指令所开立的以卖方为受益人的一种有条件的付款保证。银行承诺在提交所规定单据后，在规定的时限内按照所标明的货币向受益人支付、承兑或议付一定的金额款项。在国际贸易当中，申请人为进口商，受益人为出口商，而开证行为进口商银行。在信用证业务中，银行信用代替了商业信用。只要卖方遵守所有的信用证规定，例如在信用证所规定的时限内提交所要求的单据，那么卖方就可以获得比其他任何一种付款方式都要安全的一种付款保证。总之，在信用证业务中，银行向出口方和进口方提供了信用，使双方的利益都得到了保障。

我们在出口业务中的通常做法是在装运期前一个月将信用证开立并寄达卖方以便给他足够的时间来准备装运，例如备货和订舱。要准时装运，催开信用证是非常有必要的。

如果在信用证中发现任何卖方不同意的不符或不可预见的特殊条款，卖方应当发通知给买方，要求买方改证。信用证必须同销售合同和相关的单据保持严格一致。否则，出口商将会要求进口商改证。

为了给卖方留足够的时间来生产货物以及给银行来议付，装运时间和信用证的到期时间至少要相差两个礼拜。有时由于某种原因卖方无法按时备货装运或买方要求延迟装运时间，卖方必须请求延期信用证的到期日以及装运时间。

从出口商的利益出发，信用证要优于付款交单，即期付款交单要优于远期付款交单，而付款交单要优于承兑交单。选择正确的付款方式取决于商业伙伴的信用状况。

样函 1 要求使用信用证付款

尊敬的先生:

　　非常感谢您第 12 号订单订购 5000 件桌布,但遗憾的是我们无法接受您的付款条件。

　　我们在上一封信中给您寄了一份样本合同,其中清楚地标明了我们的一般销售条款。如果您看了样本合同,应该注意到我们通常的付款条件为保兑的、不可撤销的、以我方为受益人的、以即期汇票开立的信用证,并应于装船前一个月到达我处,而且一直到所规定的装船时间的第 21 天在中国保持有效,并允许转船和分批装运。

　　我们在 8 月 15 日的信中也提到一些欧洲的公司已经按照上面的条件跟我们进行了业务往来。我们希望您能在这方面同意我们的条件,并尽快顺利完成我们双方的第一单生意。

　　一旦收到您的肯定回复,我们将给您寄去我们的合同,以便留有足够的时间来备货。

　　盼早回复。

谨上

(签名)

样函 2 通知开立信用证

尊敬的先生:

　　我们写信告知您我们已经通过非洲商业银行开出以你方为受益人、金额为 15000 美元的、保兑的、不可撤销的信用证,有效期至 10 月 15 日。货物装船后,您有权通过加纳的银行开立 60 天汇票。银行将会要求您提供下列单据以承兑汇票:

(1) 提单,一式 3 份。

(2) 商业发票,一式 5 份。

(3) 装箱单。

(4) 保险单,一式 2 份。

(5) 原产地证。

我们期待于 9 月底收到您的货。

谨上

(签名)

样函3 请求修改信用证

尊敬的先生:

我方已收到您 9 月 19 号的来信,信中告知我们已根据我方第 56 号销售合同开立 L89 号信用证。然而,我们遗憾地发现有一些不符,跟合同有出入。在此我们将这些不符点列出提请您的注意:

1. 受益人名称应写作 Qingdao Arts & Crafts Imp. & Exp. Co.,而不是目前出现在信用证上的 Qingdao Crafts Imp. & Exp. Co.。

2. 请将 with partial shipments and transshipment prohibited 修改为 with partial shipments and transshipment allowed。

我们假定上述错误由笔误所致,并希望您能尽快修改并传真,以便我方及时装船交货。

希望得到您的早日回复。

谨上
(签名)

样函4 请求延期信用证

尊敬的先生:

我们遗憾地通知您我们直到今天才收到你方关于上述销售确认书的信用证。上述合同当中清楚地规定信用证应不迟于 11 月底就到达我处。虽然你方信用证迟迟未到,鉴于我们长期的业务关系,我们仍将安排你方订单的发货。

不过,由于信用证所造成的延误,我方无法按照销售确认书中的时间进行发货。你方应对信用证进行展期如下:

1. 将装运时间延期至明年 1 月底。

2. 将信用证的有效期延期至 20××年 2 月 15 日。

请确保在今年 12 月底之前完成上述信用证的修改,否则我们仍将无法按照延期的时限进行装运。

期盼您尽早回复。

谨上
(签名)

样函 5　信用证请求延期回复函

尊敬的先生：

　　我们已经收到您 12 月 11 日的来信，要求我们将信用证延期至 20××年 2 月 15 日，将装运期限延至 20××年 1 月底。

　　我们认识到如果我们最晚无法在 12 月底将信用证发给你方，你方将无法赶上销售确认书中规定的最终期限。但是由于我们必须通过一定的程序才能申请到进口许可证，我们无法更早开立信用证。进口许可证的有效期只能到 20××年的 1 月初。

　　我们将竭尽全力提供支持，但在目前的情况下我们无法将进口许可证的期限延期，我们很遗憾，但无法将上述信用证延期。

　　恳请您尽力按时装运，我们将非常感谢您在此所做的努力。

谨上

(签名)

样函 6　催开信用证回复函

尊敬的先生：

　　我们已经收到你方 9 月 16 日的来信，要求我们开立上述订单的信用证。

　　对于信用证延期开立以及所造成的不便，我们深感抱歉。延误主要是由于我司的沟通出现了差错。不过，我们在收到你方上一封信后已经立即通过中国银行开出了相关的信用证。我们相信你方现在应该收到该信用证。

　　请允许我们再次表示歉意，并且我们在此承诺，在未来的业务中将不会再犯类似的错误。提前再次感谢您的理解。

谨上

(签名)

样函 7　要求承兑交单的付款方式

尊敬的先生：

　　感谢您 7 月 7 日的来信。

　　你方能够按时装运，我们感到非常高兴，不过我们感到惊讶的是，你方仍然要求我们付款交单。经过多年的良好合作，我们认为我们有权享有更便捷的付款方式。实际上，我们的很多合作伙伴都采用承兑交单 60 天的付款方式。如果您在这一点上能够效仿，我们将非常感谢。

期望得到您肯定的答复。

谨上

(签名)

样函 8　催开信用证

尊敬的先生：

我们想通知您 76 号销售确认书项下的货物备好一段时间了。根据销售确认书的规定，应该在 5 月或 6 月进行装运。我们两周前给您写信督促开立相关信用证。但是让我们失望的是，至今没有得到任何回复。所以我们再次提请您关注此事。

装运期限已经迫近。我们必须指出的是，除非您的信用证于本月底之前到达我处，否则我们将无法按照所规定的装运期进行装运。

我们希望这封信能得到您的及时关注。

谨上

(签名)

第八单元 包 装

导 读

　　包装是国际贸易的必要组成部分，它是交易双方磋商的重要贸易条件之一。因此，卖方应特别注意包装的特征和外观。

　　包装分为外包装(运输包装)和内包装(销售包装)。

　　外包装应具备以下特征：

(1) 美观坚固。

(2) 容易装卸。

(3) 适合长途运输。

(4) 能防止损坏。

(5) 能防止偷窃。

(6) 防水/防震。

(7) 标准化。

　　内包装应做到：

(1) 新颖美观。

(2) 小巧玲珑。

(3) 有吸引力。

(4) 适合橱窗陈列。

(5) 易于宣传推广和销售。

　　按买方包装指示包装完后，出口包装上要标明包装标志，它主要包括：

(1) 运输标志或叫唛头。

　　它标明进口商的名字，目的港，货物的原产国，订单号码，货物的重量和尺寸等。

(2) 指示性标志和警告性标志。

　　为了确保货主和承运人双方的利益，在包装上须印刷搬运方式、装货方式、起吊方式等指示性标志和警告性标志。

　　包装信函包含以下内容：

(1) 开头句：对先前收到的信件表示感谢并提及包装事宜。

(2) 中间部分：具体陈述货物的包装要求。如果有必要，还应陈述理由。

(3) 结尾句：希望对方及时做出回应。

样函 1　买方对于包装和运输标志的要求

敬启者:

兹谈及我方 123 号订单中的 200 箱玻璃制品,我方请你们注意以下事项:

由于玻璃制品极易破碎,因而货物必须包装在塑料袋里,然后装入标准出口木箱里,箱内四周填充泡沫材料,以能经受住运输途中的野蛮装运。

关于外包装,请在三角形内刷上我公司缩写名称 ABC,其下应刷货物原产地、目的港及我方的订单号。为预防起见,请在外包装上注明"易碎物品"和"小心轻放"的字样。

上述说明供你方参考,希望收到表达你方意见的回信。

谨上
(签名)

样函 2　洽谈包装和标志

敬启者:

你方包装指示收悉,谢谢。今歉告,我方难以满足你方的包装要求。

鉴于我们长期的贸易关系和友好的合作前景,我们建议你方接受以下意见:

(1) 床单 10 打装一盒,4 盒装一纸板箱,8 个纸板箱装一板条箱。

(2) 贵公司名称缩写印刷在菱形内,而不用全称。

(3) 板条箱外面除印有毛重和净重外,还须印有"中国制造"的字样。

你方尽早回复将使我们不胜感激。

谨上
(签名)

样函 3　对包装要求的回复

敬启者:

感谢贵方 10 月 15 日的订单,现欣然告知除包装外,我方接受所有的条件。

我方建议贵方采用我们最新的包装,它既经济又坚固。贵方订单提及的包装是我们几年前采用的老式包装。从那以后,我们已经改进包装,其结果是我们的客户对最近几批货物完全满意。

我们的男式衬衫现在是以塑料袋包装的,每件装一袋,然后再装进纸板盒里,每 5 打纸板盒装一纸板箱,每个纸板箱毛重大约 25 千克。每个纸板箱衬以塑料纸,以防内装货物受潮。

我们期待贵方及时回复，并告知是否同意我方建议。

谨上

（签名）

样函4 包 装 要 求

敬启者：

很遗憾通知贵方，贵方 8 月 1 日发往伦敦的 100 箱钉子中，有 15 箱严重损坏，当然，这不是贵方的过错。

兹写信与贵方商谈有关钉子包装之事，我方认为为了我们今后的交易，须向贵方解释清楚包装方法。

发往伦敦的钉子用双层麻袋装，每袋重 50 公斤。发往鹿特丹的钉子用木箱装，净重 112 磅，每箱内装 16 袋各为 7 磅的钉子。法国市场上，我们的客户喜欢采用纸板箱包装，每箱重 30 公斤。

请求贵方告知能否满足这些要求。

谨上

（签名）

样函5　出口商通知包装、唛头和装运情况

敬启者：

我们很高兴地通知你们，笔记本电脑已装运，详情如下。

包装：20 箱，每箱 15 台。

唛头：菱形图标内标上 BD123，纽约。重量和尺寸见附件。

装运：中国对外贸易运输总公司"风庆"号货轮，4 月 1 日从上海启航，预计 4 月 20 日到达纽约。

根据信用证条件，我们已将全套提单、一式三份的发票和保险单，连同金额 30000 美元的即期汇票提交给了花旗银行，该行已如数议付。

请在货物运抵后通知我们，我们将非常感激。

谨上

（签名）

样函6　关于包装不当的索赔

敬启者:

　　我们按时收到了你方运来的机器，但遗憾地提请你们注意这种情况：货物到达时，我们发现木箱完全压扁了，大部分的机器零部件已损坏，这显然是由包装不当造成的。你方使用的木箱不够坚固，不适于包装这么沉重的机器。

　　在这种情况下，我们别无选择，只好向你方提出索赔，希望你方对此迅速予以处理。

谨上
(签名)

第九单元 保 险

导 读

国际贸易容易遭受到许多风险。轮船可能会沉没，货物在运输途中可能受到损坏，汇率可能会变化，买方可能背信弃义拒不付款，政府可能突然实行禁运。因此，进出口商必须进行保险，使自己避免遭受许多这样的风险。

就国际贸易而言，与我们关系最密切的仍然是海上保险，因为大部分的国际贸易以海洋运输为主。

出口商或进口商是根据货物类型和具体情况来办理运载货物的投保险别。海运保险的标准险别种类很多，基本的有以下三种。

(1) 平安险。

(2) 水渍险。

(3) 一切险。

一般的附加险通常有：偷窃和提货不着险、淡水雨淋险、短量险、钩损险、包装破裂险等。应该注意的是，在中国，所有这些附加险均包括在"一切险"内。

不包括在一切险中而需要单独投保的特殊附加险主要有：交货不到险，战争险和罢工、暴动、民变险。

当签有 CIF 合同的出口商或签有 FOB 合同的进口商想要投保时，他应该采取的第一个步骤，就是和保险公司取得联系。保险公司的代理人(通常称作保险经纪人)会送来一份印制好的保险申请书，然后投保人填写申请表并交给保险公司。当保险公司接受了申请，应依法出具一张保险单，上面列有所签订合同的各项条款，由保险人填写，它包括商品的所有权、货物名称、投保金额、保险费、投保时间跨度、所承保的风险等。经过签字的保险单是具有法律效力的合同或文件，是保险人和投保人之间协议的证明，也是货运单据的一部分。

一般来说，投保的金额是根据商业发票的金额而定。所建议的最低投保金额为货物 CIF 总值再加上 10%，算作进口商的其他费用和正常利润。要投保更高比例的金额也可以，不过需要支付额外的保险费。

保险信函的内容主要由以下三部分构成。

(1) 开头句：感谢对方关于投保的来信并对投保的货物予以确认。

(2) 中间部分：如果有必要，可分成若干段落，完整地陈述投保的细节问题。

(3) 结尾句：希望对方及时做出回应。

样函 1 询问保险费率

敬启者:

我们最近将有一批价值 5000 英镑的皮鞋货物,成本加保险、运费到新港,预备由伦敦班轮有限公司的船只从伦敦起运。

我们希望将这批货物从我方上述地址至新港投保一切险,请报来保险费率。

谨上

(签名)

样函 2 回复关于保险的询问

敬启者:

兹确认收悉贵方 8 月 1 日来函,特此感谢。很高兴贵公司选择我公司为这批由国际航运公司运输、从纽约至上海的 20 箱男式衬衫的货物承保。

根据惯例,在没有得到你方明确指示的情况下,我们为货物投保水渍险和战争险。保险费率是申请投保金额的 1.5%。现随函寄去我公司的有关文件供你方参考。我们相信,贵方会发现我们的费率是非常优惠的。

如贵方认为我方的费率可以接受,请及时通知我们,以便我们可以尽快给你们寄去我公司的保险单。

期盼早日回复。

谨上

(签名)

样函 3 要 求 保 险

敬启者:

我方想对以下 50000 美元的货物投保一切险和罢工、暴动、民变险:

10000 码水洗丝。

这批货物由"长风"号货轮运载,预计 5 月 15 日从大连启航,6 月 2 日抵达伦敦。

由于此事紧急,贵方及早回复我们将不胜感激。

谨上

(签名)

样函 4　答复保险要求

敬启者：

　　兹谈及你方 8 月 1 日询问保险的信函，我们希望通知你方如下事宜：由于货物按 CIF 条件出售，我公司将按发票金额 110%承保一切险和战争险。你方若要投保更多险别，所需额外保险费用由你方负担。货物抵达保险单指定的目的地并送交收货人后，保险即告终止。被保货物在终点卸货港，从海轮卸下至收货人仓库这段时间内，保险责任期为 60 天。

　　我们的承保人——中国人民保险公司在公正迅速处理理赔方面享有极高的声望，如果货物发生损坏，可向你处中国人民保险公司代理提出索赔，他们将负责赔偿你方所遭受的损失。欲了解详情，请与中国人民保险公司或该公司在贵地的代理人联系。

谨上

(签名)

样函 5　进口商请出口商代办保险

敬启者：

　　兹谈及我方第 231 号订单下 1000 箱玩具，此笔交易按 CFR 成交。

　　我方希望贵方在当地对此货物投保，如蒙贵方代表我方按发票金额的 120%投保一切险(金额为 100000 美元)，我方将不胜感激。

　　当然，一收到贵方的收款清单，我方将向贵方付清保费。若贵方愿意，也可向我方即期提取相同的金额。

　　衷心希望贵方能满足我方的要求。

谨上

(签名)

样函 6　保险单证明

保险单 No.12345

兹证明该公司代表中国纺织品进出口公司已向青岛分公司投保。

金额：200000 美元。

品名及数量：3000 箱 "白猫" 牌混纺毛毯。

自青岛至汉堡。

船名:"东风"号货轮。

启航日期:20××年 9 月 20 日。

险别:一切险。

如发生损坏,由威廉检验公司检验,在青岛支付索赔。

本保险单于20××年 9 月 7 日在青岛签发,一式两份。

中国人民保险公司

青岛分公司

(盖章)

第十单元 运 输

导 读

    运输是国际贸易非常重要的组成部分，这是因为卖方销售的货物必须运送给国外的买方，而货物的送达要靠运输服务才能实现。为了安全、快捷、准确、经济、有效地完成出口运输任务，国际贸易商必须掌握全面的运输知识，比方说，运输方式、装运条款、装运过程和装运单证等。本单元仅关注装运过程。

    国际贸易中，装运要按照买方的装运指示(以海洋运输为例)，首先依船期表选择货轮，然后进行预订舱位的申请。完成商品的出口包装，加盖唛头之后，在启航前两三天须将商品搬入船公司仓库。同时，卖方还要开立发票，领到出口许可证，发出船公司致该货轮船长的装运指示才可将货物装入该船。完成装船后，应立刻向买方发出装运通知。装运通知不仅起到告知对方已完成装运的作用，并且也能提醒对方要及早准备货款。最后非常重要的一点就是，装运必须完全按照信用证的指示，清楚地确认装船日期、是否可以转运或分批装运等事宜，否则，买方可以拒绝付款。

    与装运相关的函电内容包括：

(1) 讨论装运条款或修改装运条款。

(2) 向卖方发出装运指示。

(3) 敦促及早、迅速、准时地装运。

(4) 发出装运通知或装运单据。

样函 1 要求修改装运条款函

    尊敬的先生：

    我方已经收到你方20××年1月10信函以及DC-125号关于406号合同项下的信用证：商品为衬衫，货号为01。

    关于装运港，我方要说明的是，我们不能在中国的青岛港装运，因为我方的生产厂家在沈阳，离大连港最近。为了降低国内运输成本，最好选择接近产地的港口装运，这一点也是广为接受的原则。此外，大连的港口设施先进，装货效率也很高。因此，我方要求你方将装运港由青岛改为大连。

    关于最迟的装运期，我们遗憾地通知你方2月5日时间太紧，因为，1月下旬中国的春节有7天的假期，我方不可能在2月5日前备好货物。

    如果你方能将最迟的装运期改回原合同的规定，即20××年2月20日，我方将不胜感激。

同时，请将信用证的有效期延展至 20××年 3 月 5 日，以便我方有足够的时间将单据提交银行议付。

对于你方的合作，预致谢忱。盼望收到你方的修改通知。

谨上

(签名)

样函 2　买方给卖方的装运指示函

王先生：

很高兴收到 888 号订单项下的 5 万瓶青岛啤酒的 666 号销售合同一式两份。尽管所报的是"货交承运人"价格，我们想请你方按照通常条件与承运人签订运输合同，而风险和费用则由我方承担。

当你方订到舱位时，请通知我方船名及航次、提单号、预计离港时间、预计抵达时间，以及其他一些对我方在我地办理保险所必需的信息。

由于啤酒瓶易碎，请用特别制作的箱子包装，以经得起野蛮装卸。

如蒙你方在上述方面的密切合作，我方将不胜感激。

谨上

(签名)

样函 3　催促尽快或按时装运函

王女士：

关于 102 号合同项下的 1000 箱圣诞蜡烛，我们希望提请你方注意：装运应在 10 月份进行。然而，至今我们没有收到关于该批货的任何消息。由于圣诞季节即将来临，我方客户在圣诞假期急需该批蜡烛，现要求你方按时发货以使我方赶上销售的旺季。如果你方未能按照 102 号合同以及 A436 号相关的信用证的规定发运货物，我方将就我方所遭受的损失向你方提出索赔。在此情况下，就不可能再有订单了。

请马上通知我方你方是否已经发货以便我方提前做出安排。

谨上

(签名)

样函 4　发装运通知(对样函 3 的回复)

罗宾逊先生：

感谢你方 20××年 11 月 1 日催装圣诞蜡烛的信函。非常抱歉延误发出装运通知，原因是我需要照顾卧病在床的母亲，7 天不在单位。我希望该延误没有给贵方带来太大的不便。

关于 102 号合同，我们高兴地通知你方货物已于 20××年 10 月 25 日装运，详情如下：

你方信用证号码为：A436。

商品名：圣诞蜡烛。

数量：货号 201，500 箱；货号 301，500 箱；共计 1000 箱。

包装：货号 201，200 根/箱；货号 301，100 根/箱。

毛重：19810 千克。

净重：18810 千克。

体积：55234 立方米。

船名："东风"轮 085 航次。

开航日：20××年 10 月 25 日。

装运港：中国上海。

目的港：加拿大温哥华。

预计抵达时间：20××年 11 月 15 日。

运输标志：

现随函附寄一套副本装运单据供你方参考。我方相信货物将完好无损地抵达你方港口。

盼望明年这个时候再次收到你方的订单。

谨上

(签名)

样函5　道歉延迟装运(对样函 3 的回复)

敬启者：

你方 20××年 11 月 1 日催装圣诞蜡烛的信函，我方倍感抱歉。我方固然知道已远超过交货时间，但工厂作业因地震而中断了数周。

但是，我方正竭尽全力于一周内交货，目前正在安排装运。同时，就延迟造成贵方不便之处，深表歉意。

谨上

(签名)

样函 6　买方通知货已收到

敬启者：

　　你方 20××年 11 月 1 日发来的那箱瓷器已于昨天到货。我们马上打开箱子检查，没有发现破损。事实上箱内货物状况良好。

　　我们正安排将箱子由运输公司退还给你方，运费未付。如果你们在你方的发票上把为此索要的金额记入我方账户的贷方，我们将非常高兴。

谨上

(签名)

样函 7　询问运费率及船期

敬启者：

　　我们不久将准备把 10 箱陶器从伦敦运往悉尼。箱子的大小是 1.25 米×1.25 米×1 米，每箱重约80千克。

　　请报来你方的运费率并将你方的船期及整个航程通常所需的时间等详细情况告诉我们。我们知道，"西方之星"货轮定于 6 月 25 日起航。但是如果可能的话，我们希望船期更早一点。

谨上

(签名)

样函 8　对样函 7 的回复

敬启者：

　　感谢你方 5 月 3 日的询问。

　　"维多利亚公主"轮，6 月 10 日—15 日(首尾两天包括在内)在第 4 号码头装货。接着是"西方之星"轮，6 月 20 日—25 日(首尾两天包括在内)在第 7 号码头装货。到悉尼的航程通常需要 14 天。木箱包装的瓷器的运费率是每吨 60 英镑。

　　我们将乐意在这两艘船中的任何一艘为你方的 10 箱货物订舱位，并附上我们的订舱单。请填上此单并尽快寄回。

谨上

(签名)

样函 9　询问集装箱服务情况

敬启者：

　　我了解到贵公司在南安普敦至开普敦航线经营集装箱业务。若你方能寄来有关此项服务的详情，包括使用此项服务的费用，我们将非常高兴。我是个皮鞋制造商。

谨上

(签名)

样函 10　对样函 9 的回复

敬启者：

　　感谢你方 10 月 6 日的询问。我们提供的航运集装箱有两种尺寸，即 3 米和 6 米长，分别可装 2 吨和 4 吨的货物。它们可以两头开启，因此可以同时装卸。对于运送易受潮或受水损坏的货物，集装箱具有不漏水或不漏气的优点。必要时，集装箱可以在工厂装货和上锁。因此，偷窃是不可能的。

　　当打算运往同一个目的港的分开的货物用同一集装箱装运时还可节省运费。同时，由于对集装箱装运的货物索取的保险费较低，另外还可以节省保险费。

　　随信附上我们的价目表一份，盼望收到你方的通知。

谨上

(签名)

第十一单元　投诉、索赔和调解

导　读

在执行合同的过程中，买卖双方都必须遵守合同的条款，严格地履行各自的义务。如果一方违约，就可能给另一方带来麻烦，或使其遭受损失。在这种情况下，受影响的那一方可以要求过错方保证此类事情不再发生，这就是投诉，或者要求其按照合同规定的相关条款补偿损失，即索赔。而当另一方接到投诉或索赔时，他可以按情况或者理赔或者拒绝。

索赔涉及的各方应公正友善地解决索赔事宜。尽可能通过友好协商解决索赔问题，最好不要诉诸仲裁或法院。进行索赔的时候，索赔方切记要在合同规定的时效内提出要求，否则，索赔是无效的。而且，索赔必须要有充分的证据(如检验报告)支持以说明问题。

写此类信件，语气要礼貌得体，用词要坚定、有说服力。一般会用到这样的句型："根据合同的规定(贵方应该……)"，"我们感到非常抱歉，我们的错误给贵方带来了很大的麻烦，我们将(改正我们的错误)"。写信方通常要引用合同或单证中相关的条款来证明观点，但在引用时要记住前后信件的条款要一致。此外，信里引用的文件号、日期、句子或要求必须完全正确。否则，就会使自己陷入尴尬的不利局面，给生意带来麻烦。

样函 1　投诉货物质量低劣

王先生：

我们 8 月 10 日订购的布料与样品所示品质不符。

兹于昨天下午收到货物，但经检验布料与样品不符，我们对此感到非常诧异。实物的质量不如样品，显然无法达到我方客户的要求。

我们订购的布料是用于生产定制套装的，原计划布料一到立刻投入生产。但是，由于贵方送来的布料品质低劣，我们不得不推迟客户的原定订单。这给我们带来了很多不便。

不知贵方是否能将此批货物收回并更换为我方订购的货物？请在 10 天内备好货物。不管出于何种原因，如果贵方无法保证在 10 月 1 日前交货，我们将要求退还全部货款以及赔偿我们所产生的所有损失。

贵方如能及时处理，对我们双方均有利。

谨上

(签名)

样函2　对送错货物的投诉信的回复(对样函1的回复)

克林·普莱斯利先生：

20 天内正确的布料将运抵贵方。

很感谢贵方 9 月 1 日寄来的信件。对于布料和样品不符，我们感到很抱歉。经过仔细检查，我们发现我们将你们的订单与另一份和你们的货截然不同但名称只有一字之差的订单弄混了。我们已经安排了正确的发货，货物将于 9 月 24 日抵达你处。

作为对发错货的补偿，我们将给予整批货物 5%的折扣，希望贵方能满意这样的安排。

谨上

(签名)

样函3　货物受损或有瑕疵的索赔

季先生：

有瑕疵的 A 级 U 盘(订单号 254334522)

兹于今天下午收到 A 级 U 盘 2,000 个。

然而经验收发现此 U 盘无法正常使用。由于某种原因这些 U 盘无法储存资料，因而完全失去使用价值。

敝公司原定从周一开始进行这批光盘的促销活动。而实际上我们事先已接了许多订单，现在由于贵方质量控制不严，我们不得不延迟交货，这将给我们带来极大不便。

谨希望贵方于下周内用功能完好的 A 级 U 盘更换此批货物。不管出于何种原因，如果无法保证交货，我们将要求退还按此订单已经缴付的全部货款。

谨上

(签名)

样函4　对货物受损或有瑕疵的投诉信的回复(对样函3的回复)

蔡先生：

现就您 10 月 10 日来函做出回复。您在信中提到我们近期提供的 U 盘的质量问题，引起我们的注意，非常感谢。我们十分同意您的看法，严格的质量管理至关重要。

我们向本公司的供应商作了核实，确认他们将一批不良U盘错发给本公司。显然，质量问题是在生产过程中产生的。供应商目前正在全数追回这批批号为761b的产品。

对于此事给贵公司造成莫大不便，本人深表歉意。我向您保证今后本公司将尽力避免此类错误再次发生。

我们素来重视客户意见。本着这一原则，本公司非常乐意更换这批不良U盘，并将立即安排发运。若贵公司能退还不良光盘，本人将不胜感激。本公司愿意承担运费。

为贵公司添加麻烦，谨再次致歉。

谨上

(签名)

样函5　单据有误的投诉

主题：发票号 P5643/9

马克先生：

兹收到贵方就20××年5月4日发出的一批图书开具的上述发票。这批图书是敝公司举办的中国当代摄影师作品展展品的一部分。

然而，贵方发票显示这批图书含水文兴著《中国在前进》240册，而实际只交付200册。您可以核查本公司订单正本(随函附上复印本，订单号为4378528)，我们订购的数量仅为200册。

我们希望尽早结清账款，相信您能尽快做出安排，开具正确的发票。

谨上

(签名)

样函6　对单据有误的投诉信的
回复(对样函5的回复)

万先生：

关于您20××年5月27日来函指出我们开具的发票(P5643/9)有误一事，谨此做出回复。首先，我们非常感谢您提出有关事宜引起我们的注意。

我们向本公司的供应商作了核实，贵公司收到的发票内容有误，确系本公司之责任。因为本公司近期引进电脑化库存管理系统，启用之初出现了诸多问题。随函附寄修改后的正确发票。

希望本公司的差错未给贵公司造成太多不便，并衷心期望今后能继续保持合作关系。

谨上

(签名)

样函 7 拒绝更换的拒绝函

米切尔先生：

从您 5 月 6 日的来函中我们了解到您非常关心您的 4050 软件。我们非常愿意尽可能地把事情办好。

通过您的描述和我们职员的仔细研究，我们发现您采用的电脑网络有些问题。

操作指示中已经明确，这个型号的软件只能与 Windows XP 兼容，和 Windows 98 是不同的。而且在您使用软件之前，必须安装盒子里的驱动系统。但实际上您并没有安装。

因此，请先安装驱动系统，然后在 Windows XP 下试用。其他的步骤请严格按照我们的使用指南小册子上的要求进行。

我们希望该软件能让您感到非常便利，受益无穷。

谨上

(签名)

样函 8 拒绝赔偿损坏材料的要求

威尔逊先生：

每一位客户都有权从 Caring 塑料材料公司获得最好的产品和服务。每一种 Caring 的材料都经得起时间的检验。

我已将您 8 月 10 日的信件连同照片一起送到了本公司的生产部门。经过本公司实验室的仔细检查，我们发现贵方要求退还货款的 0150 系列材料显然经过了长时间的暴晒。而我们从一开始做广告的时候就已经提及，0150 系列材料不能长时间暴露在阳光下。

不过，2115 系列材料可以经受日晒。该材料拥有 0150 系列材料的所有优点，同时还能防晒、防水，价格也比较经济。如果贵方需要了解更多的细节，我们愿意提供帮助，请致电 01-45-4318188，或给我们发送电邮至 *caringmaterial@yahoo.com*。

谨上

(签名)

第十二单元　代　　理

导　　读

对于大量的国际贸易不仅可通过买卖双方的直接谈判来进行，还可以通过代理的方式进行。指定国外代理的一个很重要的原因是由于他了解当地的情况，了解他自己的市场。对于什么样的产品最适合他自己的市场以及什么样的价格当地市场能够接受，他都相当了解。在国际贸易的开拓发展过程中，代理和中介通常起到很重要的作用。

拥有代理的出口商被称为委托方。委托方和代理方之间的关系是建立在佣金基础之上的，在做出代理的筛选决定之前，出口商应该仔细了解代理在以下几个方面的情况：

(1) 业务状况和财务状况。

(2) 相关领域的销售经验。

(3) 处理经销产品的技术能力。

(4) 个人素质。

根据委托方所赋予的权利范围可以将代理分成以下三种：

(1) 总代理：这种代理得到委托方的全权授权，不仅能够直接代表委托方签署合同，而且能够在特定的区域内处理其他的商业活动。

(2) 独家代理(排他性代理)：这种代理方式只能在特定的期限内，在特定的区域内，对某种商品享有独家销售的特权。

(3) 佣金代理：这种代理不能完全享有某种商品的独家销售权。委托方可以在相同的期限内，在相同的区域内通过几个佣金代理商来进行促销。

我们的进出口公司经常通过指定一些外国的公司作为代理来销售我国生产的产品。代理条款有时是通过双方的函电进行确定的。不过，如果双方的业务量大，就有必要签一个正式的协议。协议中应该包括以下全部或部分内容：

(1) 代理的性质和期限。

(2) 所涵盖的区域。

(3) 代理方和委托方的责任。

(4) 购货和销货的方法(例如：代理方自行购买还是"寄售")。

样函 1　请求做独家代理函

尊敬的先生：

我们在中国有一个发展良好的销售组织，在中国的很多地方都有代表处。他们的报告显示，市场对你们工具的需求非常大。而据我们所知，你方在中国没有直接代表处，所以我方愿意提供服务，成为你们的独家代理。

你方产品有一个很好的赢利前景。如果能将具体的条款确定下来，我们相信，我们在该产品上 20 年的经验将能让我们建立一个双方受益的业务关系。

鉴于我方所拥有的销售网络和丰富经验，我们认为您应该同意净销售额的 5% 作为佣金是合情合理的。

您一定希望了解更多的我方的信息。请您向您所在城市的中国银行查询，我们确信他们将向您提供所有必要的信息。

希望得到您肯定的答复并就条款达成一致。

谨上
（签名）

样函 2　同意做独家代理的请求

尊敬的先生：

感谢您的来信要求做我们的独家代理。经过向您所提供的证明人认真咨询，我们相信您应是我们能够委托的合作伙伴。

我们已经起草了一份代理协议，附在这封信上。请看一下价格和条款，你方是否能够接受。

我们真诚地希望我们双方能够建立一个令人高兴而且双方都能受益的业务关系。

谨上
（签名）

样函 3　拒绝独家代理请求

尊敬的先生：

感谢您请求做我们的独家代理，在你们国家销售我们的产品。

经过慎重考虑，我们认为目前就做出这样的决定为时尚早，目前的业务量只能说是一般。

请不要误解我们的上述意思，绝不是说我们不满意。实际上，我们对您给我们所带来的业务感到非常满意。然而，我们认为需要达到一个更大的业务量来证明代理是有必要的。

鉴于以上所述，我们认为最好是在你们未来的销售达到这一步的时候再考虑代理的事情。我们希望您在这一点上跟我们达成共识并继续跟我们合作。

谨上

(签名)

样函4 请求就代理协议进行面谈

尊敬的先生：

我们已收到你方11月25日的来信，并在仔细考虑了来信的内容之后，我们对你方提出的担当我们的代理一事印象甚好。

我们曾经跟好几家公司商谈过，但目前对此事尚未做出决定。然而，如果条款能够商妥，我们认为你方正是我们想要找的代理人。我们相信你们在整个行业中有着很强的销售网络，而且看来进一步发展业务的时机已经成熟。

当然，这件事的关键在于你方在获得并履行的订单上需要多少佣金。既然你方的罗德里格先生即将在一周内来到上海，我们认为与其通过电子邮件等待并修改，不如当面同他讨论这些细节问题。

我们等待罗德里格先生的来访。

谨上

(签名)

样函5 阐述代理协议的要点

尊敬的先生：

我们很高兴确认上个月在我们共同洽商期间达成的协议，并希望我们能够建立一个愉快和卓有成效的业务关系。在起草正式协议书以供签署之前，我们想强调一下，我们双方一致同意的要点如下：

1. 自今年1月1日起你方为我方独家代理，为期两年。

2. 我方按照你方推销我方产品的销售额的3%付给你方佣金。

3. 你方承诺不为自己也不为别的供应商销售其他厂方的竞争产品。

4. 你方每月要向我方提供销售报告，并承兑我方按应得的净金额向你方开出的汇票。

5. 你方要保持把我方的全部产品在你处陈列室展出。

一收到你方来信确认这些要点，我方将安排拟好协议书并寄给你方签署。

谨上

(签名)

样函 6 独家代理协议

当事双方在平等互利的基础上发展业务，按照双方同意的下列条款，特订立本协议。

1. 当事双方

供应商(以下简称甲方):

代理商(以下简称乙方):

兹甲方委托乙方作为他的独家代理以销售下列商品。

2. 商品和数量

方铰链

双方同意由乙方负责在本协议有效期内销售上述商品不少于 50 万对。

3. 地区

加拿大

4. 协议的有效期

本协议一经双方签署将从 20××年 11 月 1 日起至 20××年 10 月 31 日止保持有效 12 个月。期满后如未通知对方，此协议将自动延长 12 个月。

5. 确认订单

乙方应完全按照甲方提供的规格和贸易条款向其他方报盘，未经甲方许可乙方不得擅自做任何更改。每笔交易的佣金需经双方通过商议而定，在甲方收到该交易的全部款项后付给乙方。每笔达成的交易只有在甲方确认后才成定局。

6. 市场情况报告

乙方应有责任每 3 个月向甲方提供当时的市场情况和客户意见。如果市场有什么特殊变化，乙方也应将全部细节及时用书面向甲方报告。

7. 付款

货款要用保兑的、无追索权的、不可撤销的信用证支付，在向加拿大议付银行提交装运单证时，凭汇票，见票即付。每笔订单的信用证，无论是代理开的或是客户开的都应于装运日前 21 天到达甲方。

8. 其他条款

(1) 在本协议有效期内，甲方不得把上述商品在上述地区的销售给除乙方以外的任何其他客户。乙方保证不为其他国家担任同样商品的代理或销售同样商品。

(2) 乙方必须负责在本协议有效期内向甲方订购并准备以甲方为抬头开出信用证，首期6个月不少于25万对。如果乙方在首期6个月内未能向甲方订购25万对，甲方则有权将同一商品销售给任何其他客户。

(3) 本独家代理协议不涉及下列方式达成的交易。

① 甲方以其政府名义为一方与乙方政府为另一方达成的交易。

② 甲方与其在加拿大的其他买家为把货物再出口至其他国家而达成的交易。

(4) 交易由甲方确认后，乙方必须负责履行。

(5) 甲方有权按照当时的市场情况修改或更换其销售价格，并及时把更换之事通知乙方。

(6) 在本协议有效期间，如果任何一方被发现违反了本协议的规定，另一方有权书面通知违反方，中止本协议。

甲方(供应商)   乙方(代理商)

(签名)   (签名)

第十三单元　社交信函

导　读

在日常生活中，人们为了加强联系、交流信息和联络感情，往往需要进行广泛的社会交往。社交信函则是他们进行交际的重要形式。

通过努力，掌握一些社交信函的一贯格式并不难，而且稍加练习就可以运用自如。但是要写出一封适合目的的有效的信函就需要技能。本单元所列的各式信函示例专门用于演示如何有把握地处理各种信函。

最常见的社交信函有：感谢信、邀请信、祝贺信、慰问信、推荐信、介绍信、道歉信和申请信等。

撰写本单元的另外一个目的是基于一个认识，那就是国际贸易不仅仅是流程和程序的问题，也是人与人之间的业务关系和人际关系问题。因此，在许多情况下，上述各种社交信函对于加强国际贸易和人际关系起到很重要的作用。

样函1　感　谢　信

亲爱的史密斯先生：

我写此信是想告诉您，我是多么感激您在我太太上周访问贵国时给予她的热情款待。

您给予她的协助和宝贵意见以及为她安排的情况介绍，使她有机会成功召开几次十分有用的会议，这一切都因您的帮助才得以办成，我对此真是感激不尽。

谨上
(签名)

样函2　祝　贺　信

布莱克先生：

今日获悉您晋升为贵公司销售部经理，甚感欣慰。

根据您在贵公司的资历和经验，我认为您很适合这项工作。

除了向您表示祝贺外，还要向贵公司总经理先生道喜，他真是慧眼识英才。据我所知，您是该领域这一职务的最佳人选。再次祝贺您的升迁。

谨上
(签名)

样函3　道　歉　信

尊敬的先生:

我方的延期交货给你们造成很多不便,深表遗憾,敬请接受我们致歉。

我公司业务迅速发展,为此我们将制定一系列的流程以确保此类事故不再发生。

对于贵公司在此事上表示的理解和耐心,我们深表谢意,我们很高兴今后继续向你们提供服务。

谨上

(签名)

样函4　邀　请　函

尊敬的先生:

我公司新厂将于12月28日开始投产,敬请您出席新厂开工典礼。

如您所知,新厂的投产是本公司的一个里程碑,而这正是海内外客户对本公司产品不断需求的结果。因此,我们将邀请所有对本公司做出贡献的人士。我相信您一定会赏光。

如确能光临,请来函告知您到达的时间,以便我们安排接待工作,费用由我方支付。

敬请您在百忙之中抽出时间出席本次庆典。

谨上

(签名)

样函5　约　见　函

尊敬的先生:

感谢您12月8日的传真。我们热忱欢迎你来访并参观我们的生产流水线。您建议12月12日周一上午9:00会面,这个时间没问题,届时恭候光临。

正如您希望加深相互了解并加强彼此合作,我们也真诚地希望能在平等互惠的基础上与你们经营业务往来。我深信,我们的会谈将是具有建设性意义的,并将促成对双方都有利的交易。

盼望早日见面。

谨上

(签名)

样函6　投　诉　函

尊敬的先生：

  贵公司寄来我第 237 号购物确认书项下的手机，经仔细检验后，我们不能不对其质量低劣深感惊异。该货并不符合我方以此确认订购单的样品，随函附上有关照片一张和实物数件，供贵公司核对。

  此种不符合我客户需求的货物，我们只能要求贵公司予以收回。按照贵公司同我们双方签约时的约定，费用由你们承担。

  希望贵公司及时处理此事，并告知我们。

谨上
(签名)

第十四单元　贸易合同

导　读

贸易合同是一份具有法律效力的协议书。它可以是正式的，也可以是非正式的。但在国际贸易活动中所采用的贸易合同则是正式的文字合同。

用英文拟写协议或合同比拟写信函的难度要大一些，但只要掌握写作的要领和基本知识，就能拟写出好的协议和合同。一般来说，只要能用中文拟写合同，并具有良好的英语基础，就能按照协议、合同约定好的条款拟写出英文版本。还可以先拟写出中文合同的版本，再将其翻译成英文。拟写合同的过程中，表述应全面、清楚、条理化，符合逻辑，并且要遵循英语的语法规则。

国际贸易中的贸易合同种类繁多，主要包括：销售合同、销售确认书、购货合同、购货确认书、进口合同、出口合同、代理协议、寄售合同、寄售协议和补偿贸易合同。

一、合同和协议的格式

合同或协议没有统一的、固定的格式。对于一份完整、有效的合同或协议来说，一般分为三个部分，即约首、约文和约尾。

1. 约首

约首包括如下内容：

(1) 合同或协议的标题，如销售合同、购货确认书、进口合同或独家代理协议。标题标明合同或协议的性质。

(2) 合同或协议的编号。

(3) 签约日期和签约地点(有些合同或协议的签约日期和地点放在尾部)。

(4) 合同或协议的序言。即在合同或协议的开头用一段话介绍双方当事人的名称，并注明甲方和乙方，或买方和卖方，说明签约的原则和目的。例如：

美国纽约 ABC 公司(以下简称甲方)与中国纺织品进出口有限公司哈尔滨分公司(以下简称乙方)在平等互利的基础上经过友好协商达成以下协议。

2. 约文

约文是合同的主体部分，可以用条款式或表格式或条款加表格式写明双方议定的内容。例如，销售合同或购货合同的一般条款为：商品名称及规格，数量、单价和总值，包装、装运、支付、保险、检验、索赔和仲裁等。其他合同或协议(如代理协议、合资企业合同、投资协议、技术转让协议等)的内容复杂，条款各不相同，但也已形成一定的程序，在拟写此类协议或合同时，可参考相关例文。

3. 约尾

约尾主要有下列内容：合同或协议的份数和保存，使用的语言文字，双方机构的全称及盖章等。如有附件，还需写明附件的名称和份数，作为合同不可分割的一部分。

二、书写合同和协议的要求

(1) 合同或协议的内容须符合平等互利、共同协商的原则。

(2) 条款必须全面、具体、清楚、无疏漏，以免发生不必要的经济损失。

(3) 用词准确、条理清晰、逻辑性强、表达无误。

为使读者熟悉各种不同的贸易合同，现将一些实例列举如下。

(销售确认书、销售合同、购货确认书和销售代理协议的实例系英汉对照，此处略去)

参 考 文 献

[1] 赵银德. 外贸函电[M]. 3 版. 北京：机械工业出版社，2021.
[2] 兰天. 外贸英语函电[M]. 9 版. 大连：东北财经大学出版社，2021.
[3] 王美玲. 外贸函电[M]. 北京：机械工业出版社，2013.
[4] 葛萍，周维家. 外贸英语函电[M]. 上海：复旦大学出版社，2007.
[5] 陆墨珠. 国际商务函电[M]. 北京：中国商务出版社，2006.
[6] 武振山. 国际贸易英文函电[M]. 大连：东北财经大学出版社，2004.
[7] 甘鸿. 外经贸英语函电[M]. 上海：上海科学技术文献出版社，2004.
[8] 束光辉. 新编商务英语函电[M]. 北京：北京交通大学出版社，2007.
[9] 黄水乞. 外贸英文信函范例与常用精句[M]. 广州：广东经济出版社，2006.
[10] 林叙仪. 新贸易书信宝典[M]. 广州：广东科技出版社，1995：193-264.
[11] 胡鉴明. 商务英语函电[M]. 北京：中国商务出版社，2005：198-227，258-269.
[12] 胡英坤，车丽娟. 商务英语写作[M]. 北京：外语教学与研究出版社，2005：62-109.
[13] BILBOW G T. 朗文商务英语致胜英文书信[M]. 北京：外语教学与研究出版社，2001：167-208.
[14] 兰天. 外贸英语函电[M]. 大连：东北财经大学出版社，2007.
[15] 诸葛霖. 实用外贸英语书信手册[M]. 北京：商务印书馆，1998.
[16] 杨文慧. 现代商务英语写作集萃[M]. 广州：中山大学出版社，2005.
[17] 张干周. 国际贸易函电[M]. 杭州：浙江大学出版社，2007.
[18] 张玉柯，李树杰. 英文函电[M]. 保定：河北大学出版社，1998.
[19] 徐美荣. 外贸英语函电[M]. 北京：对外经济贸易大学出版社，2002.
[20] 尹小莹. 外贸英语函电[M]. 西安：西安交通大学出版社，2004.
[21] 冯祥春. 外经贸英语函电一本通[M]. 北京：对外经济贸易大学出版社，2003.
[22] 陈永生，等. 国际商务函电与合同[M]. 北京：华语教学出版社，2004.
[23] 范红. 英文商务写作教程[M]. 北京：清华大学出版社，2000.
[24] 冯祥春. 外经贸英语函电一本通[M]. 北京：对外经济贸易大学出版社，2003.
[25] 丁溪，候银霞. 对外贸易英文函电[M]. 哈尔滨：哈尔滨工业大学出版社，2004.
[26] 黎孝先. 国际贸易实务[M]. 北京：对外经济贸易大学出版社，2007.
[27] 吴百福. 进出口贸易实务教程[M]. 上海：上海人民出版社，2003.
[28] 徐景霖. 国际贸易实务[M]. 大连：东北财经大学出版社，2006.
[29] 陈永生，等. 国际商务函电与合同[M]. 北京：华语教学出版社，2001.
[30] 葛亚军，等. 合同英语[M]. 天津：天津科技翻译出版公司，2002.
[31] 吕昊等. 商务合同写作及翻译[M]. 武汉：武汉大学出版社，2005.
[32] BILBOW G T.. Write for Modern Business[M]. 北京：外语教学与研究出版社，2001.
[33] GILLIES, MIDGE. Business Writing[M]. New York: AMACOM, 2000.
[34] 凌华倍. 外经贸英语函电与谈判[M]. 北京：中国对外经济贸易出版社，2004.
[35] 李雅静. 涉外经贸英语函电[M]. 青岛：中国海洋大学出版社，2006.
[36] 唐桂民. 新编经贸英语核心教程[M]. 北京：机械工业出版社，2006.
[37] 冯修文. 实用英语写作[M]. 上海：上海交通大学出版社，2007.